Turbulent Seasons

Also by Charles C. Alexander

Turbulent Seasons

Baseball in 1890–1891

Charles C. Alexander

Sport in American Life
C. Paul Rogers III, series editor

SOUTHERN METHODIST UNIVERSITY PRESS
Dallas

Requests for permission to reproduce material from this work should be sent to:
    Rights and Permissions
    Southern Methodist University Press
    PO Box 750415
    Dallas, Texas 75275-0415

Cover image: The 1890 Boston Players' League team (*National Baseball Hall of Fame Library*)

Jacket and text design: Tom Dawson

Library of Congress Cataloging-in-Publication Data
Alexander, Charles C.
    Turbulent seasons : baseball in 1890–1891 / Charles C. Alexander. — 1st ed.
            p. cm. — (Sport in American life)
    Includes bibliographical references and index.
    ISBN 978-0-87074-572-0 (alk. paper)
    1. Baseball—United States—History—19th century. 2. American Association (Baseball league :
1882–1891) 3. National League of Professional Baseball Clubs. 4. Players League (Baseball
league) I. Title. II. Series: Sport in American life.
    GV863.A1A425 2011
    796.3570973'09034—dc22
                                                                                    2010051941

Printed in the United States of America on acid-free paper

10   9   8   7   6   5   4   3   2   1

To the Memory of Phillip N. Bebb,
1941–2007

Contents

Preface

The seasons of 1890 and 1891 were two of the most turbulent and strife filled in nearly a century and a half of professional baseball. Although baseball had long been hailed as the National Game and the National Pastime and was played nearly everywhere by all kinds of people, the game itself was in a process of rapid evolution, with significant changes in playing and scoring rules being instituted almost annually. By 1890, however, the game on the field was comparable to today's game. What was understood as major league baseball–the baseball played in the National League and the younger American Association–was a relatively small form of business enterprise in which relations between club owners (or "magnates," as they liked to be called) were highly personal and often antagonistic. In their attitudes and practices, however, the men who owned and operated the baseball franchises of the time mirrored those of the late-nineteenth century's titans of industry and commerce.

Harold Seymour and Dorothy Seymour Mills as well as David Quentin Voigt have produced pioneering works on what might be called the structural or institutional history of the 1890–91 seasons, and Robert F. Burk has detailed the struggles between players and owners within a larger labor-versus-management context. They as well as others have written of the squabbles among club owners, the rise and revolt of the Brotherhood of Professional Ball Players, the formation and failure of the 1890 Brotherhood or Players' League, the resumption of conflict in 1891 between the National League and the American Association, and the outcome of that conflict.

The subsequent labors of members of the Society for American Baseball Research (SABR) have added greatly to our knowledge of late-nineteenth-century baseball. We now have a substantial body of writing on the pre-1900 game in the form of team histories, studies of particular seasons, and especially biographies, and we know a lot more about the period than we did even twenty-five or thirty years ago. Up to now, however, relatively little attention has been given to the actual baseball played in those remarkable 1890 and 1891 seasons—to what was happening on the field as the pennant races progressed, the makeup of teams, players who excelled and who didn't, the equipment they used, their backgrounds and ethnic makeup, the ballparks they played in, and so on. Many of the men who performed in the American Association and the Players' and National leagues in those seasons were splendid athletes who could have held their own in any period in baseball's history.

Although baseball's national following—what were later called "fans" but then were called "kranks" or "cranks"—had grown rapidly, professional baseball remained an intimate universe. Relations between owners, managers, and players on the one hand and the sporting press on the other were far more personal than in today's corporate baseball world, as its doings are reported in the omnipresent "media." As of 1890 or so, baseball journalism was still nascent, and reporters who covered the game were just beginning to acquire an identity of their own, even if many of them still lacked a byline. But what they wrote in the daily and weekly press was characteristically colorful, funny, sarcastic, and above all candid–in fact often brutally frank regarding club owners' arrogance and backbiting, umpires' incompetence, and players' misconduct, especially their all-too-frequent bouts with alcohol. To read the baseball coverage of the time is to encounter a style of journalism that wouldn't be permissible today. One of the things I've tried to do in this book—by quoting extensively from such writers as Tim Murnane, Joe Murphy, Jacob Morse, and W. F. Arnold—is to convey a sense of that very different style. With the possible exception of Murnane, the baseball reporters of the 1880s and 1890s are forgotten figures, as opposed to such men as Grantland Rice, Damon Runyon, Heywood Broun, and Paul Gallico, of the "Golden Age" of sports reporting in the decades between the two world wars.

Today's sportswriters and sports broadcasters persist in dating the beginning of "modern" baseball from 1900 and know or care little about the rich and complex history of the sport in the pre-1900 era. It's an attitude without justification, as the quantity of published work and ongoing research in late-nineteenth-century baseball should demonstrate. I hope that this book will add significantly to the enterprise of many others whose contributions are indicated in my notes and bibliography. And I also hope that what I've written here will appeal to both serious researchers and to those who just enjoy reading about baseball when, much more than today, it was truly the National Game.

I'm again indebted to Tim Wiles and the staff of the Giamatti Research Center at the National Baseball Hall of Fame Museum and Library, as well as to Eileen Canepari at the Society for American Baseball Research lending library. I also appreciate the assistance of the staffs of the microfilm departments at Ohio University and Miami University; of Valerie Elliott and Terry Beck of the Brown Regional History Center, Lane Library, Oxford, Ohio; and the interest and encouragement I've received from John Thorn, Rick Huhn, Steve Steinberg, and other fellow SABR members. Again it's been a pleasure to work with the people at SMU Press, one of the finest small university presses in the country and an ornament to Southern Methodist University. Finally, I've about run out of ways to acknowledge the two women in my life: JoAnn, my wife, and Rachel, my daughter. So I'll just say to them, "Thanks for everything."

Charles C. Alexander
Hanover Township, Butler County, Ohio
October 2010

Turbulent Seasons

CHAPTER 1

1889: The National Game

As a form of athletic competition in which adult males participated, baseball was only a few decades old. Yet almost from its beginnings as such in the 1830s and 1840s, it had been hailed as "America's National Game" and the "National Pastime"—never more so than at the end of the 1880s. Whether played before thousands of people in cities in wooden structures called "parks," "fields," or "grounds"; on vacant lots in towns and cities; in school yards; or even in cow pastures, baseball was omnipresent. Americans of all ages, ranging from the preadolescent to the sexagenarian, played baseball (then usually written as "base ball"). A St. Louis newspaper estimated that each summer Sunday, at least six hundred men and boys competed for organized amateur and "semipro" clubs on baseball diamonds across the city.

Whether for participants or spectators, baseball had no real rivals as the nation's favorite sporting activity. A "sporting crowd" of young men who liked to drink, carouse, and gamble on the bloody matches followed prizefighting, which was still in its toe-the-mark, bare-knuckle period. John L. Sullivan, acclaimed as the world's champion, might be a hero to vast numbers of his fellow Irish Americans, but the higher class of the population still viewed prizefighting with contempt and disgust. The sport was still illegal in nearly all the states (of which there were forty-four by 1890). To a great extent the same negative attitudes related to horse racing, which depended on gambling and thus carried an unsavory reputation for having fixed outcomes. Football, still evolving out of English rugby, was already the dominant collegiate sport; but with a college education beyond the reach of the great majority of Americans, football still lacked widespread popular appeal. Football's following consisted mainly of the minority who could afford college, while the well-to-do elite of an increasingly stratified society were just taking up tennis and golf.

If baseball was played nearly everywhere and nearly every kind of American played it, by the 1880s the professional game defined baseball at its best. (In contrast to college football, which was supposed to be wholly amateur, despite the money and other inducements given covertly to players at Yale and Harvard, the collegiate powers of the day.) The Cincinnati Red Stockings' sensational 1869 season demonstrated the superiority of a club of hired professionals matched against the nominally amateur clubs that they overwhelmed in the East, Midwest, and finally the Pacific Coast, which the club reached by the newly opened transcontinental railway route.

Two years later, professionalism came to full flower with the formation of the National Association of Professional Base Ball Players. Lasting from 1871 to 1875, the National Association suffered from a variety of ills. It was just that—an "association" of previously independent clubs, numbering anywhere from eight to thirteen from season to season. Although the clubs had local financial backers, the National Association was a loosely run outfit in which players scheduled "matches" with players of other clubs for dates that were sometimes kept, sometimes not. The National Association was also handicapped by the absence for three years of the Chicago club, whose lakefront ball grounds were destroyed, along with most of the rest of the city, in the great fire of 1871. Popular interest lagged from 1872 to 1875, as Boston, under captain William Henry "Harry" Wright (who had built the Cincinnati Red Stockings), finished on top every season. The Boston club thus retained title to the pennant-shaped banner symbolizing the championship. Finally, National Association matches were often characterized by open gambling and rowdy and drunken behavior on the part of both spectators and players. Players were also known to bet against their own clubs and sometimes take bribes to lose.

The National Association wasn't necessarily a bad scheme; with a few reforms it might have survived as the country's foremost baseball organization. It didn't survive, though, because a group of men representing six of its cities plus two others was able to bring off what was in effect a coup d'état that ended the National Association. The group's driving force was William A. Hulbert, president of the Chicago White Stockings. Anxious to build a powerhouse club in Chicago that would prove both a profitable enterprise as well as a stimulant to general business activity in the still-rebuilding city, Hulbert persuaded the representatives of the other seven cities to join him in forming a radically restructured baseball organization. On February 2, 1876, at the Grand

Central Hotel in Lower Manhattan, they brought into being the National League of Professional Base Ball Clubs.

The key words in the title of the new organization were "league" (not "association") and "clubs" (not "players"). That wasn't a matter of semantics; the way things were put together left no doubt that the owners would be in charge. Each club was to contribute $100 per year toward maintenance of a permanent central office, with a president and a secretary-treasurer. Hulbert persuaded Morgan G. Bulkeley, a prominent Hartford financier and president of the local baseball club, to accept election to the presidency of the new league; Nicholas E. "Nick" Young, a congressional clerk, kept the job of secretary-treasurer he had held in the National Association. (Bulkeley had little interest in the presidency; at the end of 1876 he was succeeded by Hulbert.) The National League's charter members were Chicago, New York, Philadelphia, Louisville, Cincinnati, Hartford, St. Louis, and Boston.

Hulbert had loaded his White Stockings with much of the best baseball talent of the day. From Harry Wright's Boston club he lured four players, including Albert G. Spalding, the National Association's top pitcher; and from the Athletic Club of Philadelphia he added a powerful young first baseman with the imposing name of Adrian Constantine Anson. Not surprisingly, the White Stockings copped the first National League pennant with a 52–14 record. After that season, Spalding gave up pitching for first base and then, at age twenty-seven, retired from playing altogether. Besides purchasing stock in the White Stockings, Spalding with his two brothers established a sporting goods store in Chicago. It was the modest beginning to what would become a virtual monopoly in the manufacture and sale of sports equipment.

Still in his forties, Hulbert died of a heart attack in the spring of 1882. Albert G. Spalding succeeded him as White Stockings president and, within a short time, chief stockholder. At his death, Hulbert's vision of a stable organization that returned profits for all its clubs was far from being realized. The National League's membership had undergone yearly reshufflings. New York City and Philadelphia, its two biggest markets, were kicked out at the end of the first season for violating schedule commitments, by refusing to make their final trips to the western cities. For the next two years, the National League operated with only six member clubs. Hartford, St. Louis, and Louisville dropped out following the 1877 season. Louisville had done all right financially, but revelations that several of its players had thrown games toward the end of the season left Hulbert no choice but to ban them from the League forever. St. Louis left at the same time, and Cincinnati was voted out in 1880 for violating two of the league's cardinal operating rules.

To distance themselves from what they considered the unsavory features of the National Association and appeal to a respectable clientele, Hulbert and associates fixed a minimum admission price of fifty cents and prohibited games on Sundays and the sale of liquor. The Sunday rule was irrelevant in the eastern cities, where Protestants had imposed ordinances banning a variety of commercial amusements on the Christian Sabbath. But the western cities, with their large Irish Catholic and German immigrant populations, had no such ordinances. So in 1880, Cincinnati, languishing in last place, scheduled Sunday home games and offered nickel-a-glass beer to the thirsty locals. That was too much for Hulbert, who convinced a majority of his colleagues that the city boasting of having given birth to professional baseball had to go.

Between 1877 and 1882, clubs representing Indianapolis, Milwaukee, Providence, Buffalo, Syracuse, Cleveland, Troy, and Worcester competed in the National League at one time or other. Most came and went; a few stayed, at least for a while. The League regained some strength by re-admitting New York and Philadelphia in 1883, but during its early years, putting money into any of its clubs was no way to get rich.

Yet there have been few times in baseball's long history when potential investors were scarce. By the late 1870s, several other professional leagues, structured along the lines of the National League, had been formed in the northeastern and middle-western states. Most belonged to the League Alliance, an arrangement whereby "minor" leagues placed themselves under the National League's protection with regard to contracts, territorial rights, and other matters. Then, in the fall of 1881, Oliver Perry Caylor, sports editor of the *Cincinnati Commercial-Gazette*, led a group of well-to-do baseball enthusiasts who met in the Queen City and formed the American Association of Professional Base Ball Clubs. The new circuit began play the next spring with clubs in Cincinnati, Louisville, St. Louis, and Philadelphia, all onetime National League cities, plus Baltimore and Pittsburgh.

The American Association adopted essentially the same playing rules as the National League and copied its constitution, but in other ways it was going to be a very different circuit. Sunday baseball was explicitly authorized in the three cities where Sabbatarianism didn't hold sway: Cincinnati, Louisville, and St. Louis. Majority stockholders in four Association clubs owned breweries and/or operated saloons, so liquor would be sold inside the playing grounds, prompting the self-righteous National League to sneer that the Association was a "beer and whiskey league." Besides offering Sunday ball and booze on the grounds, the Association sought to attract working-class patrons by setting a base admission price of twenty-five cents. Finally, the Association would have a regular staff of paid umpires, unlike the National League's practice of hiring local men to officiate.[1] (The National League soon formed its own umpiring staff.)

The Association men remained noncommittal on one aspect of National League operations. In 1879 the League's club owners had secretly agreed to something called the "reserve rule." Its purpose was to curb "revolving"—players moving from club to club for more money, which was common in the National Association and had continued in the League. Under the reserve rule as originally agreed to, each club retained exclusive rights to re-sign five players for the coming season and for as long as the club chose to.[2] At first, reserved players took pride in being considered valuable enough to be reserved, but it didn't take long for them to realize that they were held in a form of serfdom, deprived of the right to put their skills to advantage in a free market. In the next few years, moreover, the owners steadily extended their reserve lists to include everybody they had under contract, typically fifteen or sixteen men. Eventually they inserted the reserve rule into the standard player's contract as the "reserve clause."

Until the drastic alteration of the reserve clause in the mid-1970s, baseball owners and officials justified its existence in two ways—one public, one private. Publicly they argued that in an open market for players, the richer teams would buy up the best players, with the result that a few clubs would dominate the competition and kill off patronage for the also-rans. James "Deacon" White, they pointed out, starred for the champion Chicago club in 1876, then the next year went back to Boston for more money, led the league in batting, and helped that club win the pennant.

The private justification for the reserve was that restricting the market held down players' salaries and made clubs if not profitable, at least financially stable. In that regard, the investors in the relatively small-time business of professional baseball were following the prevailing conviction in big-time American capitalism: profits could be maximized only if labor costs were strictly controlled. So the men who built the great commercial and industrial entities of the period constantly fought against workers' efforts to form unions, and supported an open immigration policy that brought into the country huge numbers of hungry Europeans willing to work for low wages.

The absence of the reserve in the Association was an open invitation for National League players to jump to the new organization for better pay. Only one unexceptional player did that, but the advent of the Association caused other National League players to demand and usually get salary increases. Baseball's first inter-league war—the first of six that would take place over the next four decades—threatened to cost everybody a lot of money. Being typical businessmen of their time, club owners in both leagues quickly moved to stabilize the situation. Following the 1882 season—in which Cincinnati won the first Association pennant—Abraham G. Mills, Hulbert's successor as National League president; Dennis McKnight, head of the Association; and Elias Mather of the Northwestern League, a strong minor league circuit, met in New York City and formed a "National Agreement." The National League accepted the Association as an equal "major" league (at least nominally); the two circuits agreed to respect each other's player contracts; the Association adopted the same ball marketed by A. G. Spalding and Bros. used in the League (albeit under a different label); and the Northwestern and other minor leagues would retain the protected status they had under the defunct League Alliance.

With the competition for players at an end, the coming of peace made for the most prosperous circumstances professional baseball had experienced up to then. The Association added clubs in Columbus and New York City. (Given the elegant nickname "Metropolitans," the New York team quickly became the "Mets.") Tight pennant races in both circuits brought out record crowds. The Athletics of Philadelphia beat out St. Louis in the Association; in the League, Boston ended Chicago's three-year run at the top.

In the fall of 1883 news came out of Pittsburgh that still another league was being formed with the intent of challenging the two existing "major" organizations for players and patronage. Spearheaded by Henry V. Lucas, a young St. Louis heir to a railroad fortune, the Union Association established clubs in six League and Association cities as well as Washington and Altoona, Pennsylvania. Encouraged by the League, the American Association expanded to twelve clubs to preempt the Unions' movement into any new territory.

Although Lucas and his associates pledged to respect League and Association player contracts, they specifically disavowed the reserve and urged players not already under contract to join their new venture. The Unions were somewhat more successful than the Association was in 1882 in persuading players to jump. Two of the foremost jumpers were infielder Fred Dunlap, who came over from Cleveland to lead the Union Association with a .412 batting average, and Charlie Sweeney, a hard-drinking San Franciscan who deserted Providence in midseason, in time to win twenty-four games.

Both Dunlap and Sweeney performed for Lucas's St. Louis Maroons. Lucas had more money than the other Union investors and simply hired more good players. The result proved disastrous for the Union Association as a whole. The Maroons ran away with the pennant, finishing with an .832 winning percentage (94–19). The lopsided race quickly killed off interest; several clubs had to be moved elsewhere. A total of twelve cities fielded teams in the Union Association at various times, after which the whole thing became little more than a footnote in baseball history.

For 1885, the American Association cut back to eight clubs, dropping Toledo, Richmond, Indianapolis, and Washington but keeping Brooklyn, which had joined the Association the previous year. Meanwhile the National League replaced Cleveland with Lucas's St. Louis Maroons. The Union Association had offered a clearly inferior brand of ball, of which the Maroons left no doubt by finishing on the bottom of the League. After that one season St. Louis, along with Buffalo, was gone from the League, replaced by Kansas City and Washington.

The American Association, with its twenty-five-cent admission, Sunday ball, and liquor sales, attracted about 817,000 customers in 1885, some 200,000 more than the National League. Players' salaries had increased steadily in the past few years; by the mid-1880s the top players were being paid in the $3,000 to $4,500 range, at a time when the typical industrial worker made less than $500 per year. Holding down expenses—especially labor costs—remained an imperative for the "magnates," as the press referred to the club owners. In 1885 they agreed on a $2,000-per-player salary limit, but most of them weren't willing to enforce it.

In other ways, though, the magnates made sure players (whom they commonly referred to as "the boys") remained subservient. Owners freely levied fines for anything from drunkenness—which was widespread among players, as it was in the general population in the nineteenth century—to bad table manners in hotel dining rooms. Then, as now, players bought their own baseball shoes (cleated high tops made in Philadelphia by the Clafin Company) and what other equipment they used. But some owners also required players to buy their own uniforms and pay to have them cleaned, and usually refused to cover medical bills for the treatment of injuries suffered on the playing field. On the road, stingier owners booked teams into third-rate hotels (with players sleeping two to a bed). At home games, when they weren't in the lineup, players took tickets at the admission gates. Arthur H. Soden—who with John B. Billings and William H. Conant constituted Boston's famed "Triumvirate" of owners—ordered his players to go into the stands to retrieve foul balls. (Balls, which Spalding and Bros. supplied for $1.25 apiece, were considered property of the home club and were kept in play if at all possible.)

Among the club owners, Soden in the National League and Christian Frederick Wilhelm von der Ahe, owner of the Association's St. Louis Browns, represented polar opposites. Born in 1843, Soden was an old-line New Englander who had made his money respectably in the roofing business. An investor in the Boston club since the National League's formation, Soden affected an aloof, haughty manner. According to Tim Murnane, sports editor of the *Boston Globe*, he rarely spoke to his players; at most he might nod to them on the street.

Born in 1851 in the German state of Saxony, "Chris" von der Ahe came to the United States at age sixteen and made his way to St. Louis, where he became wealthy selling groceries and operating a saloon. He purchased a controlling interest in a local independent professional club, renovated a baseball facility on Grand Avenue, renamed it Sportsman's Park, and gained a franchise in the aborning American Association. Von der Ahe spoke with a pronounced German accent (which the baseball press liked to parody) and at least in the beginning, knew little about baseball. But he was a shrewd businessman and a born promoter, and he spent freely to make his St. Louis Browns a winning team. He also attended to the comforts of his customers as few owners did, including installing toilets for women and a beer garden in right field. (Balls landing in the garden remained in play; right fielders charging in among brew-quaffing patrons was a common sight.)

If Arthur Soden distanced himself from his players, von der Ahe loved being around "mein Prowns"—often too much so. He had no compunction about leaving his grand-stand box to argue with umpires; frequently he sat on the Browns' bench and yelled encouragements or criticisms at his players, depending on the course of the game.[3] Von der Ahe rewarded his players with gifts and wined and dined them when they won, which they did most of the time. The Browns garnered four straight Association pennants from 1885 to 1888 and narrowly missed a fifth in 1889. In 1886 they brought a large measure of credibility to the upstart Association when they defeated the mighty Chicago White Stockings four games to two in the third World's Championship Series between the two leagues' pennant winners.

Led by captain-first baseman Charles Comiskey, the Browns were fierce as well as exceptionally foul-mouthed competitors. They made life miserable for umpires, who worked games alone in both the Association and the League.[4] Ted Sullivan, who found and signed Comiskey for von der Ahe and remained Comiskey's close friend, described him as having "a volcano fire burning inside him to make himself famous." "I go on the field," Comiskey said of himself, "to win a game by any hook or crook. It is the game we are after, not reputations as society dudes."[5]

When the Browns didn't win, von der Ahe berated his men in public and imposed fines for what he thought was poor playing. In 1887 he spent $35,000 on posh railway cars and hotel accommodations for himself and his cronies during a long, drawn-out World's Championship Series with National League champion Detroit; when St. Louis lost the majority of games, he refused to share any of the gate receipts with the players. But if "der boss President" (as von der Ahe liked to refer to himself) was blustery and bombastic, by turns lovable, ludicrous, and loutish, he also owned the Association's most successful team. His peers might laugh at him behind his back, but he became the most powerful man in his league.

If von der Ahe and all the other club owners held ultimate sway over their players, the fact remained that without their investments in the business—in the construction and upkeep of ballparks and the formation and financing of clubs—professional baseball wouldn't have become what it was by the 1880s. Some players may have acknowledged that their ability to make a good living from baseball was attributable to the owners' fondness for the game and their willingness to spend their money to build it up. Yet players in general chafed under the reserve rule and shared a variety of other complaints. Discontent was especially strong on the New York National League club.

John B. Day not only owned the New York Association club; in 1883 he also financed the city's new entry in the National League. Day shifted players from one club to the other, according to which was doing better in the pennant race. Although the Metropolitans won the Association pennant in 1884 (before losing to Providence in the first World's Championship Series), they became also-rans thereafter.[6] Day eventually sold out to Erastus Wiman, a multi-millionaire Staten Island developer, who moved the Mets out of Manhattan to the St. George Grounds on the island. Handicapped by having a playing site accessible from Manhattan only by ferry, the Mets drew poorly and dropped from the Association after the 1887 season.

By then Day's League club had acquired the nickname "Giants," supposedly because manager Jim Mutrie boasted of "my big men, my giants," and local baseball writers picked it up. Mutrie also liked to parade around the ballpark in top hat and Prince Albert coat, his mustache immaculately waxed, waving his walking stick and yelling, "We are the people!" to which the crowd would roar back, "We are the people!"[7] It became the Giants' motto and their followers' battle cry.

By 1888 the Giants had the foremost concentration of talent in baseball (including five men who, long after their deaths, would be elected to the National Baseball Hall of Fame). They won New York's first National League pennant that year, then dispatched von der Ahe's Browns in the World's Series. The Giants' stalwarts were William "Buck" Ewing, who played various positions but was behind the plate most of the time; pitchers Tim Keefe and "Smilin' Mickey" Welch; outfielder Jim O'Rourke (nicknamed "Orator" because of his stilted verbiage); husky first baseman Roger Connor; and infielder John Montgomery Ward. Two of those men were licensed attorneys: O'Rourke, who had been in the National League since its first season, earned his law degree at Yale; Ward received degrees in both law and political science from Columbia.

Born in 1860, Ward grew up in the little town of Bellefonte, Pennsylvania. To the home folks he was "Monte," although in baseball circles he was "John" or "Johnny." At 5' 9" and 165 pounds, he was about average size for an infielder of his time. Earlier in his career he was an outstanding pitcher, winning forty-seven games for Providence's 1879 champions and thirty-nine the next year. In the process he ruined his pitching arm and eventually became a full-time infielder, dividing his time between shortstop and second base. Well-read and articulate, he authored a book that was partly a concise history of baseball but mostly an instructional guide to playing the game. Published in 1888 as

Base-Ball: How to Become a Player, it was a clearly written work, something a young base-ball aspirant might still find useful more than a century later.[8]

Slender and handsome, reportedly fluent in French, and educated far above the typical ballplayer of his time, Ward cut quite a dashing figure in Manhattan society (although for all his learning and sophistication, he feared cross-eyed men, who, he thought, brought bad luck). In 1886 Ward married the lovely and celebrated actress Helen Dauvray (nee Ida Mae Gibson); subsequently Tim Keefe married her sister. As the sometime captain and acknowledged spokesman for his Giants teammates, Ward became a strong advocate of players' rights. On October 22, 1885, five days after the owners announced their $2,000 salary cap, Ward, O'Rourke, Ewing, Connor, Welch, and four other Giants formed the world's first sports union, which they entitled the Brotherhood of Professional Ball Players. Ward was elected president, Keefe secretary-treasurer. The Brotherhood's announced aims were to "protect and benefit its members, promote a high standard of professional conduct, and advance the interests of the national game."[9] They also sought to foster respectable behavior and a professional attitude among their peers. As they secretly recruited members on other clubs in both the League and Association, they only accepted men who were considered sober and morally upstanding. Within a year the Brotherhood had signed up 107 players in the two leagues.

The 1880s was a period of growing labor militance and hardening resistance by employers to the formation of workers' organizations. The Knights of Labor, seeking to enlist "all who toil," had been on the scene since the previous decade; the American Federation of Labor, formed late in 1886 in Columbus, Ohio, followed an opposing policy, organizing skilled workers vertically by trade. Although the Brotherhood of Professional Ball Players borrowed the term "Brotherhood" from existing unions in the railway industry (such as the Brotherhood of Locomotive Engineers and the Brotherhood of Trainmen), Ward and associates were unwilling to call their organization a union, emphasizing instead its beneficent aspect. In fact it was a union from the beginning and would increasingly function as such in the years ahead.

The Giants players generally liked John B. Day, who paid his men well and sided with them on various issues, including salary caps and the sale of players. It turned out that the 1885 salary cap was observed more in theory than in practice, but Ward nonetheless went on the offensive, airing the Brotherhood's grievances in various magazine and newspaper articles and interviews. "Is the Base Ball Player a Chattel?" he asked in an article in the respected *Lippincott's Magazine*.[10] Although he wasn't ready to attack the reserve directly, he inveighed especially against the traffic in players. Following Chicago's loss to the Browns in the 1886 World's Championship Series, Al Spalding began breaking up his great team, first selling the colorful all-around star Mike Kelly to the Boston Triumvirs for a record $10,000. The next year Spalding sold John Clarkson, his ace pitcher, to the same people for the same amount. In neither instance, Ward pointed out, was the player consulted before the sale or given a portion of the sale price.

Selling Kelly and Clarkson made Spalding somewhat wealthier, but the main source of his growing fortune was his sporting goods business, which now included not only multiplying retail stores but a complex of manufacturing facilities. Cocksure and boundlessly ambitious, Spalding was the personification of the self-made man idolized in social theory and popular culture in late-nineteenth-century America. In 1888 he conceived a plan for a postseason global baseball tour, pitting his White Stockings against players picked from other National League teams. Spalding convinced himself that such a trip would both spur enthusiasm for baseball in other countries, thereby making the American national game the world's game, and open up new markets for his sporting goods. The trip achieved neither, but it was a *succès d'estime*, a grand adventure that captivated the imagination of great numbers of Americans, whether or not they were "kranks," as dedicated followers of the sport were called then.

Ward, who loved travel, went along as captain of the picked team. He was matched against Adrian Anson, now known as "Cap," who had led the White Stockings to five pennants from 1880 to 1886 and was rivaled only by Mike Kelly as the game's foremost everyday player. Spalding, the ballplayers, and assorted others sailed from San Francisco on November 18. (The party didn't include Helen Dauvray; citing professional commitments, she stayed behind after quarreling with Ward.) The Brotherhood leader was a smart young man, but he had no idea what the club owners, with Spalding's prior approval, planned to do in his absence.

The previous year the Brotherhood made what it considered a major concession to the owners, agreeing to the inclusion of the reserve in players' contracts. In turn, the owners pledged that if they intended to cut a player's pay, they wouldn't reserve him; he could thus put his services on the free market. Now the "magnates" threw out that understanding and, three days after the baseball tourists left the country, adopted what was called the "Brush Classification Plan."

The scheme bore the name of John Tomlinson Brush, owner of the Indianapolis franchise, which had been re-admitted to the National League two years earlier. Proprietor of Indianapolis's first department store, Brush was new to baseball and had lost money on his seventh-place finisher. But as he once said, "I run a ball club . . . for the interest I take in the game and the recreation its gives me. I sell *pants* for money."[11] Gaunt and bony, in his early forties but already beginning to suffer from a degenerative condition of the nervous system, Brush nonetheless quickly became a formidable figure among the club owners. Unlike von der Ahe and some of the other owners, he shunned publicity, choosing to operate in quiet ways. As a critic described him years later, "Chicanery is the ozone which keeps his old frame from snapping, and dark-lantern methods the food which vitalizes his bodily tissues."[12]

Under the classification plan, all players would be put into one of five categories, ranging from "A" to "E," according to how the owners viewed not only their abilities but their conduct. Nobody could be paid more than $2,500; "E" players, limited to $1,500, would also be required to sweep ballparks and do other chores. When the globe-circling baseball party arrived in Rome (by way of Honolulu, Australia, Ceylon, and Egypt), news of the classification plan finally reached Ward and the other players. Spalding professed surprise and sympathy for the Brotherhood, but in fact he and Anson had deliberately kept the group out of touch for three months with what was happening back home. From England, an indignant Ward sailed home ahead of the rest of the party and quickly went into conferences with Brotherhood members.

On April 8, 1889, with everybody back home, Spalding paid for a nine-course banquet for players, club owners, and a bevy of dignitaries at Delmonico's, Manhattan's finest restaurant. It was on that occasion that Samuel L. Clemens, then at the zenith of his persona as Mark Twain, offered his famous tribute to baseball as "the very symbol, the outward and visible expression of the drive and push and rush and struggle of the raging, tearing, booming nineteenth century."[13]

Posh banquets and stentorian tributes were fine, and it turned out that the richer club owners still wouldn't observe official salary limits. The Boston Triumvirs paid Mike Kelly a $3,000 bonus when he signed for 1889, while John B. Day kept Ward, Jim

O'Rourke, and Buck Ewing at the $4,000–$5,000 level. Day also denounced the classification plan as "wrong in the beginning" and useless.[14] Yet players' resentments continued to accumulate. Spalding would pay only a fraction of the costs for treatment of a broken leg suffered by Chicago third baseman Ed Williamson during a game in France. Mordecai Davidson, owner of the bottom-running Louisville Association club, levied so many fines on his players that they staged a two-day strike in Baltimore.

There was considerable sentiment in the Brotherhood for a general strike on Independence Day, usually the biggest revenue date of the season. That was voted down when Ward threw his influence against it. But while Ward realized most players continued to be paid pretty well, the obnoxious classification plan was still in place if the owners united to enforce it in 1890. Spalding and Ward, who had remained on friendly terms, met to talk over the situation. When Spalding put Ward off with the claim that it would be impossible for the owners to get together until the season was over, the Brotherhood president gave up trying to reason with the men who owned baseball. On July 14, 1889 (appropriately enough, the one-hundredth anniversary of the storming of the Bastille), representatives of the sixteen Brotherhood chapters secretly convened at the Fifth Avenue Hotel in Manhattan and voted to form their own professional league. The players went back to their teams to finish the season and start raising capital for the new organization. They named it the Players' National League, although nearly everybody would call it simply the Players' League.

Suspecting something was up, Spalding offered to change the classification plan, keeping its good-conduct requirement but stipulating that after three seasons a player would be freed from his classification to negotiate for more money. If sold, he would receive 25 percent of the sale price. The seventeen minor leagues in operation in 1889—a record number—would be classified according to the maximum payrolls they could carry. That all sounded pretty good, but the plan drew condemnation in the baseball press as a scheme for establishing a baseball trust, à la existing corporate trusts in various areas of industry and commerce that, the next year, would be outlawed (at least theoretically) by the enactment of the federal Sherman Antitrust Act. Nor would the Brotherhood have anything to do with Spalding's overture.

On October 10, Ward met with John B. Day and informed him that his league champions would be in the Players' League next season. So it was more than a little ironic that in the 1889 World's Championship Series, which began eight days later, the Giants players—who had given birth to the players' union and now were in full-fledged revolt against the existing baseball order—should again represent the ownership they intended to desert. After beating out Boston on the last day of the season (the first time that had happened in either major league), they met Brooklyn, which had won the Association pennant in a race almost as close with the largely reconstructed St. Louis Browns. The Giants would be defending the Dauvray Cup, the trophy John Ward's glamorous wife had donated to the World's Championship Series winner the previous year.

On October 2, in Cleveland, Boston was still in first place as Mike Kelly sat on the bench in topcoat, nursing a hangover after a night of drinking with Al Johnson, a wealthy young Clevelander. When teammate Hardie Richardson was called out trying to score, Kelly jumped up and accused umpire Jack McQuaid of being "bound to do the Bostons out of the championship." After McQuaid had park police remove Kelly from the grounds, Boston manager Jim Hart bought him a ticket so he could get back in, but the police wouldn't allow it. Kelly's outburst was a continuation of complaints by catcher Charlie Bennett that the umpires favored New York, while Hart accused the western teams of reserving their top pitchers for Boston and pitching "green amateurs" against New York.[15] However all that may have been, Cleveland's Ebenezer "Eb" Beatin held the "Beaneaters" (as the Bostons were nicknamed) to a single run, while John Clarkson, pitching his seventh straight game, gave up seven scores. New York won in Pittsburgh that day and took the lead from Boston.

The contenders switched cities to end the season. On Tuesday, October 8, New York won in Cleveland, 5–3. The *Boston Globe* had put up a $1,000 purse if the Beaneaters won the pennant; in turn Hart and John Clarkson wired Cleveland manager Tom Loftus that his pitcher and catcher could get $500 and the rest of the team a like amount if they beat New York. All to no avail. In Pittsburgh, Clarkson, worn out after pitching 620 innings and winning forty-nine games, lost for the nineteenth time, 6–1. New York finished at 83–43, Boston 83–45.[16] (The *Globe* gave the Beaneaters the $1,000 anyway.)

In 1889 Brooklyn was still a proudly independent city and, with a population of more than 800,000, the nation's fourth largest, behind New York, Chicago, and Philadelphia.[17] Drawing a record-setting 353,690 kranks at little Washington Park and on Sundays at Wallace's Ridgewood Park in rural Queens County, Brooklyn won its first pennant under manager Bill McGunnigle, an elegant dresser who directed his players from the bench by waving a bat. The "Bridegrooms" (so-called because several players had married before the season) took the Association flag by a two-and-one-half game margin over St. Louis. If not for a falling-out with their mercurial owner, the Browns might have made it five pennants in a row. When Chris von der Ahe slapped a big fine on one of his players for bawling out a Sportsman's Park employee, the Browns rebelled by playing sloppy ball in a series in Kansas City. The loss of three out of four games there probably made the difference in the race's outcome.

In what was scheduled as a best-of-eleven-game World's Championship Series, the Giants came back from a three-games-to-one deficit to win five straight from the Bridegrooms and retain the Dauvray Cup. John Ward was the Series' outstanding player, stealing ten bases, batting .417, and hitting the Series' only home run (and his only one of the season). After the Series, Ward and the rest of the Giants told John B. Day they had no ill-feeling toward him. Day then treated them all to a sumptuous lunch at Barrio's Casino and announced their shares of the Series receipts: $380 per man. As Jim O'Rourke's biographer has noted, "This would be the last cordial meeting between players and owners."[18]

With the combined attendance in the two major leagues reaching nearly 2,600,000, the 1889 season was the most prosperous baseball had seen. By then the League, which had begun in 1876 with a 70-game schedule, was scheduling 140 games, while the Association's schedule of 80 games in its inaugural season had also expanded to 140. Brooklyn, with a smaller salary list than either Boston or New York, undoubtedly made the biggest 1889 profit, although even with their relatively heavy payrolls, John B. Day and the Boston owners had done quite well. From 1883 to 1889, Tim Murnane estimated, the Triumvirate cleared close to $300,000.[19] But with the players in revolt and forming their own separate league, a year of stark uncertainty lay ahead.

Although the clash of wills between owners and players got the most press coverage, relations between the two leagues, despite the nominal peace achieved in 1883, hadn't been amicable. The National Leaguers had never accepted their Association counterparts as true equals and repeatedly sought to undermine the "beer and whiskey league." Since 1883, Pittsburgh, Cleveland, and New York had left the Association, with Pittsburgh and Cleveland joining the League in 1887 and 1889, respectively. Then, on November 11, at the Association's annual meeting in New York, Cincinnati and Brooklyn announced they were joining the National League, which became—temporarily as it turned out—a ten-club circuit. Cincinnati owner Aaron Stern was attracted by the League's fifty-cent admission, and although he would have to give up beer sales in his ballpark, the growing strength of local Sabbatarianism, supported by Mayor William Mosby, made it likely Stern would lose his Sunday home dates.

The Brooklyn ownership consisted of a lesser triumvirate: Charles Byrne, a realtor, and Ferdinand Abell and Joseph Doyle, who both operated gambling establishments. Byrne hated Chris von der Ahe and had long wanted to be part of the National League. Like Aaron Stern, Byrne believed his Sunday home dates in Queens County were threatened by Sabbatarians. Although Abell and Doyle hardly represented the kind of respectability the League wanted to project, the addition of Brooklyn gave the League a huge new market and set up a natural intra-league rivalry between the two most recent World's Championship Series clubs.

As if the loss of Cincinnati and Brooklyn to the League wasn't bad enough, the owners of franchises in Baltimore (a charter member of the Association) and Kansas City (which had only joined the Association in 1889) decided they could do better in the minor leagues. Kansas City joined the Western Association (successor to the Northwestern League); Baltimore, the Atlantic Association. Left with only St. Louis, Louisville, Columbus, and Philadelphia, the Association's club owners were even willing to consider an overture to the inchoate Players' League. On December 6, 1889, they met in the Columbus office of Allan W. Thurman, the Association's attorney, to discuss a possible amalgamation with the new organization. When word of that reached the Brotherhood's leadership, the response was a flat "no." Tim Keefe said, "All the talk of consolidating the two organizations is being done by the American Association not the Brotherhood."[20] Thus rebuffed, the Association had to take in Rochester and Syracuse, re-admit Toledo, and grant a franchise to a new group of investors in Brooklyn. Having lost much of its market, the Association was ill-prepared for its ongoing contention with the National League and now with the insurgent Players' League.

Of course the baseball kranks of that time, like "fans" a century later, were interested far less in the off-the-field strife between owners and players and squabbles among the owners than they were in the game on the field. For people who paid to watch baseball and otherwise followed the fortunes or misfortunes of their favorite teams, it was the *game* aspect of the National Game that really mattered, not what Charles Byrne said to Chris von der Ahe or John Ward said to Al Spalding.

By 1889 the baseball the kranks watched had changed significantly over the past decade. On balance, baseball had become a more attractive spectator sport—something much closer to what later generations would be watching. The annual meeting of the joint League-Association rules committee produced almost annual changes in both playing and scoring rules. In 1881, for example, the front line of the 6-feet-by-6-feet pitcher's box was set back from 45 to 50 feet, although pitchers could still move around inside the box and also take a hop step in delivering the ball (akin to the delivery of a cricket bowler). Two years later, balls caught on one bounce in foul territory would no longer be called outs. (That prompted first and third basemen to move away from their bases and out into the infield, where they could cover more ground.) Up to 1884, pitchers had been required to throw with an underhand or three-quarter-underhand motion; that off-season all restrictions were removed, which would bring the advent of the overhand "speed pitcher."

In the 1886–87 off-season the joint rules committee mandated an exceptional number of changes. The dimensions of the pitcher's box were altered to 4-feet-by-5 ½ feet. A rubber home plate (still four-sided and pointed) would replace the stone plate previously used. Which team would bat first had always been determined by coin toss; henceforth the home team had the choice. (Unlike the later assumption that the home team had the advantage by batting last, the home-team captain would often opt for first at bats, when the ball, which got smeared and softened as it remained in play, was still clean and hard.) The batter could no longer call for the pitch location—high ball or low ball—which meant that the umpire, previously positioned off to one side of home plate, would now move behind the catcher. Amid general concern about low batting averages, the rules-makers gave the batter four strikes rather than three, required five pitches outside the strike zone (defined as knees to shoulders) for a base on balls, and scored a base on balls as a base hit. Predictably, averages soared in 1887, by eighteen points in the League, thirty in the Association. Browns outfielder James "Tip" O'Neill, one of the game's top hitters in any season, averaged .492, an all-time high.

That was obviously too much offense, so for 1888 the rules-makers did away with the base-on-balls hit and returned to three strikes; the next year they finally stopped fiddling with balls-strikes combinations and settled on three strikes, four balls. They also provided that one player could be substituted for at any time during the game; previously a substitution could happen only in case of an injury, and then only with the consent of the opposing captain. And while the flat-surface pitcher's box was retained, henceforth the pitcher would have to deliver the ball with his back foot on the back line of the box. So he would actually be throwing from 55 and ½ feet.

Among the various new scoring rules adopted for 1889 were that errors would no longer be charged to catchers for passed balls or to pitchers for bases on balls, wild pitches, hit batters, and balks. One of the oddest scoring rules then in place credited a base runner with a stolen base not only when he reached second or third base ahead of the catcher's throw, but also when he advanced from first to third base or scored from second base on another player's base hit, or scored on a fly ball. (The extra-base stolen-base rule lasted until 1898.)

Also tending to make the game more attractive was better fielding. From 1883 to 1889, fielding averages improved by thirty-two points in the National League, twenty-two points in the Association. By the standards of a century or even a half-century later, teams still made a staggering number of errors. During the 1889 regular season, the two leagues combined for 7,460 miscues—an average of 466 per team. Much of the reason had to do with the condition of playing fields. Many infields were skinned, and even if they had grass, the infields of that time didn't have the big elliptical dirt area from first base around to third base that became standard on later diamonds. Instead, if one is to judge from contemporary illustrations, the dirt base lines were about two feet wide, so that infielders would usually have to field balls on the grass behind the base lines. Outfields might have at least patchy grass, but the grass was cut only occasionally using horse-drawn rigs. Not even the Spalding company had thought to produce canvas tarpaulins to cover areas of the playing field when it rained; infielders and outfielders often had to play in ankle-deep mud with a ball that was soaked and heavy after a couple of innings.

But fielding had improved, in large part because of the use of equipment unavailable until the mid- and late 1880s. John Ward's book contained several illustrations of fielding technique, with the catchers wearing fingerless gloves on each hand and infielders and outfielders catching balls bare-handed. (The accepted technique for fielding ground balls was to put one's feet together!) By 1889, though, catchers wore face masks and lightly padded canvas chest-crotch pads (but as yet no shin guards); most of them were also using big padded mitts, the design of which changed little for the next sixty years. With the big mitt, noted a contemporary observer, "came the power to hold the swiftest balls, and with the renewed confidence in having good support behind the bat, came an improvement in pitching."[21]

More fielders—sixty-one, according to an early 1890 advertisement in the weekly *Sporting News*—were using a glove patented by Arthur Irwin, an infielder for five different National League clubs over thirteen years. The Irwin glove was just that—an essentially flat, five-fingered object with some padding in the heel and thumb. First basemen might use the Irwin glove, although eventually most of them went to a version of a rounded glove invented by Harry Decker, who played various positions in four undistinguished seasons in the majors. As primitive as such assets would seem later, they helped considerably for fielders who were willing to use them.

Not all were. Pitchers worked bare-handed for at least another decade, "believing," as Cap Anson explained it, "that it would be impossible for them to caress and handle the ball rightly if they wore a glove."[22] As for other players, some simply considered wearing a glove unmanly; others believed they could field balls quicker bare-handedly. Tommy Tucker, one of the game's earliest switch hitters, led the Association in batting in 1889 and played first base for thirteen years in the majors, retiring in 1898 without ever having worn a glove. Fred Pfeffer, regarded as one of the finest players of his day, resisted using a glove almost to the end of his sixteen-year career. Pfeffer long held the record for most career assists by second basemen (and no doubt will keep the unenviable record of 980 career errors for all players).

In 1890 John "Bid" McPhee, who spent his entire eighteen-year career with Cincinnati, explained why he played without a glove: "I have never seen the necessity of wearing one; I cannot hold a thrown ball if there is anything in my hands. . . . It is all wrong to suppose that your hands will get battered out of shape if you don't use them [gloves]. True, hot-hit balls do sting a little at the beginning of the season, but after you get used to it there is no trouble on that score."[23] Six years later, McPhee began the season with an injured finger and finally donned a fielder's glove. It obviously helped; that season he recorded a fielding percentage of .978, which for twenty-nine years remained the best mark for second basemen.

What can be said of the players themselves—backgrounds, ethnicity, general circumstances? First off, in the National League and American Association, they were all white men. As of 1889, a few African Americans were still scattered through the minor leagues, although by the end of the century they would all be gone from organized professional baseball. It was a period of intense racial feeling nationwide. All of the former slave states and much of the rest of the country enacted segregation laws and ordinances.

Across the American South, black voters were disenfranchised by a variety of legal and extra-legal means. And besides being segregated in everything from schools and hospitals to public toilets and cemeteries and denied voting rights, black people—especially in the southern states, where the great majority of them still lived—were frequently victims of lynchings and other forms of white-on-black violence.

The National League and the National Association before it had always been lily white. In 1884, Moses Fleetwood "Fleet" Walker caught about half of Toledo's games in the American Association, and his younger brother Welday Walker played the outfield in a few games. Toledo's kranks seemed to have accepted having the two African Americans on the local club, but Tony "Count" Mullane (so-called because of his darkly handsome looks and high-fashion attire), Toledo's best pitcher, didn't conceal his dislike for working with Fleet Walker. In later years Mullane acknowledged that Walker was the best catcher he had pitched to, "but I disliked a Negro and whenever I had to pitch to him I used to pitch anything I wanted without looking at his signals."[24]

Toledo was gone from the Association after 1884; thereafter Fleet Walker played in various minor leagues. In 1887 he was in the International League with Newark, where he and George Stovey, an outstanding left-hander, formed an all-black battery. Five other African Americans also played in the International League that year. But when the Chicago White Stockings stopped over in Newark for a midseason exhibition game, Cap Anson refused to put his team on the field if Walker and Stovey played. Newark's manager reluctantly agreed to Anson's demand. At almost the same time, the International League's club owners agreed not to have any more "colored men" on their rosters, and two months later, despite captain Comiskey's imprecations, the St. Louis Browns refused to play an exhibition game at West Farms, New Jersey, against the all-black Cuban Giants.

That Mullane, born in Cork, Ireland; Anson, who had rarely seen a black person growing up in Marshalltown, Iowa; and the Browns, all but two of whom were northern-born, should have such strong racial prejudices simply underlines the fact that white supremacy was the national norm in the late-nineteenth-century United States. Steadily and then totally excluded from organized professional ball, African American players formed their own independent clubs, such as the Cuban Giants, and went their separate way.

If everybody playing in the National League and American Association was white, players nonetheless came from a variety of backgrounds. The majority had been born and raised in the northern states. New England, New York, New Jersey, Pennsylvania, and Ohio provided the biggest complement, although the baseball hotbeds of Chicago and St. Louis produced a number of major leaguers. A few players came from California, which was still a distant, remote land for most Americans. The game was firmly established south of the Mason-Dixon Line and the Ohio River, but as yet only a small number of southern-born players—mostly Kentuckians—had made it to the top level in professional ball.

A few players were college graduates; a somewhat larger number who had attended colleges but hadn't taken degrees were nonetheless classed as "college men." But most ballplayers in the century's last decades lacked much in the way of formal education. In many instances they came from working-class families in which they were expected to quit school after a few years and, by working, contribute to the family's income or, by moving out, reduce the family's expenses. Often they were barely literate, ill-mannered young men who had grown up in rough circumstances—products of an environment in which crime, prostitution, and saloons were commonplace. (In 1889, New York City alone numbered 7,884 saloons.) Their role models were all too often men who worked hard, earned little, drank a lot, and died early.

When the Grand Hotel in Cincinnati announced it would no longer accept ball-players, a local sportswriter could understand why. "There are ball-players on some of the clubs' pay-rolls," he wrote, "who delight in parading their low-flung instincts, and whose table manners would make a Digger Indian move away from a good meal. They are boisterous and vulgar, and when not busy trying to sneak a few drinks unbeknown [*sic*] to the manager, are out in front of the hotel squirting tobacco juice on the pavement, and trying to mash every lady who happens to come within range of their eyes and smiles." The weekly *Sporting News* even took exception to players' slang expressions, such as "new chestnuts" (a reference to first-year men), "out of sight," or "not in it." The Boston baseball writer Jacob C. Morse complained about ballplayers' poor pronunciation and grammar. While John Ward, Charles Comiskey, and Cap Anson, among others, were well-spoken, "To hear some of them talk, one would come to the conclusion that they could neither read nor write."[25] (Which some of them barely could.)

Other players took good care of themselves, spoke in approved fashion, behaved properly in public, and even attended church. Deacon White got his nickname from his abstemious, Sabbath-observing ways. When, after fifteen years in the National League, outfielder Paul Hines found himself with Washington in the Association, he was excused from playing on Sundays. Philadelphia-born Harry Stovey was never comfortable playing Sunday ball during his seven seasons with the hometown Athletics, who had games on the Sabbath not only in the West but also Sunday home games at Gloucester Point, New Jersey.

White, Hines, and Stovey were descended from Americans of the "old-stock"—people who were predominantly Protestants and had migrated to North America from England, Scotland, Wales, and northern Ireland. In fact, an ancestor of Harry Stovey had helped cast the Liberty Bell. Plenty of other ballplayers shared old-stock ancestry, but starting in the late 1870s, Irish Catholics—usually young men from cities and industrial towns—entered professional baseball in remarkable numbers. By the mid-1880s an estimated 40 percent of players in the National League and the American Association were of Irish ancestry. (Harry Duffield Stovey's family name was Stow, but he became "Stovey" because his Methodist mother didn't want the family name associated with a lot of Catholics in baseball.)

Often members of the first generation of American-born Irish Catholics, they found in baseball a way out of the disadvantaged circumstances in which most of their families still lived. By the mid- and late eighties, League and Association rosters were replete with names such as Kelly, Ryan, Duffy, Dwyer, O'Brien, O'Rourke, O'Day, Keefe, Daley, Fogarty, Healy, Farrell, Tiernan, Mullane, Kilroy, Reilly, and Fitzgerald. The 1889 St. Louis Browns were loaded with "sons of Eire": Charles Comiskey at first base, Arlie Latham at third, Tip O'Neill in left field, Charlie Duffie in center field, Tommy McCarthy in right field, and catchers Jack Boyle and John "Jocko" Milligan. Washington, still in the National League in 1889, had a young catcher from East Brookfield, Massachusetts, named Cornelius McGillicuddy, who had taken the *nom de jeu* Connie Mack. Soon baseball-connected people were theorizing that there must be something about the Irish that made them unusually adept at baseball. (Later on, the same kind of theorizing would go on about Italians and still later Latinos.)

Although the Irish were the most numerous, German Americans were also entering professional ball in increasing numbers. Players with names such as Pfeffer, Gruber, Getzein, Faatz, Zimmer, Bierbauer, Weyhing, and Ehret were on League and Association rosters in 1889. Some German Americans anglicized their names. Columbus pitcher

Hank Gastright grew up in Covington, Kentucky, as Henry Charles Gastreich. St. Louis native Charles Koenig won thirty-three games for the 1889 Browns pitching as "Silver" King (so nicknamed because of his light-blond hair).

If the late nineteenth century was a period of intense racial consciousness, it was also an intensely patriotic and imperialistic period. As the United States emerged as the world's foremost industrial power, successive Congresses and presidential administrations looked covetously toward Central America, the Caribbean, and the vast expanses of the Pacific and the markets of Asia. The popular acclaim for baseball as something uniquely and gloriously American was part of a swelling of national pride—pride in a classless game in which men with sufficient ability could rise to the top, regardless of background. (The great exception, of course, being African Americans.)

But in various ways, professional baseball remained deeply troubled. If the game on the field improved in the 1880s, the decade had also been characterized by instability in the structure of the two major leagues and a host of often ephemeral lesser leagues, squabbling among club owners, and a breakdown in player-owner relations, resulting in the creation of a players' union and, ultimately, the advent of the Players' League. The 1890 season would prove to be a strange, bitter, punishing experience for almost everybody.

1. The Association's umpires were required to dress in blue serge suits and blue caps, thus establishing the enduring image of the "men in blue."
2. Hereafter, "League," upper case, will refer to the National League; "league," lower case, will refer to baseball organizations in general.
3. There were no players' dugouts at ballparks until the early twentieth century. Players sat on open benches situated about halfway between the first and third base lines and the grandstand.
4. Although the St. Louis Browns didn't follow the practice, most teams of that era had both a "manager" and a "captain." Managers handled such everyday matters as train schedules, hotel reservations, payrolls, and park maintenance, while captains were players who had charge of the team once a game began. On some teams, though, managers, confined to the bench in street clothes, and captains on the field shared direction of the team.
5. Jon David Cash, *Before They Were Cardinals: Major League Baseball in Nineteenth-Century St. Louis* (Columbia: University of Missouri Press, 2002), 102, 171.
6. The nineteenth-century championship series between the League and Association winners was written "World's Championship Series," with an apostrophe.
7. John Montgomery Ward, *Base-Ball: How to Become a Player, with the Origin, History, and Explanation of the Game* (Philadelphia: Athletic Publishing Company, 1888).
8. David Stevens, *Baseball's Radical for All Seasons: A Biography of John Montgomery Ward* (Lanham, Md.: Scarecrow Press, 1998), 42.

9. David M. Pearson, *Baseball in 1889: Players vs. Owners* (Bowling Green, Ohio: Bowling Green Popular Press, 1993), 3.

10. John M. Ward, "Is the Base Ball Player a Chattel?" *Lippincott's Magazine*, 40 (August 1887), pp. 310–19.

11. *Sporting Life*, March 19, 1890, p. 4. Italics in original.

12. Charles C. Alexander, *John McGraw* (New York: Viking Press, 1988), 99.

13. Ibid., 52.

14. Stevens, *Baseball's Radical for All Seasons*, 85.

15. Harold Kaese, *The Boston Braves, 1871–1953* (New York: Putnam's, 1948, 1954; reprint, Boston: Northeastern University Press, 2004), 53; Marty Appel, *Slide, Kelly, Slide: The Wild Life and Times of Mike "King" Kelly, Baseball's First Superstar* (Lanham, Md.: Scarecrow Press, 1999), 144.

16. Ever since the formation of the National Association, pennants had been decided on a percentage basis; teams finishing the schedule with uneven numbers of games simply had to accept the situation. So in 1889 there was no League rule requiring the Giants to make up the two fewer games they played than Boston. If they had been so required and had lost both games, the teams would have tied for the pennant. The lack of such a makeup requirement when the league's pennant could be affected continued at least through the 1930s. As late as 2000, moreover, the Oakland Athletics won the American League's western division by finishing a half game ahead of Seattle. Nothing was made up.

17. Brooklyn remained an independent city until the adoption of the Greater New York charter in 1898, when it became one of the five boroughs constituting New York City.

18. Mike Roer, *Orator O'Rourke: The Life of a Baseball Radical* (Jefferson, N.C.: McFarland, 2005), 168.

19. By the 1880s, the U.S. government was firmly committed to a "sound" monetary policy, which meant basing the currency on the gold standard. As a consequence, the value of the dollar actually increased over the century's last two decades. Figuring monetary ratios from one period to another is always inexact, but a ratio of 1–20 from the 1880s to the present seems not unreasonable. By that ratio (and by Murnane's estimate), the Triumvirs would have cleared about $6 million.

20. Larry G. Bowman, *Before the World Series: Pride, Profits, and Baseball's First Championships* (DeKalb: Northern Illinois University Press, 2003), 173.

21. *Spalding's Official Base Ball Guide, 1891*, (Chicago: no pub., 1891), p. 129.

22. "Pop" Anson et al., "Interviews with the Old Timers: Commentaries on Past Events in Baseball History," *Baseball Magazine*, 21 (June 1918), p. 227.

23. Ralph C. Moses, "Bid McPhee," *National Pastime*, 14 (1994), p. 50.

24. Jerry Malloy, "Moses Fleetwood Walker," in Robert L. Tiemann and Mark Rucker, eds., *Nineteenth Century Stars* (Cleveland: Society for American Baseball Research, 1989), 131.

25. *Sporting News*, February 15, 1890, p. 1; May 31, 1890, p. 4; August 8, 1891, p. 1.

CHAPTER 2

1890: "Seven Stories with a Mansard Roof"

he Players' League was a unique undertaking that, had it succeeded, would
have changed the course of American baseball history—perhaps permanently. It was at once progressive and reactionary; above all it was visionary.
It was progressive in that it promised a new order in professional baseball, one in which
players would have control over their own professional lives and would no longer be
dominated by a group of "magnates," who cared more for their profits than for their
employees' well-being. Yet it was reactionary in that it sought to return to the supposi-
tions underlying the old National Association: that the players themselves were capable
of organizing, governing, and making a financial success of something as complex as a
professional baseball organization.

By mid-December 1889, John Ward and his Brotherhood associates had ninety-
seven men under Players' League contracts for the coming season. Those signed up
included most of the best players in the National League and American Association,
although several had also signed contracts with National League teams, and a number
of good ones were still unsigned by anybody. The Brotherhood's original squeamishness about players' character and conduct was a thing of the past; the idea now was to
persuade as many quality players as possible to join the new league. (Such squeamishness
hadn't meant much anyhow when it came to such high-lifers as Mike Kelly.)

Adopting the eight-club setup that had become the norm throughout professional
ball, the Brotherhood made the fateful decision to go head-to-head against the National
League in seven of its member cities: New York, Boston, Philadelphia, Pittsburgh,
Cleveland, Chicago, and Brooklyn. The Brotherhood probably should have challenged
the Association in St. Louis, where it might have competed effectively for customers

tired of Chris von der Ahe's shenanigans. Instead the Brotherhood accommodated the interests in Buffalo of Deacon White and Jack Rowe, two of its charter members.

After the National League dropped Detroit in 1888, White and Rowe, mainstays of the 1887 Detroit champions, bought the Buffalo International League franchise and intended to manage and play there, only to be forced by the National League to spend half the 1889 season with Pittsburgh. Now White and Rowe sold the International League team and put their money and their fading talents at the service of the Buffalo Players' League entry, which otherwise was stocked mostly with players from the previous season's last-place Washington National Leaguers. As one might have predicted, Buffalo would have the weakest team in the new league. (The Buffalo minor league club soon moved to Grand Rapids.) As for the Association, for all its problems, at least it would be competing against the Players' League and the National League only in Brooklyn and Philadelphia.

The Brotherhood and the Players' League weren't synonymous. Although many players invested in the league's franchises, they had no offices or playing sites. Ballparks would either have to be built from the ground up or renovated from existing recreational facilities. It was imperative that the players recruit substantial financial backing—from men willing to take a risk on something whose success was by no means guaranteed. But once they brought in the "money men," as the late Ed Koszarek pointed out in his study of the Players' League, "the basic premise of a player's league became history."[1] At that point Brotherhood idealism had to give way to the hard-nosed realities of the baseball business.

With baseball coming off its best year to date, well-to-do investors weren't hard to find. Baseball offered a tempting opportunity to make some money—if not a lot of money, then enough to add to the wealth one had already accumulated by other means. The New York club—which insouciantly appropriated the nickname "Giants"—got financial backing from, among others, Edwin A. McAlpin, a tobacco broker and real-estate developer; Edward M. Talcott, a stockbroker; and Cornelius Van Cott, a state assemblyman. John Ward also had a small investment in the New York club. But Ward also had money in the Brooklyn club, which would compete for ticket buyers with the National League's Bridegrooms and the new Brooklyn Association entry. Ward would be the player-manager of a team bearing the nickname "Ward's Wonders." The major

Brooklyn investors were Wendell Goodwin, a streetcar financier, and prominent local bankers George W. Chauncey and Edward F. Linton.

The Boston "Red Stockings," or simply "Reds," were financed mainly by Charles Prince, a Harvard graduate and wealthy attorney, and Julian B. Hart (not to be confused with Jim Hart). John Addison, who had made his money as a building contractor, was the principal investor in the Chicago "Pirates," although C. A. Weidenfeller and various players also put various sums into the operation. In Cleveland, Albert Johnson (with whom Mike Kelly had painted the town before that fateful October 3, 1889, game) was the sole financier of the team oddly nicknamed "Infants." Al Johnson was the younger brother of Thomas L. Johnson, who had become rich by inventing, patenting, and licensing a pay box for trolleys. A future Democratic congressman and reform mayor of Cleveland, Tom Johnson, with brother Al, had investments in streetcar lines in Indianapolis and Detroit as well as in Cleveland, where they competed with lines operated by Frank DeHaas and Stanley Robison, owners of he Cleveland National League team.

Four local Pittsburgh businessmen—Henry B. Love, John B. Beemer, C. F. Buiner, and M. B. Lemmon—paid for the rebuilding of falling-apart Exposition Park, which would be the home of the Players' League Burghers. The Philadelphia Quakers—competing against the National League's Phillies and the Association's Athletics—were backed by J. M. Van Slice and the Wagner brothers, who were in the wholesale meat business. The Buffalo Bisons were financed by Moses Shire, an attorney; former sheriff Frank Gilbert; a local businessman named Charles B. Fitzgerald; Deacon White; Jack Rowe; and two players who had been with Washington the previous year: catcher Connie Mack and William E. Hoy, a diminutive outfielder, who was a deaf-mute and thus inevitably known as "Dummy."

So the players would have to share governance with the men whose money made their league possible. The Players' League had a sixteen-member central governing board, consisting of a player and a financial backer from each club. As Koszarek noted, "This would invariably result in two cliques when differences arose." The board elected Edwin A. McAlpin president and named Frank H. Brunell, a sports writer for the *Cleveland Plain Dealer* and a good friend of Al Johnson, as the league's secretary-treasurer. Brunell, in Koszarek's characterization, was "this bespectacled man of stooped shoulders, this Casper Milquetoast sort of a fellow."[2] Critical of the way the Players' League was organized, Brunell nevertheless remained its loyal functionary to the end.

The board also established basic operating procedures. The Brotherhood initially favored the pooling of gate receipts, with players to be paid out of the pool and investors sharing the remainder. That wasn't acceptable to the "capitalists" (as the investors were sneeringly referred to by the National Leaguers), so it was finally agreed that gate receipts would be split 50–50, although the home team could keep receipts from concessions. The financial backers established a $20,000 league insurance fund, and each club was to contribute $2,500 to a postseason prize fund, which was to be distributed in amounts from $7,000 for the pennant winner to nothing for the last-place team. Players were guaranteed salaries at not less than what they had made in 1889. Player sales were prohibited, and a player couldn't be traded without his consent. Although the reserve clause was specifically repudiated, players would still be bound to their clubs by three-year contracts.

The Brotherhood (not the board) was supposed to assign players to different clubs, with the intent of equalizing the talent. Yet at the same time, the new league needed to be strongly represented in New York, Boston, and Chicago. Given the carryover from the 1889 National League rosters in those cities, clearly equalization wasn't followed to the letter. For example, from the 1889 roster, New York listed catcher and captain Buck Ewing; first baseman Roger Connor; second baseman Danny Richardson; outfielders Mike Slattery, George Gore, and Jim O'Rourke; and pitchers Ed "Cannonball" Crane, Hank O'Day, and Tim Keefe. From 1889, Boston's roster included Mike Kelly as its captain; first baseman Dan Brouthers; infielders Billy Nash, Arthur Irwin, Harding "Hardie" Richardson, and Joe Quinn; outfielders Tom Brown and Dick Johnston; and pitchers Charles "Ol' Hoss" Radbourn, Mike "Kid" Madden, and Bill Daley. Chicago had outfielders Hugh Duffy and Jimmy Ryan; infielders Fred Pfeffer, Charlie Bastian, and Ed Williamson; catcher-infielder Charles "Duke" Farrell; and catcher Conrad "Dell" Darling from the 1889 White Stockings, plus captain Charles Comiskey, Tip O'Neill, Arlie Latham, Jack Boyle, and Silver King from the past year's St. Louis Browns. So much for equalization.

Unwisely, as things turned out, the Players' League aped the National League in striving for respectability: no Sunday games, even in Chicago (where Sunday ball was legal), no liquor sales of any kind, a fifty-cent base admission charge. The Players also went along with a rule change the National League and Association had already adopted, permitting two substitutions during a game. But in some ways, the Players broke with existing practices in both the National League and the Association. Players' League balls would be supplied by the New York sporting goods firm of Keefe and Behannon, which Tim Keefe and his partner had established the previous year. Once the season got underway, it became apparent that the Keefe-Behannon balls were livelier than the Spalding and Reach balls the National League and Association used. As a further boost to offensive output, the Brotherhood moved back by a foot and a half the back line of the pitcher's box. With the pitcher still required to keep his rear foot on the back line in delivering the pitch, he would now stand fifty-seven feet from home plate.

Although two umpires had worked World's Championship Series games and occasionally critical games late in the pennant races, one umpire per game had always been the norm throughout professional baseball. By the late 1880s the single umpire had to be a man who could "race about the diamond in order to render [his] decisions" and "get to the appropriate bases as quickly as the players themselves."[3] However dedicated and conscientious (and agile) an umpire might be, he couldn't possibly be in position to see everything he needed to. So players often cut across the infield instead of touching all the bases and used various other tactics to deceive the umpire, whose life became more and more of a trial as the game got faster and the rules more complex.

The Players' League's most progressive innovation was to assign two umpires to work every game. (The umpires would also wear white suits and caps, as opposed to the blue serge that had become standard umpire attire.) Any reasonable person should have recognized that having an umpire in the field as well as behind the plate would make for more capably officiated baseball, but at the time many people viewed the innovation as radical and extravagant. In mid-February, Brunell announced the eight-man staff. As was the case then and for many years to come, umpires were commonly former ballplayers. Of the eight, only two hadn't played in the National League or the Association. The Players' League adopted the existing rule that umpires would first assess a fine on a player, and would eject him only if he persisted in unruly behavior. But if anybody assumed that with the two-umpire system, games would be more orderly and less marred by protracted disputes, he was going to be disappointed. Charles Comiskey wasn't likely to abandon his calculated umpire baiting, nor were his former Browns teammates.

Still another Players' League innovation had to do with the players' uniforms.

Home teams were always to wear white with blue stockings, visiting teams always to wear blue with white stockings. Why that was done isn't clear. Perhaps the idea was to deemphasize franchise affiliation in favor of the common identity of the players within the Brotherhood. The incongruity of a team called the Boston Reds wearing only blue seems to have escaped comment.

There were no bench managers in the Players' League. All the National League and Association teams had player-captains, some of whom, most notably St. Louis's Charles Comiskey and Chicago's Cap Anson, had full charge of their teams. In other instances, managers such as Brooklyn's Bill McGunnigle and Philadelphia's Harry Wright, attired in street clothes, directed their players from the bench. The Players' League consisted of investors and players (who were often, of course, also investors). Thus each team was led by a player-captain, who was held responsible for its success or failure on the playing field.

The rebel league had the support of much of the baseball press and the opposition of much of the rest. Edited by Al Wright and Will Rankin, the weekly *New York Clipper*, which gave as much coverage to the popular theater as to baseball, followed a non-committal policy (and reported only line scores, not box scores, from the Association). *Sporting Life*, published in Philadelphia since 1882 by Francis C. Richter, endorsed the Brotherhood as soon as its existence was known, published contributions from John Ward, and encouraged the formation of the new league. The *Sporting News*, published in St. Louis since 1886 by the brothers Alfred H. and Charles C. Spink, had been a strong supporter of the Association and had treated Chris von der Ahe with indulgence, while often criticizing Al Spalding and the niggardly ways of the National League owners. After some hesitation, it became a warm friend of the Brotherhood and the new league—and thereby lost Spalding's advertisements for his sporting goods.

Although people who reported on baseball enjoyed nothing like the cachet of city-beat reporters and often didn't even get bylines, some had acquired a distinct identity and a faithful readership. Most of them sympathized with the grievances of the players and supported the Players' League. That was especially true of the *Boston Globe*'s Tim Murnane, who had played four seasons in the National Association and three in the National League, and had even been a part-owner, manager, and first baseman for Boston in the ill-fated Union Association. Other prominent writers backing the Players'

League included William D. Sullivan, assistant city editor of the *Globe* and a Harvard graduate, who wrote for *Sporting Life* under the pseudonym "Mugwump"; Jacob C. Morse of the *Boston Herald*; Joseph G. Donnelly of the *Brooklyn Eagle*; Joe Pritchard of the *St. Louis Post-Dispatch*; Joe Murphy of the *Chicago Tribune;* and the New York scribes George Dickinson, William H. Harris, and Joe McDonough.

Although the Players' League managed to recruit most of the available baseball talent, some of the big names stayed with the two older leagues. The New York Players' Leaguers would have been happy to have John B. Day as an investor and Jim Mutrie as manager. "It is my opinion," said Day, "that they are making a grand mistake and that their [financial] supporters will not stand by them." Mutrie vowed to "stand by the old ship, no matter whether it sank or not." In his autobiography, published in 1900, Cap Anson recalled being approached by John Ward about joining the Brotherhood, but he "declined with thanks. . . . The truth of the matter is that I felt bound in honor to stand by my friends, even if I sank with them, and at that time the skies did look remarkably dark." By his "friends," Anson presumably meant Al Spalding as well as Jim Hart, who left Boston after the 1889 season to become Spalding's front-office second in command. Baseball's profitability in 1889, wrote Anson, "excited the cupidity of certain capitalists" who hoped to use the players "as catspaws."[4]

"The truth of the matter" was also that as a stockholder in the Chicago franchise, Anson had a financial stake in staying with the National League. Yet according to Fred Pfeffer, who had played under Anson since 1882, he bought the stock in the summer of 1889, shortly after the Brotherhood delegates secretly voted to form the Players' League. Feeling shut out of what was going on in the Brotherhood, Anson became its avowed enemy. Whether or not one believes Pfeffer's story, Anson despised the Players' League and did whatever he could during 1890 to bring about its downfall.

The failure to bring in Anson proved a definite handicap for the Players' League. Anson was a less-than-sparkling first baseman, but he was the foremost power hitter of his day, rivaled only by fellow first basemen Dan Brouthers and Roger Connor. Blond and blue-eyed, big and powerful at 6' 2" and 225 pounds, Anson would have been a prolific home run hitter in a different time. As it was, when he quit playing at age forty-five after twenty-two years in the National League (1876–97), Anson had amassed 3,056 base hits (the first 3,000-hit player), 1,880 runs batted in, and a career .333 batting average.[5] He was also universally respected as a tough but skilled field leader, having directed the White Stockings to five pennants in the previous decade. Moreover, his close relationship with Al Spalding gave him more clout in league affairs than any player.

If Anson was the biggest star the Players' League missed, Mike Kelly was the biggest it could boast of. Later generations might have a hard time understanding just how big a star Kelly was. "It is not an exaggeration," his chief biographer has written, "to say that he enjoyed a celebrity comparable to Babe Ruth, comparable to his era."[6] He was born in 1857 in Troy, New York, and lived in the off-season in New Jersey with his wife. As was typical of Irish American ballplayers, Kelly came from a working-class background, was poorly educated, and grew up in an environment where the neighborhood saloon rivaled and commonly out-rivaled the Catholic Church. To his peers he was "Kel," but to his legion of admirers he was "the Only Kelly," "King of the Diamond," or simply "the King." Strikingly handsome, with black hair and mustache, Kelly was a well-built 5' 10 ½" and 185 pounds. An immaculate dresser, he affected diamonds, top hats, and fancy walking canes, and hobnobbed with the theatrical set. He made several off-season stage appearances, including a performance in the 1888 production of *The Rag Baby*, by the prolific comic playwright Charles H. Hoyt. Kelly was also a good friend of John L. Sullivan.

Although his irresponsible behavior had continually nettled Cap Anson at Chicago and then John Morrill and Jim Hart, who tried to manage him at Boston, Kelly was a very good player who possessed plenty of what would later be called "color" and still later "charisma." Women came to ballparks just to watch Kelly, and he even inspired a musical composition based on a poem entitled "Slide, Kelly, Slide." For old-stock Americans, Kelly fit the prevailing stereotype of an Irishman—gregarious, boastful, a gambler, generous to the point of profligacy, and frequently drunk, in Kelly's case, both off and on the ball field. When Kelly complained to a young Boston reporter who had written that he drank too much champagne to be able to play good ball, the reporter asked, "But, Mr. Kelly, you do drink, do you not?" "Well, yes," replied the King. "I can't eat all the time, you know." As the author of an anonymous biographical sketch in the *Sporting News* put it, "In private life Kelly is his worst enemy, as he has a whole souled, garrulous nature that has a tendency to keep him poor."[7]

Even in a period when rosters numbered only fourteen or fifteen, and players were expected to be capable of playing different positions, Kelly was extraordinarily versatile.

Nominally a catcher, he also played everywhere else on the ball field, including pitcher, at least adequately. Kelly may have had little formal education, but he possessed an abundance of baseball intelligence. A daring base runner, he was quick to see and seize upon whatever advantage the opposition gave him. At the age of ninety-two, Arlie Latham named Buck Ewing as the best player he ever saw, but called Kelly the most brilliant. And when an aging Hugh Duffy was asked about Kelly, he reminisced, "If you had ever seen him, you would have no trouble remembering him. Kelly was in a class by himself. There has never been anyone like him since he passed away."[8]

The Players' League's quarrel was mainly with the National League, which is where Ward and the other Brotherhood leaders concentrated their efforts. They did, though, enlist a total of twenty-six players from the Association, including several of its top performers. Mark Baldwin, whose 1889 record with a poor Columbus team was 27–34, joined the Chicago Players to form a splendid box tandem with Silver King. Rotund Dave Orr, a heavy-hitting outfielder, had been Baldwin's Columbus teammate; the 250-pounder became one of Ward's Wonders. Left-hander Matt Kilroy, a twenty-nine-game winner for Baltimore in 1889, signed with the Boston Players. From the Athletics came Louis Bierbauer, a highly regarded second baseman, who joined the Pittsburgh Burghers, and Lafayette Napoleon "Lave" Cross, then a catcher and later a third baseman, who would be with the Philadelphia Quakers. The Athletics' biggest loss, though, was Harry Stovey, probably the Association's finest player.

A solid six-footer who had originally been with the National League's Worcester club, Stovey had starred for the Athletics since 1883. He led the Association in home runs four times and triples twice, but his specialty was base stealing. Credited with inventing the feet-first, pop-up slide as well as sliding pads, Stovey had topped the Association from 1886 to 1889 with an accumulative 510 steals (under the scoring rule then in place). Now Stovey joined Matt Kilroy on Mike Kelly's talent-laden Boston Reds.

If the term "pure hitter" had been around in that day, it would have been applied to Louis "Pete" Browning, a Louisville native who left that river city's sorry club to play for the Pittsburgh Burghers (as did pitcher John Ewing, who joined older brother Buck on the New York Players). Standing 6' 2" and weighing about two hundred pounds, Browning was an outfielder; but like young Ted Williams a half century later, he had little interest in outfield play. Like Williams, Browning lived to hit. And hit he did, winning a batting title when he was twenty years old in the Association's first season, winning another in 1885, and recording a majestic .471 in 1887, the year of generally overwrought offense.

Browning was also a genuine eccentric—what a later generation of ballplayers would call a "flake." He maintained a stock of about two hundred 48-ounce, 37" bats made by J. F. Hillerich and Son, a Louisville wood shop (which later, as the firm of Hillerich and Bradsby, produced custom-made "Louisville Sluggers"). Browning thought a particular bat had only so many hits in it; when he decided it had reached its limit, he discarded it. He also believed that staring directly into the sun improved his eyes (his "lamps," as he called them), and he thought smoking cigarettes also helped his vision.

But in various ways, Browning was also an unfortunate figure. A grade-school drop-out, he was virtually illiterate (although he knew enough arithmetic to keep track of his batting average, which he wrote on his shirt cuffs). He also suffered from acute mastoiditis, which made him almost deaf and kept him in chronic pain. Long before antibiotics, he dulled his misery with drink—lots of it, especially good Kentucky bourbon. As with Mike Kelly, it was sometimes questionable whether he would show up for that afternoon's game.

In the winter of 1889–90, the otherwise mild-mannered Nick Young (Abraham Mills's successor as National League president) and the league's club owners launched an all-out campaign to discredit the Players' League and retain or win back as many players as possible. The League formed a "War Committee" consisting of Al Spalding, John B. Day, and Colonel John I. Rogers, co-owner of the Philadelphia Phillies. "We'll fight these ingrates with everything we have," vowed Rogers. "And it won't be long before we have our jumpers crawling home."[9]

In their assault on the insurgent league, the owners had the support of a number of sportswriters. O. P. Caylor moved from the *Cincinnati Commercial-Gazette* to write for the *New York Herald* and edit the Spalding-financed *Sporting Times*. Brotherhood partisans in the press viewed Caylor with utter contempt. The *Sporting News* referred to the emaciated journalist as the "Cadaver," while Joe McDonough opined, "After careful study of Caylor, I am forced to the conclusion that he has not a redeeming quality."[10] Other pro-National Leaguers included Ren Mulford of the *Cincinnati Enquirer*; John B. Foster of the *Cleveland Leader*, Harry Palmer of the *Chicago Herald*, and, most importantly, Henry Chadwick.

Born in 1824 in England, Chadwick spent his entire American life in Brooklyn.

Venerated as the game's seer, he was being called "the father of base ball" long before his death in 1908. Besides covering the game for various New York and Brooklyn dailies, he authored the first hardcover baseball book and generally did everything he could to promote baseball as a healthy, manly activity. His most important achievement was the invention of the box score, which became the essential element for amassing baseball's statistical base and thus for evaluating player performance. (In 1891 Chadwick also tried to get runs-batted-in added to other statistical categories but got nowhere. It would be 1921 before that statistic—subsequently considered vital to measuring offensive output—came into favor.)

In 1881 Chadwick took over the annual *Spalding's Official Base Ball Guide*, which he edited until he died. Like Cap Anson, Chadwick was beholden to Al Spalding, and he proved a bitter foe of the Brotherhood and the Players' League. In the 1890 *Guide*, he included figures on the salary history of various National League players from 1881 to 1889 (presumably as supplied by Spalding). Mike Kelly's salary, for example, had grown from $1,300 to $4,000; Dan Brouthers's, from $850 to $4,000; Fred Pfeffer's, from $750 to $3,000; Buck Ewing's, from $1,000 to $5,000; John Ward's, from $1,700 to $4,250; Tim Keefe's, from $1,500 to $4,500; Roger Connor's, from $900 to $3,500. According to Chadwick, under the reserve clause, only Charles Radbourn's pay had been reduced—by $250 from the $4,500 he was paid by Boston in 1888—and each time a player had been sold, his salary had gone up. "All of the players—or nearly all—are now among the Players' League Clubs," grumbled Chadwick, "and every one is not only guilty of ingratitude toward his club, but has deliberately broken his written contract with his club."[11] Of course that last charge wasn't generally true; at Ward's urging, most Brotherhood members had refrained from signing 1890 contracts with League and Association clubs.

Chadwick also had harsh words for "the class of young base ball journalists—new to base ball matters as they existed over a decade ago—who have during the period of the inauguration of the League players' strike been so free in censorious comments on certain features of past League legislation in governing the professional fraternity."[12] So for Chadwick the formation of the Players' League amounted to a "players' strike," and, by implication, one had to have covered baseball affairs in the 1870s to write knowledgeably about the current situation.

Thirty-eight-year-old Tim Murnane—whom Chadwick may have considered a "young base ball journalist"—had no patience with Chadwick's fulminations. "For a newspaper man, who claims to be fair," wrote Murnane, "he is about as far from the mark as I know. The older he gets the worse he gets." "As an intelligent man," adds his biographer, "Chadwick must have certainly understood the players' position, but he never seemed to understand or, at least to articulate, the players' side in the press, choosing instead to appeal to emotion rather than logic."[13]

As the members of the baseball press took sides, the National League's War Committee devised a war plan. Besides upping the visitors' share of the fifty-cent base admission charge from one fourth to one half in an effort to shore up the League's weaker franchises, the war plan basically came down to seeking injunctions against particular players who had signed with the Players' League and throwing money at others who were wavering. The first part of the campaign was a total failure. In each suit filed by National League clubs—most notably John B. Day's against John Ward and Buck Ewing and John I. Rogers's against infielder Bill Hallman—the courts ruled against the owners, whose attorneys based their cases on the reserve clause. Judges in New York and Pennsylvania decided that the standard player's contract lacked mutuality, in that it bound a player to his employer as long as he was wanted, whereas the player could be released with only ten days' notice. "If an injunction will not apply to them," Al Spalding had proclaimed the previous fall, "we will expel all players who enter the conspiracy."[14] As events would show, that was pure bravado.

Early in February, at Nick Engel's Home Plate Saloon on West Twenty-seventh Street in Manhattan, Mike Kelly, Tim Keefe, George Gore, and various Brotherhood sympathizers drank champagne to celebrate Ward's legal victory. The party lasted from early afternoon until 3:00 a.m. When Ward, "the Spartacus of the Brotherhood," arrived at 11 p.m., he was loudly cheered.[15] John I. Rogers, who was in town for a National League confab, dropped in at Nick Engel's, but he refused to join in a toast to the Brotherhood raised by the comic actor Edward Everett "Digby" Bell.

While joy abounded in Brotherhood ranks, Rogers and the other club owners were busy trying to keep what players they had left and to win back as many as they could. Some Brotherhood members played it cagey. At Hot Springs, Arkansas—a favorite players' spa for "boiling out" a winter's worth of food and drink—George Van Haltren, a young left-handed outfielder-pitcher, would only say, "If I do join the Brotherhood [league], I will not ask anybody about it, but will use my free will and accord in the matter."[16] Eventually Van Haltren decided to leave Anson's White Stockings and sign with John Ward's Brooklyn team.

Charles Comiskey—"Commy" in baseball circles—was one of the most sought-after players. Although he was considered a skilled first baseman, Comiskey was never a big threat at the plate.[17] He batted above .300 only once in a twenty-one-year baseball career—in 1887, the year of freaky batting records. But Comiskey carried a reputation as a field leader on a par with Cap Anson—except that where Spalding had given Anson a free hand at Chicago, Comiskey had been plagued by von der Ahe's continual interference.

At the close of the 1889 season, having yet to commit himself to the Players' League, Comiskey led the runner-up Browns on a long exhibition tour—what would later be called "barnstorming"—that began with a series with Kansas City for the mythical championship of Missouri. Then the Browns put their skills on display against minor leaguers and local semipros in Fort Worth, Dallas, Houston, Shreveport, New Orleans, Houston, El Paso, and Juarez, before crossing the desert to Los Angeles and then traveling up to San Francisco. There, after many days of rain, they met Mike Kelly's Boston runners-up in a soggy series. By the time the Browns started home (after an appearance in Portland), they had traveled 10,000 miles and played thirty-five post-season games in five states, plus Mexico.

In Los Angeles, Comiskey supposedly said, "I will be found with von der Ahe and no one else. I have determined now to stick by him."[18] But later he claimed that when John Clarkson came to his hotel room in San Francisco and offered him $12,000 to stay put, he angrily ordered Clarkson to keep away from him. At any rate, when the Browns' contingent reached St. Louis in mid-January, Comiskey announced he would sign with the Chicago Players' League club.

That he did in Chicago a few days later, at the Players' League central office, room 927 of the Opera House Block, in the presence of Frank Brunell, Fred Pfeffer, and three reporters. His contract specified $5,700 per year over the required three-year term—the same yearly salary von der Ahe had been paying him—although he was also to receive $1,300 from the club's receipts. Comiskey explained that as a native Chicagoan whose family still lived in the city, he had "a kindly liking for the place." He went on to say that if the players didn't "stand true to their colors, and maintain their organization, they will forever be at the mercy of the corporations who have been running the game, who drafted the 'reserve' rule and gave birth to the obnoxious classification list."[19]

Later in Dubuque, Iowa, where he was visiting acquaintances from his minor league days, Comiskey said he had gotten along with von der Ahe up until last year, when von der Ahe's son Eddie began to influence his father on club affairs. Von der Ahe and his son "came close to driving me and all the players crazy. I was satisfied he [Eddie] was the mischief maker."[20] He broke with the von der Ahes, said Comiskey, when they fired George Munson, the Browns' loyal secretary.

John Clarkson was a truly great pitcher. Since coming into the National League in 1883, he had won 219 games, including fifty-three in 1885 and forty-nine the past season. Born in Cambridge, Massachusetts, in 1861, Clarkson was slightly built at 5' 10" and 155 pounds; but he was a workhorse at a time when teams typically carried four pitchers and expected one or two to take the box most of the time. No power pitcher, Clarkson relied on guile, pinpoint control, and a variety of off-speed pitches—"slow balls," as they were then called.

Clarkson was also a complex, moody man who was always hard to figure. Although he had supported the Brotherhood from the start, the Boston Triumvirs co-opted him with a two-year contract for $6,500 per year, whereupon he began working actively to convince others to shun the Players' League. Pfeffer encountered Clarkson during the Boston team's stopover in Chicago on its way to San Francisco. When Pfeffer had seen his old teammate a few months earlier, Clarkson claimed to be still strong for the Players' League. Now "he became an icicle," said Pfeffer. "It chilled me through to hear him talk and I walked away from him." Clarkson might explain that he had gone against the Brotherhood for "purely business reasons," but for the Brotherhood leadership, Clarkson had become an arch villain among a growing list of villainous players.[21]

Early in February, Boston Players' League investor Julian B. Hart traveled to the Detroit home of Charlie Bennett, whose reputation as a catcher for Boston rivaled that of New York's Buck Ewing. (Bennett's throws to bases, though, were always overhand, whereas, according to baseball writer and old-time ballplayer Sam Crane, Ewing threw with a sidearm snap motion "that made the balls he threw strike a baseman's hand like a lump of lead.") Earlier Bennett had declared he would sign with the Boston Players, subscribe $1,000 in stock, and "catch some one else besides Clarkson this season. No loyal man can be anywhere else."[22] But when Hart saw Bennett, the catcher gave him the runaround, while his wife flatly opposed his signing with the Players' League. Subsequently, former Detroit manager Bob Leadley arrived to offer a guaranteed $3,500 for the season plus a $600 advance to stay with the Boston National Leaguers. The Bennetts took the deal.

An indignant Julian Hart said he was "positive" the National League had paid Leadley $1,000 for keeping Bennett in the fold and Clarkson a like amount for signing Boston infielder Charles "Pop" Smith and Charlie Ganzel, Bennett's backup. Hart also suggested that in a couple of other cases, National League people had even used "courtesans" to try to convince Brotherhood men to jump back to the League. But Mike Kelly, in an unlikely encounter with Murnane in a Boston hotel reading room, said he was convinced that in nearly every case where Brotherhood members had gone back on the Players' League, "it has been through the influence of the other half."[23]

By the early part of 1890, terms such as "ingrate," "deserter," "traitor," and "turncoat" were flying around in the little world of baseball. Wounds had been opened. Some would heal slowly; others never would. Von der Ahe proclaimed that the men who had left him "can never play on the St. Louis Club again. . . . This applies to Comiskey as well as the others." The florid Browns owner denied he would miss Comiskey, whom he slandered as "a drawback to the team" with "a very ugly disposition [who] could never gain the good will of his men." "Spalding and I do not speak," Fred Pfeffer said. "We look icily at each other." Pfeffer added that he no longer spoke to Anson, either. The Chicago captain had told him he could never return to the National League. "That," said the rugged infielder, "broke my heart." Subsequently Pfeffer sold the five shares he held in the Chicago club for $1,500, with the comment, "I wanted to have nothing more to do with the Spalding outfit."[24]

From Richmond, en route north from spring training in Savannah, the Boston Players' Leaguers, joined by New York's Jim O'Rourke, wired Frank Brunell their opposition to reinstating "a single Judas Iscariot" who had signed with the Players and then gone back to the National League. Such men, read the wire (probably written by "Orator" O'Rourke), were "creatures who are deficient in all the attributes of manhood" and of "malignantly corruptible heart and with nature itself thoroughly putrid."[25] That pretty much covered it.

Another arch villain in Brotherhood eyes was "Pebbly Jack" Glasscock, probably the game's finest shortstop. Glasscock was born in 1859 in Wheeling, in what was then still part of Virginia. He was an excellent hitter, especially for someone who occupied a position valued mainly for fielding ability; in 1889 he batted .352 for Indianapolis. Playing gloveless until 1890, he led National League shortstops in fielding average seven times. In 1940, Gay M. Smith, an old-time journalist, credited Glasscock with being the first shortstop to cover second base on steal attempts, to signal his catcher whether he or the second baseman would cover the base, and to back up second on the catcher's throws. Smith rated him even better than the great Honus Wagner at fielding balls in the "hole" back of third base and getting the ball accurately to first.[26]

Glasscock got his nickname from his supposed habit of picking up pebbles in the area around shortstop, although in an interview when he was eighty-one, he insisted he actually picked up grass blades, which he rubbed on his hands to make them sticky and get a better grip on balls. He must also have had an exceptionally foul mouth. Ella Black, a young Pittsburgh woman Francis Richter hired to write for *Sporting Life*, announced that her club of twenty-four female kranks wouldn't attend the local National League team's games with New York because of Glasscock's language.

Back in 1885, when he was with the National League's St. Louis team, Glasscock had pledged himself to the Brotherhood. Then, following the 1889 season, he signed to play another season for John T. Brush at Indianapolis and reputedly became Brush's spy inside the Brotherhood. "A regular coat of tar and feathers would be very appropriate in his case," huffed the pro-Brotherhood *Sporting News*.[27] But for the 1890 season, Glasscock played not for Brush but for John B. Day in New York.

The National League owners—with Brooklyn and Cincinnati in the fold and after much hemming and hawing—voted to drop Indianapolis and Washington. Initially the National Leaguers drew up an unwieldy schedule for ten teams, then thought better of that. In mid-March, after a session in New York lasting from midnight to 5:00 a.m., they voted to trim back to eight. The League held a mortgage on Washington and simply foreclosed on the franchise. The wily Brush held out until he got his price—$30,000. In turn, he transferred Glasscock and eight other players under his reserve to the New York club, which had been eviscerated by Players' League defections. All but two of the transferees—young Amos Rusie and Jesse Burkett, up from the Atlantic Association—had been Brotherhood members. The rest of the Indianapolis players Brush parceled out to Cleveland, Pittsburgh, Chicago, and Brooklyn.

Tim Murnane predicted that the transferred players "would be losers in a league composed of minor league players." His estimate of what the 1890 National League would be like seemed confirmed when Nick Young wrote to newspapers across the country soliciting players interested in playing in the League. Young received replies from about 150 hopefuls, of whom a few would actually appear on National League rosters at some point during the season. Cap Anson signed three players who had played in 1889 for the semipro Whitings in the Chicago Commercial League. John Ward, back in New York from a trip to Havana, reported watching an exhibition game in Jacksonville between Anson's team and Harry Wright's Philadelphia Phillies. "They played a very nice amateur game," remarked Ward smugly.[28]

Ward vowed never to serve on the same team with Clarkson, Glasscock, or any of the other "deserters"—Brotherhood members who turned their backs on the Players' League. Others were "jumpers" because they signed contracts with Players' League clubs, then went back to their old teams for more money. Frank Brunell exaggerated when he claimed that League and Association owners were offering players salaries double what they termed "ruinous" a year earlier, but in fact they were putting out a lot of money to try to cripple the Players' League.

It worked a good deal of the time, at least in terms of persuading Brotherhood men to stay with the two older leagues. Of several dozen men the *Sporting News* polled by mail in November 1889 who affirmed they had already signed Players' League contracts, ten ended up back in the National League. Besides Charley Bennett, they included Mickey Welch, a founding member of the Brotherhood; outfielder Mike Tiernan, Welch's Giants teammate since 1887; Charles "Chief" Zimmer, Cleveland's ace catcher; and outfielder Walt Wilmot, who later joined Chicago after the Washington team was disbanded.

When the Players' League was formed, Harry Wright announced, "I don't want any players on my team who is [*sic*] not with me heart and soul." Infielder Al Myers, slugging outfielder Sam Thompson, and catcher Jack Clements may not have been with Wright to that degree; but John I. Rogers and Phillies co-owner Al Reach were successful in luring back all three. (Adopting the National League's legal tactics, the Players' League sued the three players for violating contracts; once the season got underway, the Players abandoned the suits.) In at least one case, it was affection for the avuncular Wright that kept a player loyal. William "Kid" Gleason, a diminutive, twenty-three-year-old pitcher (and later infielder), explained why he refused to go with the Players: "Harry Wright gave me my chance two years ago when I was just a fresh kid playing coal towns, and I'm not running out on him now."[29]

Ed Delahanty, another twenty-three-year-old, appeared to be safely back with the Phillies, only to wriggle off the hook. Delahanty had spent the previous two seasons as a part-time shortstop and second baseman. Late in 1889 the native Clevelander signed a contract with the Players' League club in his home town, only to jump back to Philadelphia. He played the infield for the Phillies in exhibition games in Jacksonville with Chicago and Brooklyn. But when Wright and his men stopped over in Charleston, South Carolina, on their way north, a package was waiting for Delahanty from Cleveland Players owner Al Johnson. It contained a contract for $3,500 plus a $1,000 advance. Wright tried to talk Delahanty into staying with the Phillies, but Johnson's lavish enticement to an as-yet ordinary young player finally decided where Delahanty would play in 1890. Bidding Wright goodbye, he hurried to catch the next train out of Charleston— Cleveland-bound.

Through the late winter and into early spring, the wooing of players continued, sometimes almost frantically. Delahanty and a few others were triple jumpers, but the champion jumper of them all was Ed McKean, Cleveland's hard-hitting shortstop in the Association and the League since 1887. McKean first signed again for 1890 with Cleveland and the Robisons, then signed with Al Johnson, then jumped back to Cleveland. Then, in Florida with the Cleveland National Leaguers, he wired Johnson that he wanted to re-sign with the Players' League. Johnson sent him another contract, which he signed, then disregarded it and remained with his old club.

Meanwhile John B. Day was traveling from place to place trying to win back his players. He had futile discussions in Connecticut with Roger Connor and Jim O'Rourke, then went to Elmira, New York, to talk with Danny Richardson. Day and John B. Gordon, a minor stockholder, spent two days with Buck Ewing at his home in Cincinnati. The New York owner offered Ewing a three-year contract at $8,500 per year, which would have been a record salary. Day added if Ewing came back, he could also get Richardson and Connor to return. Ewing replied if Day could get those two plus George Gore and Mike Slattery, then he would return as well. When Ewing— en route from Cincinnati to Shamokin, Pennsylvania, with his new wife to visit her parents—stopped off in Pittsburgh, Al Johnson was on hand to buy him breakfast and assure everybody that Ewing was a loyal Players' Leaguer.

Ewing and Richardson took the same train to New York. When it stopped at Mauch Chunk, Pennsylvania, Edward W. Talcott was on the platform, waiting anxiously to be reassured that the pair were still steadfast in their allegiance to the new league. That still wasn't enough. When Ewing and Richardson arrived in New York, they addressed a statement "To the Base Ball Public" affirming they would play for the city's Players' League club. Ewing also wired Mike Kelly in Boston that Day had left Cincinnati "with a second-class railroad ticket," by which Ewing presumably meant Day had gotten nowhere with his offer.[30]

Yet for all his assurances and reassurances, by meeting with Day and Gordon and publicly disclosing that he could be persuaded to desert the Players' League, Ewing had cast a shadow of doubt on himself. From then on John Ward, Tim Keefe, Dan Brouthers, and other prominent Brotherhood members didn't fully trust him. When Ewing arrived in Cleveland with the New York delegation for a Players' League meeting, he greeted Frank Brunell with, "Well, I scared you fellows pretty badly, didn't I?" It was a lame joke at best, not likely to inspire confidence in the captain of the new-edition New York Giants. Commented the Chicago reporter Harry Palmer, "Buck is distrusted nowhere so much as in his own organization."[31]

By contrast, Mike Kelly said or did nothing that could possibly raise doubt about his loyalty to the Brotherhood and its league. He did, though, call at O. P. Caylor's *Sporting Times* office in New York to pick up a gold badge, his prize for being voted most popular player in a poll Spalding's weekly had conducted the previous season. (Probably the irony was lost on the King.) In Boston the Reds' captain selected uniforms for his team at the Wright and Ditson store, then dropped by the local Players offices to purchase $500 in stock.[32]

By March, the Boston Triumvirs claimed to have spent $55,000 in bonuses alone to keep or get back players. But having given up on Kelly, they gave Spalding and Jim Hart permission to try to get him to return to the National League with Chicago. When Kelly arrived back in New York, first Hart and then Spalding descended on him with lavish offers, all to no avail. "My father and mother," Kelly told reporters, "would never look at me again if I should prove a traitor to the boys."[33] Back in Chicago, Spalding denied ever having talked to him, but obviously the National Leaguers considered "the Only Kelly" to be such a gate attraction that they had to have him back.

If Buck Ewing, a founding member of the Brotherhood and one of the game's top

players, had brought suspicion upon himself, otherwise the Players' League's prospects appeared nothing but promising. At the Cleveland meeting, the Players' League
senate, over Ewing's vehement protest, voted formally to reinstate Ed Delahanty and
infielder Ed Mulvey, who had also re-signed with the Phillies before jumping back to the
Philadelphia Players, as well as first baseman Jake Beckley, who had seesawed between
the Pittsburgh League and Players' clubs. In talking with reporters in Cleveland, Brunell
resorted to architectural imagery to convey his optimism. The new league, he said, was
"Way up. Seven stories with a mansard roof. The people are with us, and we are bound
to win."[34]

Yet the loyal Brotherhood members and the Players' League's financial backers faced
more difficulties and uncertainties than they acknowledged. To be sure, most National
League and Association rosters had been badly depleted. The National League retained
thirty-seven players from 1889, the Association thirty-six. Besides signing twelve who
had been in the International League and the Western Association the previous season,
National League clubs gave contracts to fifty-six from the lower minors and amateur
ranks. The Players' League had eighty-one former National Leaguers, twenty-six from
the Association, nine from the Western Association, and eleven from the lower minors
and amateurs. So the Brotherhood fell short of its goal of attracting and keeping 90 percent of the National League's players and thereby "leaving Spalding's league an empty
shell."[35] In short, the National League, if not the Association, could still field enough
talent to put up a fairly decent brand of baseball.

If the majority of front-rank players were in the Players' League, the two older
leagues held one big advantage. With the exception of the Association's new Brooklyn
outfit, the National League and Association clubs already had playing facilities; the
Players' League had none. Obtaining places where the new league could showcase its
talent was going to be a costly process, one that neither the Brotherhood nor its financiers had thoroughly considered beforehand.

But by mid-April the hastily built playing sites were more-or-less ready. The biggest ballparks were in Boston and New York. Mike Kelly and his men would play at the
new Congress Street Grounds, located near Boston Harbor. A double-decked structure
modeled on the local Beaneaters' South End Grounds, it seated about 16,500. It was
completed on time despite a brief walkout in March by the carpenters union, which
claimed the Brotherhood had gone back on its pledge to contract with union workers in

all the Players' League cities. The New York Players rented property between 157th and 159th Streets in upper Manhattan and would play in front of a double-decked grandstand, wedged up against a boulder formation called Coogan's Bluff. Brotherhood Park, as it was called, seated about 16,000. Buck Ewing personally laid out the configuration of the playing field.

Ward's Wonders would play in the East New York section of Brooklyn near Jamaica Bay; their ballpark would be a challenging commute from where most Brooklynites lived. For their home games, the Philadelphia Quakers would perform at Forepaugh Park, owned by Adam Forepaugh, P. T. Barnum's chief rival in the circus business. Located at York (later Broad) and Dauphin Streets and previously used as a circus arena, the place had daunting outfield dimensions of 345', 500', and 385'. New York's Brotherhood park also had a deep outfield but short left- and right-field foul lines; Boston's Congress Street Grounds measured only 250' down the left-field line.

The Pittsburgh Players entry was based at Exposition Park in Allegheny, a population center north of the Allegheny River that had not yet become part of the city of Pittsburgh. Situated close by the National Leaguers' Recreation Park, Exposition Park had an even bigger outfield than Forepaugh Park but had the drawback of being regularly flooded by river overflows in the spring. In Cleveland, Al Johnson paid for the construction of a brand new facility east of downtown on Willson Avenue (later East Fifty-fifth Street). Chicago's playing site was built on the south side at Thirty-fifth Street and Wentworth Boulevard. Olympic Park, at Masten Street and East Ferry Street, would be the home of the Buffalo Bisons.

Of course all of these ballparks were built of wood. Construction consisted basically of sawing boards and posts and hammering and bolting them together. The parks usually had a section or two for the fifty-cent base-admission customers—open seating on "bleaching boards" (thus the later term "bleachers"). For twenty-five cents more, one could sit in the grandstand, which was usually covered and would have a section of "opera chairs" with backs and arms. The Players' League's parks had toilets but might or might not have plumbing.

The siting of Brotherhood Park in New York created the most bizarre circumstance of its kind in major league baseball history. Following the 1888 season, the city of New York announced plans to put a street through the Giants' ballpark at 112th Street, where occasional polo matches had been held—thus the name Polo Grounds. John B. Day first moved his ball club to the former Metropolitans' grounds on Staten Island; then in July the Giants occupied a new playing site called Manhattan Field (sometimes also called the new Polo Grounds), between 155th Street and 157th Street. So when Brotherhood Park was built under Coogan's Bluff, the two ballparks almost abutted each other, separated only by the Players' League's wooden fence and a canvas fence stretched around the top of a steep dirt embankment ringing Manhattan Field's outfield.

Meanwhile the Association's Brooklyn club—which the local press dubbed "Gladiators"—found playing accommodations at Wallace's Ridgewood Park, located in a scenic area near the village of Ridgewood in rural Queens County, about five miles east of the Brooklyn city limits. So the Brooklyn Association team's home site would be even farther out on Long Island than the Players' League's Eastern Park. (In their Association years, the Bridegrooms had played Sunday games at Ridgewood Park, a practice that, as National Leaguers, Charles Byrne and his co-owners had to give up.) Each of the other Association clubs was supposed to contribute a player to the Gladiators, but they ended up with only five, of whom four were donated by the new Rochester club. Otherwise the Gladiators consisted of over-the-hill veterans, who would be managed from the bench by Jimmy Kennedy, a former semipro player who was only twenty-two.

All three leagues scheduled 140-game seasons, although because of the rain outs and missed train connections common in that period, none of the twenty-four teams starting the season would play all 140. The Association went ahead as usual, putting together its schedule in late winter; the Players' League had its schedule fixed by late March. But the National League, having scrapped Indianapolis and Washington and its original ten-club schedule, waited until the Players' League schedule was set, then drew up a new schedule that deliberately conflicted with a big majority of Players' dates. National and Players' league teams were scheduled to play on the same day sixty-three times in New York, fifty-eight in Brooklyn, sixty in Boston, fifty in Philadelphia, and fifty-eight each in Chicago, Cleveland, and Pittsburgh. Al Spalding and associates intended to do anything they could to keep people away from Players' League parks, even if that also meant keeping as many or more away from their own parks.

George Munson, whom Chris von der Ahe had fired, lobbied hard for a Players' League club in St. Louis but couldn't change the Brotherhood's commitment to Deacon White and Jack Rowe in Buffalo. But with financial help from Al Johnson, Munson was able to organize a preseason baseball extravaganza in St. Louis, with the intent both to upstage von der Ahe and to demonstrate St. Louis's readiness to join the Players' League, presumably in 1891. A physical structure Munson named "Brotherhood Park" was built in two weeks, at Broadway and Russell Avenue on the city's west side. There a series of preseason games would be played between the Cleveland Infants and Chicago Pirates, both captained by their first basemen: Henry Larkin for Cleveland, Charles Comiskey for Chicago. Munson's idea was that the "homecoming" of former Browns Comiskey, O'Neill, King, Latham, and Boyle would excite the city and make for big crowds.

Which is more or less what happened, even if the weather didn't cooperate. On the evening of Saturday, March 29, 1890, the train carrying the two teams was greeted by a throng of local dignitaries and kranks at Union Station. Arlie Latham, half-ballplayer, half-clown, alighted to do a jig and joke with his admirers. Preceded by the Emerald Fife and Drum Corps and the Walsh Zouaves, and with the former Browns riding in a tally-ho and the rest of the players in open carriages, the procession went to the Lindell Hotel.[36]

Then came a snowstorm on Sunday, followed by a week of intermittent snow and rain, during which the Pirates and Infants lolled around the Lindell in the daytime and were entertained with lavish dinners and theater evenings. The two teams finally got to play on Saturday, April 5: an 8–7 Cleveland win (with the peripatetic Ed Delahanty at shortstop). Some 6,000 people, paying twenty-five cents apiece, filled the seats and the roped-off carriage park in center field, where, as was common in ballparks of that period, well-to-do customers could watch the action in style. Comiskey's wife, his little son Louis, and his sixty-five-year-old father came down from Chicago for the game. Cleveland won again on Sunday, in a game that was played despite Frank Brunell's telegram to the two teams reminding them that Sunday ball was against Players' League rules. Some 10,000 people stormed the place, climbing over fences and swarming the grounds. As if Munson had scripted it, that same afternoon at Sportsman's Park, von der Ahe's patched-together Browns lost 19–18 to Omaha of the Western Association before eighty people. Afterward a furious von der Ahe headed toward the Browns' dressing room, only to be cut off and calmed down by captain Tommy McCarthy.

Comiskey's Chicago team remained in St. Louis for nearly two weeks, finishing its series with Cleveland and then playing another exhibition set with the Pittsburgh

Burghers. While the Players' Leaguers were in town, Anson's "Colts"—as his team of mostly youngsters was being called—arrived for exhibition games with the Browns. The Colts also stayed at the Lindell; when Anson registered himself, his wife, and his players, he wrote in the registry book with underlined emphasis, "The Chicago Ball Club."[37] With the city's baseball following still agog over their old Browns favorites, the games between Anson's club and the new Browns aroused little interest.

Meanwhile, the Boston and Brooklyn Players' Leaguers played each other in Worcester and other towns around Boston before moving into the state capital on Thursday, April 3. A procession of tally-ho's and carriages filled with local dignitaries and well-to-do kranks went from the Tremont House to the Huntington Avenue station to greet the players' train. That afternoon an overflow crowd, which Boston Reds officials gave out as 23,900, filled the seats and stood everywhere inside the Congress Street Grounds. In pregame festivities, 150 *Boston Globe* printers marched onto the field to present bat-shaped flower arrangements to captains Mike Kelly and John Ward. General Arthur "Hi! Hi!" Dixwell (whose nickname derived from his high-pitched yell) led the crowd in cheers for the Brotherhood. A wealthy man who handed out cigars for exceptional feats on the ball field, Dixwell, like most former Beaneaters partisans, had shifted his allegiance to Kelly and his men. "The people had come to a house warming rather than a contest," effused Tim Murnane. Ward looked at the crowd and exclaimed, "It completely knocks me out!"[38]

The goings-on in St. Louis and Boston seemed to foretell success for this new league that sought to revolutionize professional baseball. Yet Al Spalding and his brethren were implacably bent on its destruction. The feeling was equally strong on the Players' League side. Asked whether the Players would consider revamping their schedule to minimize conflicting dates, Buck Ewing was adamant: "Never! I am in favor of making it unpleasant for the League in any way possible as I know they feel that way toward us."[39] What lay ahead was a season full of lies, intrigue, recriminations, and, for people who just loved baseball and wanted to see it prosper, an altogether confusing set of circumstances.

1. Ed Koszarek, *The Players League: History, Clubs, Ballplayers and Statistics* (Jefferson, N.C.: McFarland, 2006), 43.
2. Ibid.
3. Peter Morris, "A Motion as Near Flying as Any Human Being Could Attain," *Base Ball: A Journal of the Early Game*, 2 (Fall 2008), p. 21.

4. Daniel M. Pearson, *Baseball in 1889: Players vs. Owners* (Bowling Green, Ohio: Bowling Green Popular Press, 1993), 184–85; Adrian Anson, *A Ball Player's Career: Being the Personal Reminiscences of Adrian C. Anson, Late Manager of the Chicago Base Ball Club* (Chicago: Era Publishing Co., 1900), 287.

5. Anson's career statistics don't include the five years he played in the National Association.

6. Marty Appel, *Slide, Kelly, Slide: The Wild Life and Times of Mike "King" Kelly, Baseball's First Superstar* (Lanham, Md.: Scarecrow Press, 1999), xi.

7. *Boston Globe*, March 23, 1891, p. 5; *Sporting News*, July 26, 1890, p. 3.

8. Harold Kaese, *The Boston Braves, 1871–1953* (New York: Putnam's, 1948, 1954; reprint, Boston: Northeastern University Press, 2004), 41.

9. Fred Lieb and Stan Baumgartner, *The Philadelphia Phillies* (New York: Putnam's, 1953), 33.

10. *Sporting Life*, July 19, 1890, p. 3.

11. *Spalding's Official Base Ball Guide, 1891* (Chicago: n. p., 1891), 18.

12. Ibid., 24.

13. Frederick Ivor-Campbell, "Henry Chadwick," in Frederick Ivor-Campbell et al., eds., *Baseball's First Stars* (Cleveland: Society for American Baseball Research, 1996), 27; Andrew J. Schiff, *"The Father of Baseball": A Biography of Henry Chadwick* (Jefferson, N.C.: McFarland, 2008), 168.

14. *Sporting News*, November 23, 1889, p. 2.

15. Ibid., February 8, 1890, p. 2.

16. Don Duren, *Boiling Out at the Springs: A History of Major League Baseball Spring Training at Hot Springs, Arkansas* (Dallas: Hodge Publishing Co., 2006), 44.

17. After he retired as a player and became a successful club owner, Comiskey promoted the myth that he invented the practice of playing off the base toward second base. In fact, once the one-bounce out on foul balls was eliminated, all first and third basemen moved off their bases.

18. *Boston Globe*, January 18, 1890, p. 5.

19. *Sporting News*, February 1, 1890, p. 1; *Boston Globe*, February 9, 1890, p. 6.

20. *Boston Globe*, February 9, 1890, p. 4.

21. Ibid., January 5, 1890, p. 3.

22. Sam Crane article in "Fifty Greatest Ball Players in History," *New York Journal*, January 2, 1912, in William "Buck" Ewing File, National Baseball Hall of Fame Library; *Boston Globe*, February 2, 1890, p. 4.

23. Ibid., January 27, 1890, p. 8; February 11, 1890, p. 6.

24. *Sporting News*, February 1, 1890, p. 1; March 1, 1890, p. 1.

25. *Sporting Life*, April 2, 1890, p. 5.

26. William E. Akin, "The King of Shortstops: Jack Glasscock," 1977 article, no i.d.; Gay M. Smith manuscript, no i.d. [1940], both in Jack Glasscock File, National Baseball Hall of Fame Library.

27. *Sporting News*, November 30, 1889, p. 2.

28. *Boston Globe*, February 26, 1890, p. 1. Among those replying to Nick Young's circular was "George T. Stallings, catcher," a young Georgian who appeared in four games in 1890 for the Brooklyn National Leaguers. Later in the decade he managed and caught a few games for Philadelphia, then managed in various places before gaining renown as the manager of the "Miracle" Boston Braves, 1914 National League and World Series winners.

29. Christopher Devine, *Harry Wright: The Father of Professional Base Ball* (Jefferson, N.C.: McFarland, 2003), 153; Dan Lindner, "William 'Kid' Gleason," in Ivor-Campbell et al., *Baseball's First Stars*, 68. In fourteen seasons in the National League, Jack Clements proved a left-hander could be an effective catcher. Kid Gleason, of course, is remembered primarily as the manager of the infamous 1919 Chicago White Sox.

30. *Chicago Tribune*, February 17, 1890, p. 3.

31. Ibid., March 11, 1890, p. 2; *Sporting News*, March 5, 1891, p. 2.

32. A further irony was that the co-owner of the Wright and Ditson sporting goods firm was George Wright, Harry Wright's younger brother and an investor in the Boston Players' League club. George Wright's exploits at shortstop and at bat with the 1869–70 Cincinnati Red Stockings and later in the National Association justify his reputation as baseball's first genuine star player.

33. *Cleveland Plain Dealer*, February 26, 1890, p. 5.

34. *Chicago Tribune*, March 11, 1890, p. 2.

35. Mike Roer, *Orator O'Rourke: The Life of a Baseball Radical* (Jefferson, N.C.: McFarland, 2005), 175.

36. On special occasions, ballplayers might ride in parades in carriages, but as Clay McShane and Joel A. Tarr point out, the expense of actually owning a carriage "limited them to the upper classes. Most people rode carriages only twice in their lives: when they were married and when they were buried" ("Living Machines: The Horse in Ohio Cities," *Timeline*, 27 [January–March 2010], p. 37).

37. *St. Louis Post-Dispatch*, April 10, 1890, p. 4.

38. *Boston Globe*, April 4, 1890, p. 5.

39. Ibid., April 1, 1890, p. 3.

CHAPTER 3

1890: "Trying for Years to Get into a First-class League"

T
wenty-four clubs in three professional leagues, all three claiming to offer major league caliber baseball. Head-to-head competition for ticket buyers between the Players' League and the National League in seven cities, plus three-way competition in Brooklyn and Philadelphia. The American Association would try to operate with clubs in Toledo, Rochester, and Syracuse—basically minor league cities with a combined population of slightly more than three hundred thousand. Baseball followers were understandably bemused by it all; yet at the same time the concentration in the Players' League of the majority of the best players from the National League and a substantial number from the Association presented an intriguing prospect for people in the member cities of the rebel circuit.

The mood of the men who made up the Players' League rosters and who, in some instances, put their savings into their clubs, ranged from optimistic to ebullient. Mike Kelly, captain of the Boston Players' Leaguers, boasted that for the first time he had his own team to run; he wouldn't have to take orders from anybody. Big Dave Orr, who would play for John Ward at Brooklyn, was eager to show what he could do against better competition than he was used to in the Association. "I have been trying for years to get into a first-class league," he told Tim Murnane, "and now I feel as though I was just beginning my base ball career."[1]

The Chicago Players' League team looked especially strong. Joe Murphy of the local *Tribune* hailed it as "unquestionably the leading base ball organization in the known world."[2] The *Sporting News* worried that the Comiskey-led Pirates would dominate the Players' League and kill off customers' interest before the season was half over, as Henry Lucas's St. Louis Maroons had done six years earlier in the Union Association.

If the other seven National League clubs had been depleted, Bill McGunnigle found himself decidedly better off. His Brooklyn Bridegrooms, American Association champions in 1889, remained almost completely intact amid all the player traffic back and forth in the off-season. Charles Byrne and associates, coming off a year of record attendance and profits at Washington Park, had managed to get the Bridegrooms under contract as soon as the season ended, so that while the Players' Leaguers might regard them as turncoats, at least they weren't deserters.

McGunnigle still had pitching mainstays Bill "Adonis" Terry, Tom Lovett, and little Bob Caruthers and, with the exception of catcher, all of last season's regulars. They included William "Darby" O'Brien and Tom Burns, two of the League's best outfielders, and rail-thin Dave Foutz, who had moved to first base after coming from St. Louis, where he had teamed with Caruthers to pitch the Browns to three pennants. (Chris von der Ahe sold Foutz and Caruthers after the 1887 season; with new boxmen the Browns were still able to take a fourth consecutive pennant.)

But the rest of the National League's managers had to rebuild as best they could. Besides losing ten players to the Brotherhood's league, Boston also lost its manager when Jim Hart joined Al Spalding and Cap Anson at Chicago. The Boston Triumvirs hired Frank Selee, a thirty-year-old native of Amherst, New Hampshire. Selee played one game of professional ball while managing in the lower minors, but for years he had directed his players from the bench in Prince Albert coat, cravat, and derby. After managing in the New England and Northwest leagues, he spent two seasons at Omaha in the Western Association, winning a pennant in 1889. A balding, unpretentious man with what was described as "a quiet yet decisive way," Selee put the Triumvirs' money to good use in constructing a respectable team.[3]

Selee got the Triumvirs to pay Kansas City a then-staggering $6,300 for flashy shortstop Herman Long, and to pay Omaha an undisclosed amount for Charles "Kid" Nichols, who started out professionally in 1886 at age seventeen. For Selee in 1889, Nichols won thirty-six games and recorded 357 strikeouts. Many years later, Nichols described his pitching style: "I always threw an overhand ball. Never used a swing in my delivery. Always pitched straight away. Using *same* delivery when men were on base." Nichols added that he "never drank or dissipated in any way during my base ball career or since."[4] The young right-hander had the advantage of pitching to Charlie Bennett and the almost as well-regarded Charlie Ganzel, and sharing box duties with the great John Clarkson—all three of whom were branded as "deserters" by the Brotherhood.

From Baltimore, which had dropped down to the minors, Selee obtained first baseman Tommy Tucker, reigning Association batting champion, and infielder James "Chippy" McGarr. From other National League teams he acquired outfielders Paul Hines and Marty Sullivan and pitcher Charles "Pretzels" Getzein. From Hamilton, Ontario, came outfielder Walter "Steve" Brodie and from Milwaukee Bobby Lowe, a handyman who could play the infield or outfield. It was a team that not only proved capable of contending in the weakened National League of 1890, but was the nucleus for sustained success in the years ahead.

John B. Day and Jim Mutrie, president and manager, respectively, of the team that spawned the Brotherhood five years earlier, were left with little more than remnants of their back-to-back World's Championship Series victors. They had to rely on Jack Glasscock (named captain) and the other players transferred to New York from last season's seventh-place Indianapolis team, including Amos Rusie, a big right-handed pitcher who at age eighteen had won twelve games pitching for his hometown. Although the youngster often had trouble finding the plate, at 6' 1" and more than 200 pounds, he threw probably the fastest pitch anybody had seen up to then. Pitcher Mickey Welch and right fielder Mike Tiernan were holdovers from the 1888–89 champions. At twenty-three, "Silent Mike" (so-called because he rarely spoke and said little when he did) had already spent four seasons on John Day's payroll. A strong left-handed batter and capable fielder, Tiernan was one of the few front-line National Leaguers the Players' League didn't get—perhaps because of Silent Mike's loyalty to Day, or perhaps because he was paid $4,000 to stay.

The 1889 Louisville Association team was one of the worst ever. Managed by four different men, it won 23 times, lost 111, and carried out a one-day strike against its overbearing owner, who was forced out of the league after the season. Although Louisville lost Pete Browning and four others to the Players' League, with a new ownership and a virtually new manager in Jack Chapman, it seemed the team might fare better in what was conceded to be the weakest of the three leagues. The team even had a new nickname; after a tornado swept through the city on March 28, killing close to one hundred people, local sportswriters started referring to the former "Colonels" as the "Cyclones."

Chapman had some pretty good players, notably outfielder William Van Winkle "Chicken" Wolf, the only holdover from Louisville's first Association season; first baseman Harry Taylor; and pitchers Phillip "Red" Ehret, a Louisville native, and Scott Stratton, who grew up in the eastern Kentucky mountains. Chicken Wolf was a good hitter and a decent outfielder, but for some reason the local sporting press consistently took him to task for being overweight, although he was nowhere near as wide-girthed as Dave Orr.

Chris von der Ahe had to scramble to put together a contending team in 1889, and now he was worse off than ever. No Association club was hit as hard by defections to the Players' League. Von der Ahe's sole remaining first-rate regular was center fielder Tommy McCarthy, whom "der boss President" named captain. The Browns did have two quality pitchers: Jack Stivetts, who had come up from the minors late the previous season in time to win eleven games, and Thomas "Toad" Ramsey, a left-hander who had once been Louisville's ace. The 1890 season would be the last in the major leagues for Ramsey, whose heroic drinking matched that of any of his peers.

The Players' League's season openers left little doubt that the league's Keefe-Behannon ball—together with the additional foot-and-a-half pitching distance and, in most cases, the rugged condition of the new playing fields—was going to produce the offensive boost the Brotherhood and the league's financial backers intended, so as "to reduce the number of small score games in answer to a public demand," as league secretary Frank Brunell put it.[5] All three leagues opened on Saturday, April 19, with the New York, Boston, Philadelphia, and Brooklyn teams playing in conflict with each other. The four Players' League openers produced a total of sixty-five runs, including Buffalo's 23–2 drubbing of Cleveland. The sole well-played game was in Boston, where Harry Stovey's home run over the short left-field fence won it for Matt Kilroy, 3–2. George Van Haltren took the loss for John Ward's Brooklyns. In pregame festivities, both teams rode in tally-ho's and barouches to the ballpark, then lined up at second base and marched to the grandstand as a band played "Slide, Kelly, Slide."

(A couple of months later, some of Jim Mutrie's players, using the Keefe-Behannon and Spalding balls, conducted an experiment at Brotherhood Park: "The difference was astounding," reported a New York writer on the scene.[6] The biggest New York batters couldn't hit the National League ball as far as the smallest men hit the Players' League ball. One batter hit the Players' ball one hundred feet farther than he hit his own league's ball. Frank Brunell dismissed talk of a livelier ball in the Players' League, insisting that bigger scores were a consequence of the lengthened pitching distance and poor weather, plus the concentration in the league of such hard hitters as Stovey, O'Neill, Orr, and Browning. Inexplicably, Brunell also mentioned the league's bigger playing fields. Presumably he meant outfielders had to run farther to catch up with long hits.)

The New York Players' home opener with Philadelphia prompted the weekly *New York Clipper* to extol their new playing site, even though carpenters were still banging away on the structure: "A prettier location could not have been secured on Manhattan Island. The high bluff to the west of the grounds and in the rear of the grand stand lends an additional charm." A white banner with a blue border, waving from a tall flag pole in front of the club house in center field, bore the legend, "The Only World's Champions."[7] The Quakers spoiled the day for Buck Ewing's "Giants" by winning 12–11, with the teams combining for seventeen errors and making it rough going for both winning pitcher Charlie Buffinton and loser Tim Keefe.

While Players' League clubs piled up runs, the four National League openers produced only twenty-three scores. On the other side of the wooden and canvas fences separating Brotherhood Park from Manhattan Field, Philadelphia's Kid Gleason pitched a three-hit shutout, besting New York's Rusie, 3–0. In that and the other National League openers, spectators watched many players they had never seen before.

Cap Anson's "Colts" won 3–2 in Cincinnati in that city's first National League game in ten years. Bill Hutchinson, a thirty-year-old Yale University graduate, outpitched Jim Duryea. In Pittsburgh, the Musical Mutual Protective Union, affiliated with the American Federation of Labor, announced it was boycotting the National League Alleghenies because they employed the Great Western Band, affiliated with the Knights of Labor. So few people had attended the Alleghenies' exhibition games that president William Nimick transferred their opening game to Cleveland. Although the Alleghenies won in Cleveland, their season would bring few good days.

After Hutchinson, on his way to a big year, pitched the Colts to a 6–1 win over the Alleghenies in Chicago's home opener, Pittsburgh captain and first baseman Guy Hecker grumbled about the work of umpire Tom Zacharias. While the *Tribune*'s Joe Murphy agreed that "Zacharias has miserable judgment, particularly on balls and strikes," he thought Hecker ought to forget about the umpires and "try to get some ball-playing out of the team he has. His team plays like a crowd of wooden men, seeming to have no ambition at all."[8]

When the Players' League's Pittsburgh entry opened at home with Chicago, captain and center fielder Edward "Ned" Hanlon and his Burghers were escorted to Exposition Park by two Musical Mutual bands. The bands rode in wagons emblazoned with streamers proclaiming "Patronize the Brotherhood Ball Club, The Only Employees of Union Labor and Union Musicians." The Players' League's two-umpire system didn't impress Joe Murphy as any improvement. Murphy described the officiating of Bobby Matthews and Tom Gunning as "simply awful. . . . Even the audience at last entered a vigorous protest against the way the Chicago club was being treated." For all that, Comiskey and his men prevailed, 10–2. But on Monday they lost to the Burghers, 5–2. Irish-born John Tener, a big pitcher who also served as the Pittsburgh club's secretary, watched from the stands until he left in disgust over the umpiring. When Gunning called three balls on Mark Baldwin that were apparent strikes, Arlie Latham yelled "How's that?" and did a triple somersault at third base.[9]

Two umpires or one, it was going to be another trying year for the men in blue (or white). The baseball writers of that day didn't hesitate to criticize the way games were officiated, and they readily printed castigations of umpires by club owners, managers, and players. On the second day of the Association's season, a Sunday in Louisville, umpire Terrence Connell declared a forfeit to the home team when the Browns wouldn't quit raging at him. Connell allowed a Cyclones batter who hit into the overflowed crowd in left field to circle the bases, instead of ruling a ground-rule double. Excoriated in the St. Louis press, Connell quit the Association staff a week into the season. Shortly thereafter, Frank O'Brien's work in a series in St. Louis with Louisville moved a local scribe to comment, "Mr. O'Brien may have been told he was an umpire, but if so he was misinformed."[10]

On April 21, at Boston's Congress Street Grounds, John Ward hit two home runs and Dave Orr hit one in a 10–7 Brooklyn win over Mike Kelly's club. Tim Murnane thought umpires Jim Gaffney and Ross Barnes repeatedly called plays in captain Ward's favor. Murnane was especially hard on Barnes, who had been an outstanding player in the National Association and the early National League. "Well," wrote Murnane, "if you had seen him umpire yesterday's game of ball you'd think he'd never seen a game before." A month later, after the Chicago Players lost 10–2 in New York, Joe Murphy wrote, "All the boys from Comiskey down charge today's defeat upon the unhappy Mr. Barnes."[11] After another month Barnes had endured enough. He was replaced by Jack Sheridan, who came all the way from California to begin a major league career stretching intermittently over twenty-five years. Shortly thereafter Tom Gunning also quit. Al Leach was hired in his stead.

In an April National League game at the South End Grounds, Mickey Welch and John Clarkson were locked in a 2–1 duel in the seventh inning when "Smilin' Mickey" quit smiling and ranted at length at umpire Michael "Sandy" McDermott. McDermott told him to shut up and pitch; when he would do neither, McDermott gave the game to Boston by forfeit. And at the end of a Sunday, May 4, Association game in Toledo, won by Columbus, 11–3, police had to stop local kranks from mobbing umpire Lawrence O'Dea. A few days later, after more complaints about O'Dea's work in the Columbus series in Toledo, league president Zachary Phelps fired the beleaguered umpire. So it would go all season, which would see heavy traffic in umpires, especially in the Association.

John Ward may have enjoyed that big day at bat in Boston, but his personal life had become something of a mess. His marriage to Helen Dauvray had always been a difficult one, strained by separate professional careers and by extended absences. They had quarreled on their European trip during the recent off-season; Ward ended up following her from place to place until they finally made up and sailed home shortly before the season opened. The season was only a couple of weeks old when Helen filed for a legal separation, while Ward was named in a divorce suit brought by George McDermott, a New York City employee and prominent figure in the Tammany Hall political machine. The thirty-five-year-old McDermott charged Ward with having had an adulterous relationship with his wife Jessie, twenty-two, an aspiring actress reputed to be even more beautiful than Helen Dauvray.[12] Ward's estranged wife remained discreet about her marital troubles, but not only the baseball press but general newspaper coverage was rife with speculation and innuendo regarding the troubles of a Gilded Age version of the Beautiful People.

Ward nevertheless managed to keep his mind on his duties as captain of his team and on his own game. But given the distance of Eastern Park from Brooklyn's city center, the Wonders were drawing fewer people than the National League's Bridegrooms. Hardly anybody seemed to be interested in watching the Association team's assortment of no-names, who quickly settled into last place.

The Association—with its Sunday baseball, twenty-five-cent base admission, and liquor sales—had always sought to appeal to working-class kranks more than had the National League, which catered to the "carriage trade," or tried to. Although there is no way of knowing for certain, the Players' League may also have been more attractive to the working class than the National League, especially for Saturday dates. That was the one day when most wage earners could see a ball game—as opposed to well-to-do and professionally affiliated customers and their spouses who could attend weekday games, which typically started at 4:00 or 4:30.

In general, attendance figures reported by Association clubs were taken at face value, but from the beginning the National and Players' leagues shamelessly exaggerated the turnouts at their games. In May, Al Spalding told Harry Palmer, his ally at the *Chicago Herald*, "From this point out it will simply be a case of dog eat dog, and the dog with the bull dog tendencies will live the longest."[13] Thus phony attendance figures—along with conflicting schedules and ongoing efforts to lure Players' Leaguers back to their old clubs—became a key stratagem in the conflict between one league determined to survive and another bent on destroying it.

It was a grim business at the time, but twenty years later Spalding could look back on it all with humor. "All eyes were centered on the question of attendance," he wrote in his history of baseball, published near the end of his life. "Along with other practices peculiar to the Ananias Club, both sides then engaged in that of 'faking' attendance reports."[14] Spalding suspected the round figures being given out by the Players' League and had "inspectors" stationed at the Chicago Players' League grounds to count each person coming through the turnstiles.

As to his own phony figures, Spalding recalled that after a game at his West Side Park that drew a scattering of people, he was talking with his club secretary, a man named Brown, when a reporter asked about the attendance. "Twenty-four eighteen," replied Brown. When the reporter was gone, Spalding asked Brown how he could possibly say that. Brown blithely replied that he counted twenty-four people on one side of the stands, eighteen on the other, adding "If he reports twenty-four *hundred* and eighteen, that's a matter for *his* conscience, not mine." Spalding's verdict: "If either party of this controversy ever furnished to the press one solitary truthful statement as to the progress of the war from his standpoint . . . a monument should be erected to his memory."[15]

Besides falsifying attendance totals, Players' and National League clubs began early to resort to various gimmicks to put more people in the seats. The pro-Brotherhood *New York World* bought up a huge block of tickets from the local Players' League club at twenty-five cents each and printed them as coupons for a May 9 game with Boston. That promotion produced the biggest crowd of the season at Brotherhood Park, a reported 13,213. About a third of the crowd paid the regular fifty-cent charge. Boston won 4–2 behind Addison "Ad" Gumbert and realized its biggest share of visitors' receipts for the season, about $3,000. Meanwhile in Chicago, Spalding started staging "Professional Days" at West Side Park; actors, musicians, and others in designated occupations got in free. Other clubs inaugurated Ladies' Days on particular weekdays, with women allowed in free of charge. Tim Murnane accused John B. Day of simply giving tickets away at locations around Manhattan.

The *New York Times*, neutral in the war between the leagues, insisted on gathering its own attendance figures at the local Players' and Nationals' ballparks. On Saturday, May 10, for example, the *Times* reporter counted 1,042 for Boston's 3–2 win over Jim Mutrie's collection of mostly former Indianapolis players. The following Saturday, 1,327, the biggest turnout since opening day at the National League park, were on hand to see Rusie pitch New York to victory over Cleveland. According to the *Times*, the usual weekday gatherings at Manhattan Field numbered about two hundred. On Monday, May 13, the New York Players beat Boston, 9–5 in front of 1,141; a week later only 528 paid to see Buck Ewing's company outhit Buffalo, 12–11. Although the Bisons had won four of their first five games, they quickly became a hapless crew that attracted small crowds both at home and away. When they left Manhattan and went over to Brooklyn, eighty people showed up for a Tuesday loss to Ward's Wonders.

Things weren't any better in the Association (which the *New York Clipper* treated as little more than a minor-plus league). On April 22 in St. Louis, despite Chris von der Ahe's elaborate pregame doings, only 808 turned out for the Browns' home opener with Toledo. The next afternoon, von der Ahe surveyed the few dozen people on hand and announced that the field was too wet for play, although the *Sporting News* thought it was "dry as a chip."[16]

Consistently drawing in three figures at home with a bad ball club, the Pittsburgh National Leaguers quickly ran into financial trouble. President Nimick had spent heavily to persuade veteran second baseman Fred Dunlap and catcher George "Doggy" Miller (also called "Foghorn" for his booming voice) to break their Players' League contracts.

Carrying a payroll reported to be $42,000, Nimick got permission from the league office to drop the base admission to twenty-five cents and continued to transfer scheduled home games to other league cities. By May the club was behind on its payroll. It was also $3,000 in arrears in rent on Recreation Park, and attorneys for the Denny estate, which owned the property, had secured a landlord's foreclosure warrant. The Central Hotel was suing for a $500 room-and-board bill, while the *Pittsburgh Sunday Globe* was suing for unpaid advertising fees. Nimick resigned in favor of J. Palmer O'Neill, who moved to cut expenses by releasing Dunlap and thereby unloading Dunlap's $3,700 salary. (Dunlap joined the New York Players but quit and went home to Philadelphia after only one game.)

Ella Black, *Sporting Life*'s Pittsburgh correspondent, couldn't resist appraising the looks of the men on both the Pittsburgh Players' League team and the Alleghenies. She named catcher Fred Carroll as the Burghers' most handsome, although first baseman Jake Beckley had rugged good looks. When the Boston Beaneaters' Paul Hines took the field "in a shirt that fit him like a kid glove," she thought "his appearance in that shirt would have brought a blush to the face of many a fair maid."[17]

Black also believed she could give some useful advice to the Alleghenies' ownership, as well as to Burghers captain Hanlon and pitcher-secretary Tener. "But I suppose," she wrote resignedly, "they would laugh and think it all nonsense to talk base ball to a woman. Everyone seems to think that all a woman knows how to do is work around the home, talk dress and fashion." But Ms. Black could also be sarcastic about the misfortunes of the Alleghenies. "Prepare to be shocked," she wrote a few weeks later. "Get your smelling salts and then while the office boy fans your brow, have it broken to you gently, our National League club has won a game."[18]

By mid-June the Alleghenies' record was 9–31. After Chicago's Hutchinson beat them three straight days, including a 16–3 drubbing in the third game, Joe Murphy couldn't contain his contempt: "There is a group of ball tossers moving around the country called the Pittsburgh club which should be called in, as the most careful search fails to uncover any reason why it should be kept alive."[19]

Besides the Alleghenies, various other clubs were in trouble. Cleveland's National Leaguers drew only a little better than Pittsburgh and stayed out of last place only because the Alleghenies were worse. Although Arthur Soden disclosed that the Beaneaters were losing about $100 per day, the Triumvirs were well enough off to ride out their losses.

But the Brooklyn Association team couldn't meet its expenses despite playing Sunday games at Wallace's Ridgewood Park. Columbus manager Al Buckenberger stated flatly that he didn't want to take his team to Brooklyn and that the Association had made a big mistake bringing in that city. Von der Ahe and some of the other Association owners provided a little financial assistance, but it was far from enough. In desperation, Brooklyn club officials arranged with John B. Day for the Gladiators to play weekday games at Manhattan Field when the National Leaguers weren't in town.

That brought in a little rent money for Day, but the plight of his club remained the most critical situation in the National League. If New York went under, then the whole league might follow. Day (whom the *Sporting News* took to calling "John Busted Day") had a mediocre team that in June somehow managed to lose five times in a six-game series in Pittsburgh. Day also carried a sizable payroll, mostly inherited from John T. Brush, whom he still owed $25,000 for Jack Glasscock and the other Indianapolis players. Day inherited Glasscock's $5,000 salary and third baseman Jerry Denny's $4,000, but he also gave Mickey Welch and Mike Tiernan substantial raises not to go with the Players' League. Day's club was simply unable to compete with the star-studded "real champions" who played next door on almost every home date. It didn't help that Jim Mutrie had trouble putting a regular nine on the field. In a 12–8 home loss to Cincinnati at the end of May, only two men were at their usual positions because of injuries and the absence of captain Glasscock, whose sister had died in Wheeling. To the irritation of Day and Mutrie, Glasscock was away from the team for weeks.

In July, Day secretly appealed to the league owners for help, saying he needed $80,000 or he would have to sell out to the Players' League. Al Spalding organized a rescue mission. He and his brother J. Walter purchased $25,000 worth of stock from Day and gave some of it to Anson, who already owned a small portion of the Chicago club. Arthur Soden also took $25,000 in stock, and Al Reach of Philadelphia and Ferdinand A. Abel of Brooklyn bought $6,500 each. John T. Brush's contribution was to cancel the $25,000 Day owed him. Day kept $20,000 in stock and the franchise presidency, but the man who had once owned two New York ball clubs was no longer even the biggest stockholder in one.

Over in the Association, Chris von der Ahe suffered through the smallest crowds at Sportsman's Park since he organized his beloved "Prowns" eight years earlier. He also had to suffer with miscreant players. On May 15 the Browns played in Syracuse. That night Tommy McCarthy and four other St. Louis players, as well as infielder Joe Battin and outfielder Mike Dorgan of the local club, attended a Military Ball put on by the Fifth Separate Militia Company. By the time the ball ended at 5:00 a.m. with a "Razzle Dazzle Quadrille," they were all quite drunk. George Frazer, who both owned and managed the Syracuse club, promptly got rid of his two transgressors; von der Ahe, traveling with the team, called his hungover players to his hotel room, hit McCarthy, pitcher Bill Whitrock, outfielder James "Chief" Roseman, and catcher Billy Earle with fines ranging from $25 to $50, and told first baseman Pat Hartnett he was released. Von der Ahe had already relieved McCarthy as captain; over the rest of the season, three other players plus McCarthy again would attempt to direct the team in the face of von der Ahe's incessant meddling.

For the first half of the season, the Athletics of Philadelphia led the Association, but Athletics manager Bill Sharsig had his own player troubles. About a month after the Military Ball episode in Syracuse, Sharsig publicly charged that Players' League people (whom he didn't name) had taken out outfielder Curt Welch and third baseman Denny Lyons—both known to be heavy imbibers—and gotten them drunk before offering them money to jump to the Brotherhood circuit. Welch showed up for work the next day; when Lyons didn't show up, Sharsig fined him a hefty $100. No denial of the bribe attempt issued from Players' League quarters; the whole thing called into question how much high ethical ground John Ward and his Brotherhood fellows actually occupied.

The Players' League had an abundance of talent, especially on the Boston, New York, and Chicago teams. Brooklyn had fewer star players, but John Ward was having one of his best years and getting strong hitting from Dave Orr and George Van Haltren, who played the outfield when he wasn't pitching. Gus Weyhing, a slightly built right-hander who had won thirty games for the Association's Athletics in 1889, was Ward's ace. For most of the season the Wonders were close to first place and occasionally led the league.

Boston's everyday lineup included the brilliant Stovey and future Hall of Famers Kelly and Brouthers. Left-hander Matt Kilroy, who had long been Baltimore's ace in the Association, had about worn out his arm and rarely went to the box after midseason. To carry the pitching load, Kelly relied on Bill Daley (another left-hander), Ad Gumbert, and the aging, cantankerous "Ol' Hoss" Radbourn. Radbourn (another future Hall of Famer) had one last good year remaining in a right arm that had produced 269 National

League wins, including fifty-nine in 1884, when he pitched Providence to a pennant and World's Championship Series victory over the Association's New York club.[20]

The thirty-six-year-old Radbourn threw with a three-quarter-underhand motion, whereas John Clarkson pitched sidearm, as did Tim Keefe. All three had begun their careers well before the legalization of overhand pitching, and they continued to pitch the way they had learned as youngsters. By contrast, Nichols and Rusie had entered professional ball pitching overhand; their success had much to do with the additional leverage they gained by throwing a ball that traveled downward toward the batter.

The New York Players' Leaguers had a power-packed lineup and several future Hall of Famers, but shaky pitching. The staff of Keefe, Hank O'Day, John Ewing, and Cannonball Crane looked strong, but at thirty-three and having pitched nearly 4,200 innings over the past ten seasons, Keefe was no longer the workhorse he had been. He missed several turns late in the season after he suffered a broken finger on his pitching hand; when he returned, he had lost much of his effectiveness. Although O'Day pitched consistently well, John Ewing and Crane were consistently inconsistent. After two terrible performances by Ewing in Philadelphia and Brooklyn, the *New York Times*'s reporter was unsparing: "Perhaps 'Long' John Ewing thinks he is a pitcher. The Brooklyn Players' League team say he is of no earthly use in the box. Likewise sayeth the Philadelphia Players' team." The same reporter wrote of one of Crane's outings, "Crane was in the box for the home team, and he made a sorry mess of it."[21] It didn't help the team's fortunes that captain Buck Ewing suffered injuries to his side and hand and missed most of the season's first half.

The *Sporting News* had worried that the all-star Chicago Pirates would run away from the rest of the league, but on their first trip east they dropped six-straight games. Over the first ten weeks of the season, Comiskey wasn't able to get his team above third place or much above the .500 mark. In June, Philadelphia briefly occupied second place, despite a bitter falling-out between club president Henry M. Love and captain Jim Fogarty, who accused Love of using abusive language toward Fogarty's players. When Love wouldn't apologize, Fogarty resigned his captaincy; thirteen games into the season, pitcher Charlie Buffinton took over the team. Although Fogarty threatened not to play at all, subsequently he returned to his outfield position.

Relations between most of the Players' Leaguers and those who hadn't joined them—or had initially joined them, then reneged on their contracts—remained strained if not outright hostile. For example, early in June, when the Boston National Leaguers were in New York, John Clarkson and club secretary George Floyd dropped by Nick Engel's Home Plate Saloon (whose proprietor they knew to be a Brotherhood partisan). The New York Players' George Gore refused to speak to them; other customers simply turned their backs.

Yet for all the enmity between loyalists and deserters, feelings toward Harry Wright remained cordial on both sides of the baseball war, despite Wright's harsh words about players who left him for the Players' League. Besides captaining the legendary Cincinnati Red Stockings, Wright had led teams to four pennants at Boston in the National Association, two at Boston in the National League, and another at Providence before coming to Philadelphia in 1884. Batting and infield practice and backing up bases on outfield throws were among various innovations Wright had brought to the emerging game of baseball. Soft-spoken and warmhearted, he was also something of a surrogate father to many of his players. (He was actual father to seven children.)

Wright was fifty-five in 1890, although with his gray beard and courtly ways, he seemed older. Early in the season, he became afflicted with an eye condition—diagnosed in the medicalese of the period as "catarrh of the eyeballs"—that rendered him nearly blind. He was bedridden for a time; when he returned to the ballpark, he wore smoked spectacles and sat in a carriage in the outfield with Phillies owners Al Reach and John Rogers, who gave him a running account of the game. On Wednesday, May 28, the Chicago and Philadelphia Players' Leaguers subordinated their enmity toward the National League to their affection for Wright. An unusually large weekday crowd of nearly 3,000 bought tickets for a game at Forepaugh Park, won by Chicago, 6–5. All receipts went to Wright and his family.

Like everybody else, Tim Murnane greatly respected Harry Wright. But he had little respect for the kind of baseball being played in the National League and none at all for the eastern newspapers supporting the League. By early May he had already seen enough of what the National League was offering and read enough of what pro-League scribes had to say in its behalf. For Murnane, "The struggle of the national league writers to make star ball players of some of the youngsters and old-timers who have no particular merit is at once picturesque and amusing."[22]

The migration of most of the National League's best into the Players' League created roster openings for young players who otherwise would have spent more time in the minor leagues, but often they weren't even ready for the diminished quality of play in 1890. One such was Alfred E. Lawson, a twenty-one-year-old British-born right-hander who had pitched at the bottom of the minors in 1889 at Wellsville, New York (where he was a teammate of a squirty infielder named John McGraw). Lawson worked one game for Frank Selee's Boston team and two for Pittsburgh, gave up 27 hits in 19 innings, walked 14, and ended his short major league career with a 0–3 record.[23]

But the National League did start the season with three youngsters who were future Hall of Famers. Billy Hamilton had spent 1889 with Kansas City in the Association, batting .301 and, under the scoring rules in place, getting credit for 111 stolen bases. When Kansas City dropped out of the Association, Philadelphia owners Reach and Rogers paid $5,000 for the 5' 6" outfielder's contract. A left-handed batter and right-handed thrower, "Sliding Billy" became an immediate star and one of the main reasons the Phillies were able to remain in contention for most of the season.

New York's Amos Rusie threw so hard, wrote Joe Murphy, "that a Gatling gun is not necessary to kill men when the New York pitcher is around."[24] By early May, Rusie had won only two games while losing four, but he had already struck out forty-four batters, more than any other team's entire pitching staff. On Monday, May 12, 1890, before a few hundred people at Manhattan Field, Rusie, not yet twenty, was matched against Boston's twenty-year-old Kid Nichols, who made his major league debut three weeks earlier with a six-hit, 5–2 victory over Brooklyn. A couple of inches shorter and about thirty pounds lighter than Rusie, the boyishly handsome Nichols nonetheless threw pretty hard himself.

What followed was perhaps the most remarkable game of baseball up to that time.

As O. P. Caylor wrote in his detailed account of the game in the *New York Herald*, Rusie "soon demonstrated that the Boston men could not hit the shots from his catapult arm," while Nichols baffled the New Yorkers "with his speed and curves and change of pace."[25] Nichols easily retired the home team, which opted to bat first. In the bottom half of the inning, the Beaneaters almost scored but were thwarted by a spectacular double play. Boston tried a double steal, with Chippy McGarr taking off from first base and Tommy Tucker running from third. Catcher Dick Buckley threw to Jack Glasscock, who tagged out McGarr and in one motion returned the ball to Buckley, who put the tag on Tucker.

Neither team got that close to scoring for another eleven innings. Caylor thought

Boston shortstop Herman Long "played an astonishing game," fielding everything the New Yorkers hit his way and keeping the game scoreless.[26] Next door, the Boston Players defeated New York, 12–2, in an hour and thirty-four minutes. With their game over, a substantial number of people gathered to hang on the fence inside Brotherhood Park and watch what was happening in Manhattan Field.

In the top of the thirteenth inning, Nichols had retired two New York batters when Mike Tiernan came to the plate. Tiernan fouled a ball into the grandstand, where, according to the obligatory practice, a spectator picked it up and threw it back onto the field. As it rolled toward Nichols, umpire Phil Powers opened a box and extracted a new ball. Nichols wanted to pitch with the old ball, but Powers replied that the new ball was "on the field first, and you'll have to use it." "Oh, all right," said Nichols, and tossed the old ball in to Powers.[27]

The introduction of a new baseball was a significant development in any game. The whole point of the home team's choosing first at bats was to try to score some runs before the ball became discolored and soft, as it invariably did as the game progressed. Nichols's next pitch came in shoulder-high. Tiernan connected solidly with the clean, hard ball, which streaked on a line over the dirt embankment in center field, over Manhattan Field's canvas fence, and either into Brotherhood Park, against the Brotherhood park fence, or into a ditch between the two fences (accounts vary). Tiernan trotted around the bases to the cheers of spectators in both ballparks. Nichols got the next batter out, and when Rusie set down the Beaneaters in short order in the bottom of the inning (Caylor wrote), "All who were there rubbed their eyes to make sure the game was not a dream."[28]

Rusie allowed the Beaneaters three hits while striking out eleven and, showing unusual control, walking only two batters. Tiernan's home run was the fourth hit off Nichols, who struck out ten and, showing his usual good control, walked a single batter. It had been an epic duel. Rusie and Nichols pitched in a National League that was decidedly weaker than the 1889 version, but at least they added excitement and a degree of luster to two otherwise ordinary ball clubs. Nichols became the ace of Frank Selee's staff, while Rusie continued to overpower batters. Five days after his thirteen-inning masterpiece, he struck out fourteen Cleveland batters in a 6–2 victory in New York.

The Players' League's Cleveland Infants had a pitcher who was even younger as well as a lot smaller than either Rusie or Nichols. Born in Atlanta, Georgia, William Vaness

"Willie" McGill grew up in Chicago and pitched in the city's Commercial League before signing with Evansville in the Central Interstate League. In 1889, at the age of fifteen, he threw a no-hit game, one of five wins he recorded against six losses for Evansville and Burlington. A left-hander, stockily built at 5' 6" and 170 pounds, McGill was one of the handful of players who were recruited out of the lower minors by the Players' League. Al Johnson, sole investor in the Cleveland club, personally signed McGill shortly after the start of the 1890 season.

On Thursday, May 8, little Willie, now all of sixteen, went to the box for his first major league start, in Cleveland versus Buffalo. Only about seven hundred spectators were on hand to watch two teams with few pennant prospects. Cleveland had won three of ten games, Buffalo five of eleven. McGill's box opponent was George Haddock, who had posted an 11–19 record with tail-end Washington the previous season. Haddock had little going for him that day. Cleveland batters made fifteen hits, walked seven times, and scored fourteen runs. McGill walked seven as well and hit one batter, but he struck out ten and held the Bisons to four runs. McGill thereby became the youngest player before or afterward to pitch a complete game in the major leagues.

That outing solidified the diminutive left-hander's place on the Cleveland club, although captain Henry Larkin used him carefully. In his next start, in Buffalo, McGill again benefitted from Haddock's ineffectiveness. Cleveland won 15–4 despite McGill's nine bases on balls and six wild pitches. On June 16, at South Side Park in Chicago, he outpitched Mark Baldwin for a 7–6 victory. But it wasn't always going to be easy. Three days later McGill was again matched against Baldwin. This time he was cuffed around for twenty-one base hits, which along with his teammates' nine errors gave Comiskey's club twenty runs, while Baldwin allowed nine. With his father watching the ordeal from the grandstand, McGill pitched the whole game, as pitchers were usually expected to do back then.

Willie McGill pitched for a better team in a better league than Cleveland's National League entry, which had the veteran Ed McKean at shortstop; Chief Zimmer behind the plate; George Davis, a talented nineteen-year-old in center field; and little else of any quality. Yet Al Johnson was losing money in the Players' League at a rate that even he couldn't sustain indefinitely. That was the situation with nearly every ball club in all three leagues. Pittsburgh, drifting in the bottom half of the Players' League, had unilaterally dropped its base ticket price to twenty-five cents, while the Alleghenies had become mostly a traveling team.

On June 20, John Clarkson ended Cincinnati's thirteen-game winning streak. At that point the Reds led the National League by four games over Brooklyn. Cincinnati retained a nucleus of Bid McPhee at second base, Tony Mullane (who often played infield or outfield when he wasn't pitching), first baseman "Long John" Reilly, and outfielder James "Bug" Holiday; and they were getting brilliant pitching from first-year right-hander Billy Rhines. Aaron Stern had taken the Reds out of the Association because he feared local Sabbatarians and liked the National League's fifty-cent ticket price. Now, though, home attendance for Stern's league-leading club was running substantially behind what the Reds drew in the Association. As the St. Louis writer Joe Pritchard pointed out, Cincinnatians were used to twenty-five-cent baseball, baseball on Sundays, and beer with their baseball; the National League offered them none of that.

At the same date, Kelly, Brouthers, Stovey, Radbourn, and crew led the Players' League with a 31–17 record. John Ward's Brooklyn club, at 29–17, held second place despite the Wonders' chronically sloppy play afield. On June 24, for example, they committed fourteen errors (including three by Ward) in a 22–3 debacle in Chicago. "Muffed flies, fumbled grounders, and wild throws were executed with the ease and grace of a trained acrobat," wrote Joe Murphy.[29] A week later, in Buffalo, the Wonders erred thirteen times and blew a five-run lead to lose 13–9.

The Athletics, at 32–15, led the Association, trailed by two teams that were big surprises. Rochester was a close second with players who had nearly all been in the minors the previous year. The other surprise was Louisville. The worst team in Association history in 1889, Louisville, with a new nickname but most of the same players, had climbed to third place at 25–20.

Chris von der Ahe's efforts to put a respectable team on the field were little short of frantic. When the Detroit franchise in the International League folded, he signed six of its players, who did him little good. He also took to sitting on the Browns' bench, where he harangued his players and countermanded the instructions of whoever happened to be serving as the team's captain. That prompted the *Sporting News* to editorialize that the Browns' owner should stay off the bench or, even better, stay away from Sportsman's Park.

On June 12 the Browns made eight errors, losing at home to Columbus, 13–6. Not a single Columbus run was earned. Afterward, von der Ahe released third baseman Jim Davis and suspended pitcher Elton "Ice Box" Chamberlain, who had won thirty-two games for St. Louis in 1889 and, together with Silver King, almost pitched the Browns to a fifth consecutive pennant. In the current season, working for a team that was markedly inferior to last year's, Chamberlain pitched indifferently on the rare occasions when he went to the pitcher's box, winning one game, losing three. Although his unique nickname had to do with his unruffled demeanor in the box, Chamberlain's relations with von der Ahe were anything but unruffled. After he deserted the team and returned to his home in Buffalo, von der Ahe sold him to Columbus.

Efforts by National Leaguers to sabotage the Brotherhood circuit were unrelenting. Having organized a salvage operation for John B. Day in New York, Al Spalding hadn't given up hope of bringing Mike Kelly back to the National League. Without its biggest attraction, Spalding believed, the Players' League couldn't carry on.

On June 25, Kelly and his league-leading club, accompanied by chief booster "Hi Hi" Dixwell, arrived in Chicago for a four-game series with Comiskey's Pirates. Before the June 27 game, Kelly (out of the lineup with a split finger) received floral tributes from Chicagoans who remembered his exploits with the old White Stockings; a few miles away, at West Side Park, Anson was honored by members of two local theater companies. It was a bad day for both captains. Silver King not only shut out Boston, 2–0, but drove in both runs himself. Anson's Colts were beaten 7–2 by Brooklyn, which was moving up rapidly on Cincinnati at the top of the National League. Boston also lost the next two games, after which Dixwell threatened to stop handing out cigars if the team didn't play better. Finally Radbourn outdueled Mark Baldwin in ten innings, 6–5. Early in that game Boston center fielder Tom Brown ran over Comiskey's foot, and Chicago's renowned captain had to be helped from the field. He faced an extended absence from the lineup.

While Boston was in town, Spalding sent word to Kelly that he would like to see him, and Kelly came to Spalding's hotel room. According to what Spalding related in his book twenty-one years later, the two engaged in some small talk before Spalding asked how things were going in the Players' League. Kelly replied that "everybody's disgusted; clubs are losing money; we made a foolish blunder when we went into it." At that point Spalding showed Kelly a check for $10,000 and offered him a three-year contract at whatever salary Kelly wanted—all that if the King would quit the Brotherhood and rejoin the National League. Stunned and confused, Kelly asked for time to think over Spalding's proposition. "There is mighty little time," urged Spalding. "If you don't want the money, somebody else will get it." Kelly said he would be back in an hour and a half and left. When Kelly returned, he told Spalding he couldn't accept the offer. Sure, he wanted the $10,000, but he "couldn't go back on the boys. And neither would you." Spalding shook his hand. They talked for a little longer before Kelly, who was usually either flush or broke, asked to borrow $500. Spalding gave it to him, thinking, as he wrote about it later, "that it was little enough to pay for the anguish of the hour and a half, when he was deciding to give up thousands of dollars on the altar of sentiment in behalf of the Brotherhood."[30] (When he died in 1915, Spalding still hadn't revealed whether Kelly ever paid him back.)

Meanwhile what Buck Ewing said and did again called into question his loyalty to the Brotherhood and the Players' League. At the end of June, Ewing traveled to Cincinnati, his home town, purportedly to see his family's physician about the injury to his side. While there, according to what he subsequently told a *New York World* reporter, he encountered Aaron Stern, who offered him an $8,000 salary to manage the Cincinnati ball club, plus a half-interest in the franchise. Ewing turned that down, then proceeded to the ballpark, where he met John B. Day, who was traveling with his erstwhile Giants. Day told Ewing the National League's Pittsburgh and Cleveland teams were about to go under and proposed an amalgamation with the Players' League, with the leftover players to be assigned to the American Association. He asked Ewing to discuss the matter with the New York Players when he rejoined them in Cleveland. Ewing agreed to pass along Day's proposal, but when he did, "They promptly sat upon it, just as I knew they would."[31]

Asked about his meeting with Ewing when he returned to New York, Day described it as "purely of a friendly nature" and denied he had said anything about amalgamation. Undoubtedly the meeting was friendly; Day and Ewing had always liked each other. But apparently Ewing took seriously Day's proposition, at least to the extent that he was willing to take it up with his teammates. When Ewing heard about Day's denial, he qualified his story. No, Day hadn't talked amalgamation "in so many words but his talk allowed that conclusion to be drawn." To which Arthur Soden scoffed, "The League has as much notion of amalgamation with the Players' League as I have of jumping off Long Wharf." "Ewing," Joe F. Donnelly snidely observed in *Sporting Life*, "appears to have supplanted Ward as the talker for the Players, and the substitution cannot be said to be a good one."[32]

Soden proved right—prevailing sentiment in the National League was still to try to drive the Players' League out of existence. The principal significance of the Day-Ewing encounter, like Kelly's gloomy remarks to Spalding (which of course weren't made public at the time), was to suggest that the Brotherhood's bright hopes of the spring had started to dim.

The Brotherhood was supposed to be just that—a common cause in which each Players' League club, while in competition with the others, was also to work for the shared interests of all. But a shabby deal on the part of the Boston and Buffalo clubs demonstrated that self-interest could figure as much in Players' League operations as it did in the older leagues.

At that time—and for close to a century thereafter—three scheduled doubleheader dates were standard throughout professional baseball: Decoration Day, Independence Day, and Labor Day.[33] Usually played morning and afternoon for separate admissions, the three holidays were nearly always good attendance dates for the home clubs. League-leading Boston was scheduled to be in Buffalo on Independence Day, but the local Bisons, buried in the cellar, rarely drew more than a few hundred at Olympic Park. So Buffalo's nonplayer investors arranged with chief investors Charles Prince and Julian Hart in Boston to transfer the July 4 games to Boston.

To reach home in time to host the Bisons, Boston forfeited the finale of a series in Pittsburgh. On Thursday, July 3, amid widespread press criticism of the forfeit and the transfer, only 213 disgruntled Buffalo kranks bothered to attend the local club's 13–3 loss to Brooklyn. At the Congress Street Grounds the next day, the Buffalo club played unusually well. A downpour halted the morning game with the score 6–6; Buffalo won the afternoon game, 7–6. Instead of the big visitors' payday the Buffalo officials had anticipated, the attendance for the two games was a reported 7,800, which was probably exaggerated.

The forfeit to Pittsburgh and then the doubleheader tie and loss in Boston left Mike Kelly and friends in first place by only a half game over a Chicago club that had recently gotten red hot. Buck Ewing finally returned to the lineup in Chicago, but Silver King and Mark Baldwin pitched two tight wins on Independence Day. After another victory over the New Yorkers on July 5, Chicago left for Brooklyn having won seven games in a row and twelve of its last fourteen. But if the Chicago club continued to play that kind of ball, it would have to do it without Comiskey, watching from the bench as Dell Darling took his place at first base.

At dusk on July 4, 1890, following a doubleheader split with Philadelphia, Cincinnati led the National League with a sparkling 41–19 record. The Phillies and Brooklyn were tied for second place, five games behind. But Bill McGunnigle's Bridegrooms faced several weeks without Darby O'Brien. During the Bridegrooms' recent series in Chicago (scheduled, of course, in conflict with games on the South Side between Ward's and Comiskey's clubs), O'Brien had gone over to Peoria, supposedly to visit family and friends. In fact he got drunk and managed to break his hand in some kind of altercation.

The Athletics, with a 42–22 record, still led the Association, which in the current season was getting little attention or respect outside of its member cities. Rochester had dropped into the second division along with Syracuse and Toledo, but Louisville and Chris von der Ahe's motley band, tied for second at 37–25, were making it an interesting race.

The Browns' afternoon win over Brooklyn on the Fourth at Sportsman's Park was still another forfeit. Jack Kerins, a veteran Association player, had been hired to umpire in the Association's ongoing shuffle of game officials. When Kerins wouldn't reverse a call against Brooklyn, manager Jimmy Kennedy took his team off the field, whereupon Kerins gave the game to St. Louis. Two weeks later Association president Phelps fired Kerins, who shortly signed a contract to play out the season with the Browns. Such bizarre happenings weren't uncommon in the history of the freewheeling Association.

Baseball interest was at an all-time high in long-suffering Louisville, where the biggest crowds in the city's history were coming to Eclipse Park on the west side. In other cities in the Association and the National League—St. Louis, Columbus, New York, Philadelphia, and especially Cleveland and Pittsburgh—interest was at or near all-time lows. The ill-advised Buffalo franchise had become the poorest relation in the Players' League, but despite inflated attendance numbers, nearly every club in the rebel organization was losing money. Many of the Players' League's financial backers were having sober second thoughts about having invested in something that more and more looked like a bad idea.

As early as May, R. W. Wright, *Sporting Life*'s Cleveland contributor, thought he knew what was going to happen. The National League owners, Wright believed, would be "gamier losers" than the backers of the Players' League, "who have been induced to invest their money on the roseate hopes of over-sanguine players. It is a matter of profit and loss for the Brotherhood backers. They are not in the game for sentiment, and like other businessmen will not stay in it and go down in their pockets every month when the prospects are daily growing less promising."[34]

1. *Boston Globe*, April 21, 1890, p. 8.
2. *Chicago Tribune*, April 20, 1890, p. 2.
3. *New York Clipper*, April 8, 1891, p. 373.
4. Autobiographical Manuscript, pp. 8, 12, Charles "Kid" Nichols File, National Baseball Hall of Fame Library.
5. *Sporting Life*, May 17, 1890, p. 6.
6. *Sporting News*, June 14, 1890, p. 1.
7. *New York Clipper*, April 19, 1890, p. 89.
8. *Chicago Tribune*, May 1, 1890, p. 6.
9. *New York Times*, April 19, 1890, p. 2; *Sporting News*, April 26, 1890, p. 1; *Chicago Tribune*, April 23, 1890, p. 3.
10. *St. Louis Post-Dispatch*, May 8, 1890, p. 6.
11. *Boston Globe*, April 22, 1890, p. 7; *Chicago Tribune*, May 23, 1890, p. 2.
12. Jessie McDermott later became a renowned actress under the stage name Maxine Elliott—so renowned that a theater in New York City was named for her. One of Ward's biographers speculates that inasmuch as the only grounds for divorce in New York State were adultery, Ward may have been a convenient target for George McDermott's suit. David Stevens, *Baseball's Radical for All Seasons: A Biography of John Montgomery Ward* (Lanham, Md.: Scarecrow Press, 1998), 123.
13. Peter Levine, *A. G. Spalding and the Rise of Baseball* (New York: Oxford University Press, 1985), 61.
14. Albert Goodwill Spalding, *Baseball: America's National Game* (Chicago: American Sports Publishing, 1911), 286.
15. Ibid., 285, 288. Italics in original.
16. *Sporting News*, April 26, 1890, p. 4.
17. Jean Hastings Ardell, *Breaking into Baseball: Women and the National Pastime* (Carbondale: Southern Illinois University Press, 2005), 42.
18. *Sporting Life*, May 10, 1890, p. 10; June 21, 1890, p. 8.
19. *Chicago Tribune*, June 16, 1890, p. 6.
20. Long thought to be sixty wins in 1884, Radbourn's record has recently been corrected. See Edward Achorn, *Fifty-nine in '84: Old Hoss Radbourn, Barehanded Baseball, and the Greatest Season a Pitcher Ever Had* (Washington, D.C.: Smithsonian Books, 2010).
21. *New York Times*, June 9, 1890, p. 2; June 19, 1890, p. 2.
22. *Boston Globe*, May 5, 1890, p. 5.
23. Lawson's talents lay elsewhere than baseball. Later in his life he was a lecturer on the Chautauqua circuit, published a religious novel, and became an aircraft pilot and designer and publisher of an aviation magazine. In the 1930s he founded a movement called "Lawsonomy," one of several organizations touting the ability of technical experts to bring the country out of the Great Depression.
24. *Chicago Tribune*, June 10, 1890, p. 2.
25. *Spalding's Official Base Ball Guide, 1891* (Chicago: n.p., 1891), 75.
26. Ibid.
27. Ibid., 76.
28. Ibid.

29. *Chicago Tribune*, June 25, 1890, p. 6.
30. Spalding, *Baseball: America's National Game*, 295–97.
31. *Cleveland Plain Dealer*, July 2, 1890, p. 5.
32. Ibid., July 2, 1890, p. 5; July 3, 1890, p. 5; *New York Times*, July 2, 1890, p. 2; July 3, 1890, p. 2; *Sporting Life*, July 5, 1890, p. 8.
33. First celebrated in New York City in 1882, Labor Day had come to be widely observed across the country, although Congress didn't make it an official holiday until 1894.
34. *Sporting Life*, May 31, 1890, p. 3.

CHAPTER 4

1890: "Rotting as Fast as Nature Will Let Them"

Much of the baseball press accepted the figures reported by the three leagues indicating that close to 140,000 people attended the twenty-four games played in the three leagues in the morning and afternoon on July 4. But some writers and daily newspapers were tiring of the phony numbers the National League "magnates" and Players' League "capitalists" were giving out. From the beginning, the *New York Times*'s baseball man (who didn't get a byline) looked with a cold eye on the inflated figures, observing facetiously, "The figures in many instances are not correct, but they are as accurate on one side as on the other."[1] By midseason his skepticism was being shared by Cleveland reporters, perhaps disgusted with the inept play of the two local teams, which had Pittsburgh and Buffalo to thank for keeping them out of last place.

For the games in New York and Brooklyn on Monday, July 8, the *Times* reported Players' League attendance as 764 for New York and Buffalo and about 500 for Brooklyn and Chicago, and National League attendance as 528 for New York and Chicago and 724 for Cleveland and Brooklyn. The next day the *Cleveland Plain Dealer* reported 680 on hand at Brotherhood Park for New York-Buffalo, and 450 at Eastern Park for Brooklyn-Chicago. On July 10 about 375 showed up at Eastern Park; at Manhattan Field a throng of 227 watched Jim Mutrie's club slaughter the wretched Alleghenies, 14–5. Mutrie told Joe McDonough, *Sporting Life*'s New York correspondent, that he wanted it understood he wasn't responsible for the bogus attendance reports.

A few weeks later Al Spalding told reporters his figures showed the Chicago Players' League club's attendance claims were 50 to 75 percent exaggerated. "The whole thing is a farce anyhow," he said resignedly. "But we—the league—readily admit that we are in the soup and are losing money hand over fist," while the Players' League was lying about making profits. "The fact of the matter is they are rotting as fast as nature will let them and nothing will save them." But Spalding denied Players' League charges he and other owners in his league were padding attendance by giving out free tickets at police stations, hotels, newspaper offices, barber shops, and saloons. George Munson, serving as secretary of the Chicago Players' League club, called Spalding's statements "the harangue of an individual sick at heart and sorely distressed in mind."[2] Shortly thereafter, proclaiming the National League would accept nothing short of the Brotherhood's unconditional surrender, Spalding sailed for Europe.

For public consumption, National League president Nick Young exuded confidence. "It is all coming about as I predicted in the spring," he assured everybody. The tide had turned; customers were coming back to National League ballparks. The Players' League, Young maintained, was losing $2,000–$2,500 daily, whereas National League clubs, paying their new players only $200–$250 per month, were holding down expenses. "There is no prospect of any of the league clubs going under," he added.[3] Yet right then Al Spalding and other League owners were bailing out John B. Day's New York franchise.

While sunny pronouncements continued to issue from the Players' League, rumors flew that the Buffalo franchise would be transferred to Cincinnati, and that Brooklyn would relocate to Baltimore. Buffalo was simply a bad team, while the Wonders, despite their good showing under John Ward's captaincy, were having trouble getting people to come out to Eastern Park. Some Players' League clubs were already in arrears on players' salaries; some of its umpires hadn't been paid up to date. On July 17 the Players' League's central board met at the Colonnade Hotel in Philadelphia behind closed doors (and closed transoms, one reporter noted). League president Edwin A. McAlpin gave out a statement that all the clubs were doing well except the local club. Squabbling among its investors had hurt the Philadelphia team and kept attendance down. Now, though, J. Earle and George Wagner, who sided with Jim Fogarty in his quarrel with Henry M. Love, were buying out Love, and the club's affairs were being straightened out. The board voted to assess each club $2,500 for "campaign purposes." Moreover, Buffalo was to be strengthened by the donation of four players from other teams.

Although the Players' League's bylaws specified that a player couldn't be traded or sold without his consent, apparently the bylaws said nothing about players being loaned out, with or without their consent. The unfortunate quartet consisted of pitcher

Ellsworth "Bert" Cunningham, from Philadelphia, and three players from Cleveland: outfielder-pitcher Larry Twitchell; first baseman Jay Faatz (who hadn't played thus far in the season), slated to supplant Jack Rowe as the Bisons' captain; and catcher Charlie "Pop" Snyder, one of the small handful of remaining National Association veterans. At thirty-four, Snyder decided against joining a team that was losing three of every four games. He announced his retirement; shortly thereafter he replaced Bobby Matthews on the Players' League umpiring staff. Jack Kerins had moved from umpire to player in the Association; now Snyder moved from player to umpire in the Players' League.

Snyder soon found what it was like to be on the other end of a disputed call. He was behind the plate in the opener of a Brooklyn series in Chicago, with Comiskey back in the Pirates' lineup. Early in the game Silver King hit George Van Haltren in the ribs; Van Haltren retaliated by throwing his bat toward the Chicago pitcher. Snyder got things under control then, but in the top of the eleventh inning, Comiskey scored on a base hit and then stood on the plate, interfering with Gus Weyhing's efforts to retrieve a wild throw from the outfield and get the ball to catcher Tom Kinslow. Fred Pfeffer also came home to make the score 7–5, Chicago. When Snyder did nothing about Comiskey's interference, the Brooklyn players stormed at him. Captain Ward was sent to the bench after calling Snyder crooked. Weyhing, in Joe Murphy's description, "became so excited that he lost his voice and only the convulsive twitching of his lips indicated that he was trying to say something. It was exciting, I tell you."[4] Although Brooklyn scored a run in the bottom of the eleventh, the game went to Chicago. Pop Snyder may have been well liked as a player, but that wasn't going to help him in his new occupation.

The runs continued to pile up in the Players' League. By July, Players' Leaguers had hit 106 home runs to 62 in the National League and 45 in the Association. Henry Chadwick, who owed his livelihood in part to Al Spalding, didn't like anything about the Players' League. He especially objected to the league's "elastic ball," which was producing "a plethora of home runs, the least skillful style of play in batting."[5] On July 23, in a 22–3 drubbing in Chicago of Comiskey's touted team, Boston's Harry Stovey became the first player in baseball history to reach the one hundred home run mark.

On August 4, however, Silver King and New York's erratic Ed Crane dueled for fourteen innings in the best-pitched game of the year in the Players' League. Chicago scored once in the top of the fourteenth on Duke Farrell's sacrifice fly to give King a 3–2 lead, which he was able to preserve in the bottom of the inning. Each pitcher gave up only six hits. By then Boston led the Players' League, but just barely; Brooklyn, Chicago, New York, and Philadelphia were all bunched close to the top. But the Chicago roster no longer included Arlie Latham, who had gotten his release a week or so earlier.

Walter Arlington Latham, who turned thirty just before the 1890 season, was one of the great characters in late-nineteenth-century baseball. A slender 5'8" and 150 pounds, the New Hampshire native was never a major threat at bat except in 1887, the statistically skewed season when walks counted as base hits. Nor was Latham anything exceptional around third base, especially after he hurt his arm in a foolish throwing contest with a teammate. What made Latham a sought-after player was his crowd appeal.

Latham was first and last an entertainer—a hyperkinetic, acrobatic, mischievous scamp of a man who was a favorite wherever he played. When he was ninety-two years old, he claimed that in his whole playing career, he never sat still during a game. He had to be on the coaching lines, ragging the opposition, yelling at umpires, turning hand springs and somersaults. Latham also liked to pull pranks, one of which may have contributed to his release. Earlier in the current season, the Chicago team's train, en route to open a series in Brooklyn, made a lunch stop. Latham finished his meal, then went outside the station and yelled "All aboard." Everybody ran for the train, leaving behind food, drink, and $19 in unpaid charges.

Joe Murphy, who was close to the team, explained Latham's release as a falling-out with Comiskey over Latham's having overdrawn on the advance money he received when he signed with the Players' League. When he pressed Comiskey for more money and was turned down, he began playing indifferently, particularly shying from hard-hit ground balls. However that may have been, Latham was sufficiently popular that he wasn't unattached for long.

Like most others who had gone with the Players' League, Latham was still under reserve to his 1889 club, which of course was the St. Louis Browns. Seven years of Latham were enough for Chris von der Ahe, who began negotiations for his sale with Cincinnati manager Tom Loftus. But under National Agreement rules, before he could be sold to anybody in the National League, the other Association clubs would have to waive (pass upon) the player. The Athletics and Columbus reluctantly waived Latham when Al Johnson announced that Latham had accepted Cleveland's terms. Aaron Stern then paid von der Ahe $2,500 for Latham's contract, and Loftus named him captain. Latham's arrival didn't help the Reds. On August 4 one of Cincinnati's biggest crowds of the year was on hand to watch his debut in a 7–6 win over Philadelphia. After that the Reds went into a protracted slump and faded out of the National League race.

Back in June, when Frank Selee's Boston club was in fifth place and drawing small crowds, Arthur Soden remarked, "I have little curiosity myself even as to what the relative standing of the clubs might be."[6] By the beginning of August, though, the Beaneaters, behind the stout pitching of Kid Nichols, John Clarkson, and Charlie Getzein, were in a tight battle with Brooklyn and Philadelphia. On August 12, at Boston's South End Grounds, Nichols had his second classic duel of the season, this one with Philadelphia's John "Phenomenal" Smith, a usually run-of-the-mill left-hander. Charlie Bennett's home run in the top of the ninth inning was the only score in the game.

Bill McGunnigle's Brooklyn Bridegrooms were also strong in the pitcher's box, with a steady rotation of Adonis Terry, Tom Lovett, and Bob Caruthers. Philadelphia, which had gone on a sixteen-game winning streak and moved into first place, was getting heroic work from Kid Gleason. On August 6, though, New York pounded Gleason for nine runs at the Phillies' Huntingdon Grounds, spoiling Harry Wright's return to the bench, although the Phillies' manager still couldn't see well enough to recognize people. (Events in Gleason's and McGunnigle's personal lives were in stark contrast. In mid-August, Gleason's baby daughter died of diphtheria in Philadelphia; while in Brockton, Massachusetts, McGunnigle's wife gave birth to a boy.)

Nobody was doing much of anything heroic for Cleveland's National League outfit, now under Bob Leadley. Leadley was brought in from Detroit to replace Gus Schmelz after the collapse of the International Association (one of several minor leagues going under). Following the Alleghenies' example, owners Frank and Stanley Robison got some of Cleveland's home games transferred. Cleveland's National League followers—insofar as there were any—were left wondering where today's "home game" would be played. Leadley's charges put their limited talents on display in Indianapolis and Detroit, among other venues.

But things brightened a bit early in August, when Denton True Young, a strapping twenty-three-year old right-hander, arrived from Canton of the Tri-State League, where he had been pitching in his first professional season. A farm boy from Ohio's Tuscarawas Valley, Young compiled only a 15–15 record at Canton, but he struck out eighteen batters in one game and pitched a no-hitter in his final outing before leaving for nearby Cleveland. He had also acquired the nickname "Cy."

On August 6, sporting a wispy mustache and wearing a uniform too small for his bulky physique, Young made his major league debut in Cleveland in the opener of a weekday doubleheader with Cap Anson's Colts. His battery mate was Chief Zimmer, who that season became the first catcher to work in more than one hundred games (125, to be exact). Matched against Young was Bill Hutchinson, who experienced one of his few bad days of the season, while Cleveland's batters experienced one of their few good ones. First baseman Jake Virtue, recently arrived from the defunct International Association, homered with Ed McKean on base for two of the Spiders' eight runs. Young struck out five Chicagoans, allowed only three hits and one run, and held Anson hitless. Many years later Young called that victory over the great Anson his most satisfying.

Anson and the rest of the Chicago lineup groused all through the game about Sandy McDermott's umpiring. Thoroughly disgusted, McDermott refused to work the second game. George Strief, who was on the National League staff and happened to be in the stands, offered to do the umpiring; but Anson wouldn't hear of Strief, presumably because Strief had once played for Cleveland and resided in the city. Finally Anson and Leadley agreed on Chicago catcher Malachi Kittredge. The Colts won the nightcap, 7–1, behind Pat Luby. A few days later McDermott received his release; Strief was hired to replace him.

The reporter covering Cy Young's debut for the local *Plain Dealer* described the new pitcher's repertoire in the terminology of the time: "Young had a splendid rise, a good drop, an inshoot and a wide incurve. All of this combined with plenty of speed."[7] Three days later Young won again, outpitching Cincinnati ace Billy Rhines, 5–4. On August 13 he ran his record to 3–0, coasting to a 20–9 victory over the Alleghenies. Fred Osborn, a left-handed newcomer, staggered through all nine innings to take one of his five losses (with no wins) in his one major league season. Four days later Young lost for the first time, in Cincinnati. He was pounded for seventeen hits and ten runs, while Rhines held Cleveland scoreless.

The situation with the Alleghenies was increasingly lamentable. "The crowd at the National League games," Ella Black wryly noted, "does not vary much. The same old 150 come out every day." (Actually Ms. Black was generous; turnouts at Recreation Park frequently numbered in two figures; one day the paid attendance was seventeen.) On the night of July 31, the Alleghenies left for games in Brooklyn, Cincinnati, and Chicago that had originally been scheduled as home dates. They stayed on the road for the next eleven weeks, playing around the National League as well as in Canton, Ohio, and Wheeling, West Virginia, and losing twenty-three games in a row. They even managed to lose a Labor Day *triple*-header in Brooklyn. "Condemned like wandering Jews to travel from place to place," wrote the waggish Joe Murphy, "they have no home." Murphy joked that the Alleghenies didn't want to return to Pittsburgh because of the poor crowds, "or worse still, lest the inhabitants of the town in their wrath should rise up and drop the club into the muddy waters of the Monongahela." Manager Guy Hecker even offered to donate $500 of his salary for the club to acquire a decent pitcher. Commented Alleghenies president J. Palmer O'Neill, "I think more of him for that."[8] No doubt.

Ella Black was also unhappy with the Pittsburgh Burghers, who couldn't get themselves out of the bottom half of the Players' League. She had no patience with several players who drank and caroused, and claimed to have seen three of them staggering on the street, although she named only pitcher Ed Morris, who had just been released. It soon came out that Burghers captain Ned Hanlon had fined five other players $100 each for drinking as well as being overweight.

Complaints about players' drinking habits were plentiful. Rochester released pitcher Will Calihan and shortstop Marr Phillips for what was candidly reported as "drunkenness." When it was rumored Syracuse might sign Phillips, the local *Sporting News* correspondent warned, "For goodness sake don't; we have enough lushers on our team at present."[9] (Syracuse didn't sign Phillips.)

Chris von der Ahe had a team in St. Louis that was drawing poorly and was almost constantly in flux, but somehow the Browns remained in contention for von der Ahe's fifth Association pennant. To spur his men, the Browns owner promised them $100 bonuses and half of the World's Championship Series receipts "ef mein Prowns vin der shampionship."[10] But the big story in the decidedly subpar Association was Louisville, which threatened to rise from last year's worst to this year's best.

In mid-July, before big crowds at Eclipse Park, the Cyclones swept a four-game series from the Athletics behind the pitching of Scott Stratton, Red Ehret, and a diminutive newcomer named George Meakin. Ehret's 12–3 victory over John "Sadie" McMahon put the Cyclones in first place. They lost to Syracuse the next day, but by winning eighteen of twenty games on their home stand, they regained the lead for good. A couple of weeks later they returned from a road trip, having won eight times in ten tries, and leading the Browns by four games, while the Athletics were seven back. As David Nemec has commented, "Awful as the Colonels [*sic*] had been the previous year, they looked like a reasonably decent unit now, and in 1890, a reasonably decent team could be good enough."[11]

The ill-considered inclusion of Brooklyn in the revamped Association produced a fiasco. Already playing weekday games at Manhattan Field, the Gladiators were in danger of losing their nominal home grounds after a state supreme (district) court in Long Island City ruled that Sunday games at Wallace's Ridgewood Park in Queens County were a public nuisance. Few people seemed to care much anyway.

Dead last in the Association, the Gladiators even managed to lose to Columbus for lack of a baseball. In a Sunday game at Ridgewood Park, umpire Jimmy Peoples (recently added to the Association's revolving-door staff) allowed Hank Gastright to return to the box when Ice Box Chamberlain, who had relieved him, refused to pitch with a new ball. Then, with Brooklyn ahead 13–9, Columbus's Jack Sneed fouled a ball into the bleachers. When nobody would return the ball to the field, Brooklyn manager Jimmy Kennedy had to tell Peoples the club had exhausted its supply—whereupon the umpire gave the game to Columbus.

Finally, on August 26 in Syracuse, with the Brooklyn club behind on players' salaries five weeks or more, the Gladiators finished losing a three-game series with the Stars and simply disbanded. Given their releases, most of the players entrained for New York; five signed with other clubs, having ended their dismal season with a record of 26–72 and having attracted around 37,000 people to about fifty home games. The next day Baltimore deserted the shaky Atlantic Association, rejoined the American Association, hosted the Browns, and lost, 11–10.

By that time the Athletics had fallen out of the race, and the Browns, after losing two of three games to Louisville in St. Louis, were seven games behind the front-running Cyclones. Evidently several Browns players resigned themselves to a runner-up finish and decided to live it up in Baltimore. In any case, live it up they did. In the early morning hours, von der Ahe, who had accompanied the team, stationed himself at the bottom of the stairway in the Carrollton Hotel and confronted his wayward employees. Tommy McCarthy got off with a lecture, but von der Ahe sent Toad Ramsey back to St. Louis, fined outfielder Charles "Dusty" Miller $25, and suspended and subsequently released infielder Bill Higgins (who signed with Syracuse). The next morning he upbraided the rest of the team at length.

Von der Ahe's disposition wasn't helped any by a clash with the National League over Ed Daily, who had been Brooklyn's only decent pitcher. Daily signed with John B. Day's New York club and thereby provoked an outcry in the Association. None of the other Association clubs had waived on Daily, and both St. Louis and the Athletics wanted to acquire him. Association president Zach Phelps and von der Ahe angrily protested to Day and Nick Young and threatened the Association's withdrawal from the National Agreement. Daily, claiming Brooklyn owed him $420, said he was through with the Association, but he pitched in only two games for New York before being released again. Louisville offered him a contract, and despite his expressed disdain for the Association, Daily was only too glad to join a team that was pennant-bound.

Club owners in all three leagues persisted in their efforts to get players to desert their present teams. The Athletics had a fine catcher in Wilbert Robinson, whom Al Johnson tried without success to get to jump to the Cleveland Players. Von der Ahe wrote a letter to Jack Boyle, catcher for the Chicago Players, offering to pay him more money to return to the Browns. "I wouldn't go back to St. Louis for any money," declared Boyle.[12] Meanwhile Cap Anson spent an hour with Mike Kelly when both Boston clubs were staying at the Tremont House in Chicago, in still another vain attempt to bring the King back into the National League fold. Kelly also refused to meet with John B. Day and Spalding in New York.

But contacts between Day and Buck Ewing still went on, to the consternation of John Ward, Tim Keefe, and other Brotherhood leaders. It later came out that early in August, when New York was playing a series in Boston, Day met with Ewing at the Fitchburg Station. Rumors circulated that Ewing had promised to return to the National League at the end of the season, and that he had even tried to cajole Keefe, Roger Connor, and Danny Richardson with offers from the League. "Never in God's world," protested Ewing, "will I go back on the Brotherhood until it goes back on me." When Alleghenies owner J. Palmer O'Neill insisted that Ewing had already signed with Day, *Sporting Life* put his denial on its front page: "For the thousandth time, I say there is no truth in the report."[13] But the New York captain also said that while he was hurt by allegations he was disloyal to the Brotherhood, he remained friends with Day, and nobody could tell him whom to associate with. It appeared Ewing might be protesting too much.

Nobody could doubt Pete Browning's fealty to the Brotherhood's league. Contending with Dave Orr for the batting title, he gave an interview with the *Boston Herald*'s Jake Morse, who no doubt dressed up Browning's grammar and vocabulary. "Last season," he complained, "I was used shamefully. I was fined without reason, and there was no redress for a player. I would have left Louisville long ago had I been able, and I thank heaven that deliverance from base ball bondage has come at last."[14]

Mike Kelly not only remained loyal to the Players' League but generally took his duties as captain seriously and probably played as hard as he ever had. But years of high living were starting to catch up with him. He had put on weight, and a succession of injuries common to the catcher's trade limited him to ninety games, his fewest since 1882 (when the National League played only an eighty-five-game schedule). But whether he was in the lineup, on the bench, or on the coaching lines, he remained the most popular player in professional baseball.

Kelly had been showered with gifts and perquisites for most of his playing career, but he had never received anything as generous as what was bestowed upon him that August. A large number of well-to-do friends and admirers in Boston, New York, Chicago, San Francisco, and New Orleans raised money to purchase a five-acre property valued at $10,000 on Main Street in South Hingham, Massachusetts. The two-and-one-half-story house contained $3,500 in furnishings, a billiard room, and a bowling alley. It even had electricity. The property also included a carriage house and stable, a hennery, and a trout pond.

At the Congress Street Grounds on Tuesday, August 12, Brooklyn's Gus Weyhing held Kelly's club to a single run, while John Ward and mates scored four times on Hoss Radbourn, who was victimized by five Boston errors. Kelly caught Radbourn and made two hits. That evening some fifty people took a train out to South Hingham for a banquet at the Cushing House and the presentation of the property to the King of the Diamond. The banquet lasted about an hour and a half and included speeches by Kelly himself, John Ward, Boston's veteran shortstop Arthur Irwin, vice president Julian Hart of the Boston club, and the omnipresent Hi Hi Dixwell. The party then adjourned to Kelly's new house. After everybody had roamed through the house and over the property, the group caught a ten o'clock train back to Boston.

By winning the last two of a three-game series with Philadelphia at the Congress Street Grounds, Boston kept its hold on first place, while Brooklyn had temporarily yielded second place to Chicago. Kelly continued to play with fierce competitiveness and to enjoy being the star attraction. On August 16, before a Saturday gathering at Brotherhood Park in New York alleged to be 8,500, his prancing around, shouting orders, and contorting himself at bat drew censure from the *New York Times* reporter on the scene. The game was a wild one, even by Players' League standards, with the teams combining for nineteen errors. Roger Connor homered for New York, Dan Brouthers and Joe Quinn for Boston. Kelly, besides making four base hits, took off his catcher's gear in the top of the ninth inning and went to the box in relief of Bill Daley. After he held New York scoreless, Boston won the game in the bottom of the ninth on Buck Ewing's passed ball and a wild pitch by Gil Hatfield, a nominal shortstop brought on as New York's third pitcher. Final score: Boston 16, New York 15.

Four days later Kelly made a fool of himself in the finale of the four-game series in New York. First he clashed with umpire Billy Holbert when he was called out at first base because Holbert thought Harry Stovey had interfered with Hatfield on a double-play attempt. Then Kelly became enraged when Holbert ruled that he had blocked Buck Ewing from scoring. At that point he threw the ball over the grandstand roof and stormed off the field, while his players lounged on the grass. Evidently thinking the better of his actions, he paraded back onto the field and caught two more innings before giving way to Morgan Murphy. Interrupted twice by rain, the game ended 8–3, New York. The win kept Ewing's team in third place, just behind Brooklyn and only a few games from first, while Chicago had slipped to fourth. The scene, thought the *Times* reporter, "savored too much of the variety theatre, when one or two comedians are engaged to do a lot of alleged funny (!) business." Tim Murnane accused Holbert of favoring New York. "Holbert has been unfair to Boston every chance he has had," Murnane insisted.[15] Boston left fielder Hardie Richardson announced he never again wanted to play with Holbert umpiring.

At that point Chicago was on the front end of an eight-game losing streak, ending whatever lingering fears anybody may have had that the all-star Pirates would dominate the Players' League. In New York, moreover, Ed Williamson's throw across the diamond broke Comiskey's finger and disabled him again, this time for the rest of the season. Injuries and illnesses had hit various other players. An unlikely doubleheader loss to Buffalo at home probably hurt Comiskey worse than his finger did. Later he rationalized that he was handicapped by having too many men who had never played together (although he began the season with five players, including Arlie Latham and himself, from the 1889 Browns). He also complained that there were men on the team he wouldn't have again "if I have any voice in the management." Next year he would pick his own team.[16]

Personal conflicts also hurt the Pirates. Joe Murphy, with the team in Brooklyn, reported that it was "badly demoralized over internal trouble." Ed Williamson acknowledged that a lot of quarreling had affected the team's play, and center fielder Jimmy Ryan said on some days as many as five players weren't on speaking terms. Ryan had a nasty run-in with Tip O'Neill after Ryan ignored O'Neill's signal to slide at third base and got himself tagged out. Ryan was one of the best players around and a clean-living young man, but he also had a cranky disposition. An unnamed Chicago player commented that Ryan had no friends on the team, and "he had a bad attitude and a swell head."[17] Ryan said publicly he wouldn't try for difficult fly balls when Silver King, whom he despised, was pitching. Finally Comiskey had enough and sent him home from Pittsburgh. Summoned before the club's board of directors, Ryan appeared sufficiently penitent and gained reinstatement.

Murphy also reported that "there is some dissipation on the team."[18] Among others, Murphy may have had in mind pitcher Charlie Bartson, Comiskey's occasionally used third starter behind King and Mark Baldwin. Late in September, when the Chicago Players had an off day at home, most of them attended a National League game at West Side Park. Bartson brought along a bottle of whiskey. After a few innings he startled heckling Anson, using increasingly nasty language. Police eventually threw him out of the park; a day or so later the club's directors, who included Comiskey, gave Bartson his release.

Two months after the season ended, Murphy told his readers more about what went wrong with the Chicago Pirates. Some of the players resented what they saw as Comiskey's favoritism for the former Browns, while Comiskey believed Fred Pfeffer was trying to take over the team. During dinner at the Park Hotel in Brooklyn on their last eastern trip (when they essentially blew their pennant chances), one player (unnamed) tried to stick a fork in the face of another player (unnamed). Comiskey had a hard time persuading the hotel's manager not to eject his team. Then, in Boston, two former

Browns (unnamed) returned to the hotel drunk, took off their clothes, and chased each other up and down the hallways. Again, the Pirates were almost tossed out.

If the Chicago Players were plagued by dissension and "some dissipation," the Association's Athletics were about to fall apart. In the two years since they acquired control of the club, William Whitaker and H. C. Pennybacker had done a poor job with the club's finances—a circumstance that caught up with them in a season when the Athletics had to compete for the local baseball dollar with two other clubs. Early in September, with the club $17,000 in debt, Whitaker called the players together, told them the club's treasury was empty, and advised them to continue on the "co-op plan," taking their pay from game-to-game receipts. Anybody who wanted his release could have it. Wilbert Robinson, Curt Welch, Sadie McMahon, and Denny Lyons got their releases; the first three signed with the Association's new Baltimore entry, while Lyons took Chris von der Ahe's offer. Robinson, pitcher Ed Seward, and George Shaffer, a thirty-eight-year-old outfielder, filed court claims in Philadelphia for $377, $350, and $240, respectively, in back pay.

Left with only four players, Bill Sharsig, a minority stockholder in the franchise, recruited seven local semiprofessionals and amateurs willing to be paid on a per-game basis and took them on a road trip. He left with $245, which was soon exhausted, so Sharsig had to start paying his nondescript charges out of his own pocket. The in-name-only Athletics were overmatched wherever they played, losing seventeen consecutive games on the road trip and finishing with five more losses at home to Rochester and Syracuse. They closed the season on a Sunday at Gloucester Point, New Jersey, before about twenty people who didn't have anything better to do. By then the Athletics' ballpark on Jefferson Street (within four blocks of the Phillies' and Players' grounds) had been sold in a sheriff's auction.

Having failed in Brooklyn and seen the Athletics go bankrupt, the American Association needed help from somewhere. Moreover, Phelps, von der Ahe, and others in the Association still simmered over the National League's disregard for waiver rules in the Ed Daily matter. In the Players' League, a growing number of investors were unhappy with their clubs' sparse revenues, if there were any. A few weeks earlier, representatives of most of the league's clubs had reconvened in the St. Cloud Hotel in Philadelphia to talk over a possible merger with the Association, but in the end they voted against it. They did vote to drop the preseason pledge to distribute $20,000 in prize money at the end of the season among the first seven teams. At the beginning of September, Al Johnson was talking about a possible postseason series between Players' League and Association champions. Johnson and his colleagues were ready again to take up the merger question and requested a meeting between delegations from their organization and from the Association.

It was supposed to be all hush-hush, beginning at midnight in the Colonnade Hotel in Philadelphia, but of course word got out to reporters, who converged from various cities. Ward, McAlpin, and Johnson represented the Players' League; von der Ahe, Phelps, and Whitaker (about to declare bankruptcy) were on hand for the Association. The meeting lasted until 4:00 a.m. Then came the farcical part. To avoid reporters, the attendees left by the back way, sneaking through the hotel cellar and a tunnel, then to the roof top of another building, and down a fire escape to Sansom Street. Caught at the railroad station by Ren Mulford, von der Ahe disclosed that the Players' League committee had presented conditions the Association couldn't agree to, so nothing happened. It's hard to see how such a merger could have come about, given the differences between the two leagues on everything from Sunday ball and liquor on the grounds to the reserve clause and pitching distances.

But if a deal with the Association couldn't be worked out, then the Players' League—or at least some of its players—sought to strengthen the league for 1891 by enticing more men from the two older leagues. On September 9 the Chicago team was en route from Pittsburgh to Buffalo. Comiskey, nursing his broken finger, and Silver King left the train and took another to Rochester, where they registered at the Hotel Bartholomew under false names. When the Browns began a series with the local Broncos, they grabbed Tommy McCarthy after a game that afternoon, with the intention of persuading McCarthy as well as shortstop William "Shorty" Fuller (another former teammate) to sign 1891 contracts with Chicago, as Denny Lyons had already done for a $500 bonus. Missing McCarthy, von der Ahe sent Joe Gerhardt to bring them back, but Gerhardt had to report that by the time he located McCarthy, he was already having dinner at the Bartholomew with the two Players' Leaguers. Then von der Ahe himself went looking for McCarthy, with no luck.

According to Comiskey, his and King's excursion had been only "a pleasure trip." Whether the gambit had any kind of official sanction or whether it was all Comiskey's idea isn't known, but in any case it was a success. McCarthy and Fuller signed to play next season for Chicago in the Players' League. Of course von der Ahe was furious. For whatever reason, he apparently took no action against McCarthy, but he fined Fuller $100, allegedly for drunkenness, although the general opinion was that von der Ahe acted out of spite.

Comiskey wasn't through with his recruiting activities. Later in the month he traveled to Cincinnati, where Brooklyn was playing a series with the Reds. There he tried to talk Darby O'Brien and infielder Hub Collins into signing Players' League contracts, but neither player would go along.

Although he wasn't playing, Comiskey was much in the baseball news that September. In the middle of the month, J. Earle Wagner announced that Comiskey would sign a three-year contract with the Philadelphia Players' League club. Chicago Players president John Addison acknowledged that while Comiskey was unhappy with his team's showing, the club's directors had encouraged him to build it up (which obviously he was trying to do with his itinerant wooing of Association and National League players). Besides, Addison pointed out, Comiskey was already under a three-year contract and "will be found guarding first base for the Chicago Brotherhood club this and next season at least, all reports to the contrary notwithstanding."[19]

In a letter to the *Sporting News*, Comiskey cited Chicago's contractual hold on him in confirming that Wagner's offer was $30,000 for three years to captain the Quakers. Wagner knew the Players' League's bylaws, so presumably he thought Addison and associates in Chicago would be willing to release Comiskey if he asked for it. In any case, Wagner's behavior hardly comported with the brotherly idealism supposedly guiding the Players' League.

With all that was going on off the field, the typical krank of 1890 may have found it hard to focus on what was happening on the field. In fact, three pennant races were entering their final weeks, and some interesting baseball was being played. On Tuesday, September 9, the Boston Players opened a three-game series with New York at the Congress Street Grounds; the Brooklyn Players did the same at Philadelphia's Forepaugh Park. Tim Keefe, his broken finger only partly healed, began the game by missing the strike zone on fifteen consecutive pitches, then hit Dan Brouthers. After Boston scored five times, Ed Crane relieved Keefe and gave up thirteen more runs. Final score: Boston 18, New York 6. Boston won again on Wednesday and Thursday, while Brooklyn dropped all three games in Philadelphia. Boston now led John Ward's team by four full games, with New York in third place.

Crane continued to be a headache for captain Ewing. Three weeks earlier Crane was fined $10 in a Harlem police court for disorderly conduct and resisting arrest, and fined $100 by the club's directors for the same drunken spree. William I. Harris, *Sporting Life*'s New York correspondent, wrote of Crane as well as Hank O'Day, "Both have seen fit to play the part of the owl, and they are regarded by many as the star attractions at a number of Harlem resorts." Vice President Talcott, who had already given up hope for a pennant, laid the team's failure on injuries, especially Buck Ewing's, but also on Crane, who had pitched erratically "due to his desire to partake of intoxicating liquors."[20] A couple of weeks later Crane at least partially redeemed himself by pitching and winning a doubleheader in Buffalo.

In the National League, Brooklyn gradually extended its lead over Boston and Philadelphia, but Chicago had become the league's hottest team. The Colts won five straight games at the end of a home stand, then took nine of twelve in the eastern cities. One of their three losses in the East occurred in circumstances that must be unique in major league history.

After sweeping both games on Labor Day at Boston's South End Grounds, Chicago was supposed to play another doubleheader the next day with Frank Selee's Beaneaters, starting at two o'clock. The problem was that nobody told umpire Jack McQuaid about the doubleheader. With no umpire on the scene at game time, Anson first demanded a forfeit, then proclaimed catcher Tom Nagle the umpire, which apparently was agreeable to Selee. Nagle officiated for half an inning, at which point Wally Fessenden, the league's designated substitute umpire, arrived armed with a letter from Nick Young authorizing him to take over. Anson wouldn't agree to that and had Nagle pull a stopwatch and declare a forfeit to Chicago. Then Fessenden ordered the game to resume. When the Colts refused to take the field, claiming they already had the game by forfeit, Fessenden pulled out *his* watch, waited five minutes, and declared a forfeit to Boston, making it two forfeits called on a single game. After a wait of five or ten minutes, Anson grudgingly agreed to play the second game. Boston won 4–3, Charlie Getzein edging Bill Hutchinson.

Although they had built their record up to 62–47, the Colts came home still in fifth place, trailing Brooklyn, Boston, New York, and Philadelphia. But with Hutchinson going to the box two-thirds of the time, they sustained their fast pace, while the Beaneaters, Phillies, and New York played poorly in the West. Boston suffered a mortal blow with a doubleheader loss in Cleveland and three straight defeats in Chicago, including a 3–0 one-hitter by Hutchinson, Kid Nichols taking the loss. Winning twenty-one of their last twenty-six games, the Colts climbed into second place and got within three-and-one-half games of Brooklyn. That was as close to the top as they came. Brooklyn clinched the pennant on September 30 in Cleveland. After being rained out on October 2, Chicago ended the season with an 83–53 record. The Bridegrooms won only three more games than the Colts but lost ten fewer—and back then pennants were decided on a percentage basis. Given that Chicago had only Hutchinson and third baseman Tommy Burns from last year's team, Anson's work as a field leader in 1890 was remarkable.

A celebration of Brooklyn's second pennant in two years in two different leagues fizzled when the Bridegrooms' train, en route from Cleveland, struck a cow and delayed their arrival at Jersey City until 9:45 that night. (To get to Brooklyn, the team would have to take a ferry across the Hudson River, then cross lower Manhattan by streetcar to the seven-year-old Brooklyn Bridge, and then travel by carriage across the East River into the city of Brooklyn.) Young Charles H. Ebbets, the Brooklyn club's front-office handyman, learned the bad news in Jersey City and made the long trip back to share his disappointment with the welcoming crowd, most of which had already dispersed.

The next night, though, the Bridegrooms did enjoy a proper celebration at the Grand Opera House, where both the 1889 and 1890 pennants were put on display. They closed the season by beating up on the poor Alleghenies. Not having been paid for weeks, the players at first wouldn't board their train in Pittsburgh, then finally yielded to manager Hecker's entreaties. In the final game of their ill-starred season, the Alleghenies made thirteen errors, losing for the 117th time, 10–4. "The Pittsburghs played so badly," reported *Sporting Life*'s man in Brooklyn, "that the spectators were thoroughly amused by them."[21]

With Harry Wright directing his team for its last forty-five games, Philadelphia finished third at 78–54. Cincinnati rallied late in the season to occupy fourth place, as Boston lost ten of its last twelve games and faded to fifth. New York ended John B. Day's unhappy season in sixth place, almost twenty games ahead of Cleveland. The Alleghenies' 23–117 record was the worst yet in the history of either the National League or the Association. Of the seventy home games originally scheduled, the Alleghenies played thirty-nine. Guy Hecker used forty-six players, including twenty different pitchers. Nothing worked for a team that committed 607 errors.

Brooklyn's trio of Lovett, Terry, and Caruthers combined for 79 of Brooklyn's 86 wins, led by Lovett's 30. The Bridegrooms made only 320 errors, a low total for that era. Yale graduate Hutchinson won 42 and lost 25 for Chicago. He completed 65 games and worked a league-leading 603 innings, followed by New York's Amos Rusie with 549 innings and the Phillies' 5' 7", 158-pound Kid Gleason with 506. Gleason compiled a sparkling 38–17 record, while Rusie, often getting poor support in the field, lost 34 times despite giving up fewer than three earned runs per game. Kid Nichols won 27 games and led in shutouts (7). John Clarkson, despite facing fewer good hitters than in previous years, ended with a sub-par 25–18 record. Cincinnati's Billy Rhines won 18 of his first 20 decisions, then lost 15 of his last 25. Cy Young won 9 of 16 decisions in the two months he pitched for the hapless Cleveland outfit. His eighth and ninth wins—Cleveland's 43rd and 44th—came in a season-closing doubleheader at home with Philadelphia. In the opener he won over Tom Vickery, 5–1, then held the Phillies to three runs, while the Spiders scored seven on Gleason.[22]

The Phillies' Billy Hamilton began his National League career by batting .325 and stealing 102 bases. The league's batting champion at .336 was Jack Glasscock, who also tied with Philadelphia's Sam Thompson in base hits, 172. Chicago's switch-hitting Walt Wilmot, a hitherto little-noticed outfielder, led in home runs with 14; Mike Tiernan and Philadelphia catcher Jack Clements tied for runner-up with thirteen.

In the American Association, Louisville swept five mid-September games from the jerry-rigged Athletics and essentially put the pennant away. *Sporting Life's* Louisville's correspondent described the games as "a farce at ball playing," but at least the crowds for the one-sided games at Eclipse Park—including 8,267 on Sunday—gave Bill Sharsig, who had been digging into his own pockets for his players' pay, $1,200 out of the visiting team's share of the receipts.[23]

Louisville closed the regular season on October 15 with an 18–1 trouncing of the Browns, who, for all of Chris von der Ahe's player shufflings, ended up in third place. In bringing Louisville the only pennant it would ever enjoy as a major league city, Jack Chapman's Cyclones won 88 games, lost 44, and finished ten games ahead of Columbus. When Gus Schmelz took over from Al Buckenberger, Columbus was two games below

.500. Under Schmelz, the Solons won 38 of their last 51 games. Hank Gastright led the staff with 30 wins, while Ice Box Chamberlain was a big part in Columbus's surge, winning 12 of 18 decisions after von der Ahe released him.

For Louisville, Scott Stratton won 34 times, lost 14, and held opponents to 2.26 earned runs per game, besides batting .323 in 189 at bats.[24] Red Ehret won 27. But the winningest pitcher in the Association was Sadie McMahon, who won 29 games for the Athletics and another seven after joining Baltimore. Chicken Wolf was the Association's batting champion with a .363 average on a league's best 197 hits. Denny Lyons and Tommy McCarthy may both have been troublesome players, but they were also good ones. Lyons batted .354, McCarthy .350.

The forlorn Brooklyn Gladiators had the worst record in the Association when they folded; that was still the case at season's end. After Baltimore replaced Brooklyn, the Orioles won 15 of 34 games and officially finished seventh, ahead of Syracuse and behind Rochester. Toledo, which like most of the Association clubs fielded an assortment of 1889 minor leaguers, was in fourth place. The pathetic Athletics finished next to last, which officially registered as eighth place.

Of course for most of the baseball public, the only true major league in 1890 was the Players' League. Through September, getting steady pitching from Hoss Radbourn, Ad Gumbert, and Bill Daley, Boston maintained its lead over Brooklyn and New York. Losing two games of a three-game series in Cleveland, while Boston swept three in Chicago, badly hurt Brooklyn's chances. With thirteen games left to play, New York, with a 68–50 record, was basically out of the running for the pennant, while Kelly's team led Ward's Wonders 73–43 to 71–50.

On Wednesday, September 24, Boston won its fifth game in a row, beating Cleveland, 5–1, behind Daley. Hi Hi Dixwell made so much noise among the (honestly reported) 783 in attendance that a woman tried to get a policeman to quiet him, without success. Kelly and his men clinched the Players' League pennant the following afternoon, although they lost to the seventh-place Infants. Before 753 paying customers, Charlie Dewald, a recently acquired left-hander, held Boston to four runs while the Infants scored ten times on Gumbert and Daley.[25] But in Pittsburgh, Ned Hanlon's sixth-place Burghers beat Brooklyn, 6–4, before 453 faithful kranks. Harry Staley was the winning pitcher; Gus Weyhing lost his game in the top of the ninth inning when right fielder Jack McGeachy's fumble let in two runs.

At the end of the day Boston's record was 78–44, Brooklyn's 74–53. New York was still third at 71–53. Basking in the glow of his pennant, Mike Kelly held forth at Cleveland's Hollenden Hotel (where the New York National Leaguers were also staying). "I will probably stay right with the present team for years to come," he said, "or as long as they want me and I can play ball. Boston is the best base ball town on earth. . . . This is the first year that I ever had full control of the team, and I guess every one is satisfied with our record."[26]

On Friday, an off day in the schedule, Kelly and five others remained in Cleveland while the rest of the Boston team played an exhibition game with the Infants in Youngstown, home town of Cleveland center fielder Jimmy McAleer. On Saturday, with Kelly having left for the East, a patched-together lineup lost to Cleveland, 9–0, before a turnout of 628.[27]

While Kelly basked in his success, John Ward was determined to finish second. For all his erudition and *savoir faire*, Ward had always been a tough competitor. Although the Players' League directors had voted to forget the $20,000 split originally pledged to the first seven teams, for Ward second place was a matter of pride. Brooklyn eventually did clinch second, although it wasn't easy. On September 30 the Wonders lost a painful game in Chicago. With the score 4–4 going into the tenth inning, the Pirates scored four runs. At that point Ward demanded that umpire Charlie Jones call the game on account of darkness, which would have caused the score to revert to the previous inning and left the game tied. Jones wouldn't agree to that; Brooklyn couldn't score in the bottom of the tenth. Fortunately for Ward and his men, New York lost consecutive shutouts in Chicago at season's end to clinch the runner-up spot for Brooklyn.

The Wonders closed out with a doubleheader sweep in Buffalo, where Jay Faatz had been fired as captain, the club's foremost local investors had resigned from its board of directors, and the Players' League had taken over the club's affairs. Gus Weyhing, having led Brooklyn's staff with a 30–14 record, must have felt he had the prerogative to relax as he watched the doubleheader from the Olympic Park grandstand. Whether he was drinking wasn't clear from the news accounts; in any case, when Ward was called out at third base on a close play, Weyhing started yelling at umpire Pop Snyder, accusing him of being in Buffalo's pay. He became so abusive the police took him out of the park. Undaunted, Weyhing returned to the stands and started in again on Snyder, using "vile language in the presence of ladies in the ladies stand," according to police captain

Cable.[28] At that point the police took the Brooklyn pitcher in hand and, followed by Ward, his players, and a crowd of local kranks, hauled him to the local precinct station, where he was put in a jail cell. That night either Weyhing himself, Ward, or the Brooklyn players collectively raised $200 bail to get him out.

(Weyhing would no doubt have agreed with the verdict of the pro-National League *New York Tribune* on the Players' League's umpiring innovation: "The double-umpire system has been tried and found wanting. It has been illustrated that two poor umpires are worse than one." Players' League secretary Frank Brunell agreed that using two umpires had proved a failure, but it was "on account of the men, not the system."[29])

The baseball press of the day had few qualms about reporting players' escapades. In Pittsburgh, a contingent of Philadelphia and Pittsburgh Players' Leaguers barged into a downtown saloon at 11:30 p.m., bribed the proprietor to let them use the back room, and stayed until 4:00 a.m., drinking enough "to float a seventy four gun ship," according to the *Sporting News*'s correspondent, writing as "Reddy."[30] Burghers' captain Hanlon promised a general shakeout of the team before next season.

At the start of the season Tim Murnane described the Boston Players' Leaguers, of whom eight were married, as a clean-living group of men. Murnane didn't except Kelly, who did seem to comport himself better off the playing field than in past seasons. Whether or not the Boston Players' sober ways helped them to the pennant, they came out on top and thus gained general recognition as the best team in baseball—which they undoubtedly were. Their final record was 81–48. Brooklyn's runner-up mark was 76–56; New York was third at 74–57. Comiskey's disappointing Chicago team ended up fourth (75–62), trailed by Philadelphia, (68–63), Pittsburgh, (60–68), Cleveland (55–75), and Buffalo (36–96).

Of Chicago's 75 wins, Mark Baldwin and Silver King accounted for 64. Baldwin led the league with 34 decisions; King matched Gus Weyhing's 30. Cleveland's Henry Gruber won 22 games but lost 23; Willie McGill, still not yet seventeen at season's end, posted an 11–7 mark. George Haddock, who had toiled for bottom-dog Washington in 1889, won only nine games while losing 26 for an equally inept Buffalo aggregation. But then nearly everybody who had pitched in the National League or the Association the previous year gave up more runs in the Players' League.

What Henry Chadwick called the league's "elastic ball," together with the lengthened pitching distance and playing fields that were sub-par even by nineteenth-century standards, produced a lot of hits, runs, and errors. The league batting average was .274, versus .254 in the National League, and .249 in the Association. Players' Leaguers scored 7,278 runs; National Leaguers, 6,010; Association teams, 6,042. Three-hundred-four-teen home runs were hit in the Players' League, whereas National Leaguers totaled 259; Association clubs, only 188. Nearly 4,000 errors were recorded in the Players' League, as against 3,264 in the National League and 3,449 in the Association.

Seventh-place Cleveland led the Players' League in batting average at .286, with Pete Browning's .373 edging Brooklyn's Dave Orr for the batting title by two points.[31] New York scored the most runs (1,018) and hit the most home runs (65), of which Roger Connor slammed 14 to lead the league. But the main trouble with Buck Ewing's team was season-long unreliability in the pitcher's box. Not surprisingly, Boston's pitching staff was the most reliable, yielding the fewest runs in the league (767). It was also the most balanced, with Radbourn winning 27, Gumbert 23, and Daley 18.

Mike Kelly and associates may have been the best baseball team in 1890, but the champions of the rebel league wouldn't be meeting anybody in a World's Championship Series. Instead they played a series of "benefit games" for extra money against New York at Brotherhood Park and around New England before finishing the series at the Congress Street Grounds. A fete at Boston's Music Hall climaxed when "the Only Kel" led his players in a parade onto the stage. The next afternoon Kelly was presented with the pennant; followed by the rest of the team, he dashed to the flag pole to raise the banner to the cheers of one of the season's biggest crowds.

Meanwhile, in Philadelphia, several local Players' Leaguers and amateurs met a pickup team headed by Wilbert Robinson and Sadie McMahon at Forepaugh Park in a charity game for Bill Sharsig, who in the past three years had lost nearly all his life's savings, estimated at $18,000, in the mismanaged Association club. And in New York, Digby Bell, having bet Nick Engel his long hair against Engel's beard that Chicago would win the Players' League pennant, went to the Hotel Brunswick barbershop to have his locks shorn, escorted by Engel, Tim Keefe, and George Gore.

What about a World's Championship Series? Outside of Louisville and Brooklyn there seemed little enthusiasm for having one. Finally, Brooklyn's Charles Byrnes traveled to Louisville from Kansas City, where the Bridegrooms had played three games (losing two) with the local Western Association champions. Byrne got together with Cyclones owner Lawrence Parsons and manager Jack Chapman, and hurriedly made the arrangements. It was to be a nine-game series in a 4–4–1 format. In *Sporting Life*, Francis Richter editorialized that it was "by courtesy only called the 'world's championship' series," and would prove "nothing more than the relative superiority of the League and Association."[32]

The series was to begin on Thursday, October 16, at Eclipse Park in Louisville, but rain pushed back the opening pitch by a day. Some 5,600 people, including a considerable number of women, were on hand for the biggest baseball event in the city's history, only to be disappointed when Brooklyn jumped on Scott Stratton for three runs in the first inning and later scored six more, as Adonis Terry held the Cyclones scoreless. About half as big a crowd showed up on Saturday. Chapman called on the peripatetic Ed Daily, who had won six games since joining the Cyclones; Bill McGunnigle sent Tom Lovett to the box. Both pitchers worked effectively, but Lovett squelched a Louisville rally in the ninth inning to preserve a 5–3 Brooklyn win. A still smaller turnout in chilling temperatures was on hand for game three, which umpires Wes Curry from the Association and Jack McQuaid from the National League called in the cold and gloaming after eight innings, with the score 7–7. On October 21 even fewer paid to see game four. Behind Red Ehret, Chapman's other ace, Louisville finally won a game, 5–4.

The teams made an overnight trip east on the Louisville and Nashville railroad, arriving at eight in the morning. More bad weather delayed the series two more days, as interest waned in Brooklyn. When the series began again at Washington Park on the twenty-fifth, cold winds made for miserable conditions for the thousand or so spectators; the condition of the field made for sloppy baseball. Brooklyn won 7–2 to take a three-games-to-one advantage. Byrne couldn't help but compare the tremendous excitement the Brooklyn-New York Series had generated a year earlier with the apathy prevailing now.

Sunday ball being illegal in Brooklyn, the series resumed its fitful progress on Monday the twenty-seventh. No more than six hundred bought tickets and huddled in what a New York reporter described as "a cutting wind [that] fairly froze the blood of both players and spectators."[33] In a surprisingly well-played game, Louisville prevailed, 9–8, to cut Brooklyn's advantage to a single game. When it was over, Parsons, Chapman, Byrne, and McGunnigle convened and decided that tomorrow's game would be the last. Neither team had made expenses; attendance was dwindling; the weather didn't look likely to improve. So the series ended on October 28 before about three hundred diehards. Louisville tied the series at three games apiece behind Ehret, who pitched a four-hitter and allowed only two runs while his teammates scored six.

Thus ended what the *Sporting News* called "a gigantic failure." It was unusual in various respects, not least in that it was free of the wrangling with umpires and off-the-field controversies that had marred previous World's Championship Series. But the Series produced a total attendance of only about 12,000. No profits were made, so the players received nothing for laboring through seven games under mostly dreadful playing conditions. As the late Larry Bowman observed, "Baseball was awash with red ink in 1890, and the World's Championship receipts mirrored the trend."[34]

Awash in red ink indeed. Even with a roster of players mostly unknown outside of Louisville and environs, the regular-season turnouts for Jack Chapman's Cyclones far exceeded anything in the city's history. Drawing 206,200 people (about 40,000 more than the city's population), the Cyclones led all three leagues in attendance and, with one of the smallest payrolls among the twenty-four clubs, were the only club that definitely showed a profit. Otherwise, the financial news across baseball was generally bleak. Home turnouts for the other six Association teams lasting the full season ranged from about 50,000 in Toledo to 134,000 in Philadelphia. Chris von der Ahe's Browns drew 105,000 kranks to Sportsman's Park, some 70,000 fewer than the previous year and the smallest total since the club's inception. The Association's aggregate attendance dropped by more than a third, to 803,200. According to the *New York Clipper*'s estimates, Rochester lost $18,000; Toledo, $16,000; St. Louis, $15,000; the Athletics, $13,000; Columbus, $12,500; Syracuse, $10,000; and Brooklyn-Baltimore, $9,000.

But at that, the Association outdrew the National League, which, according to figures that were fairly accurate, could interest only 776,042 in going to its ballparks, a little more than half the league's 1889 total. Brooklyn, in competition with Ward's Wonders and, marginally, with the woebegone Gladiators in Queens, attracted about a third as many ticket buyers as the record attendance at Washington Park for last year's Association champions. Philadelphia and Boston were the attendance leaders with 148,366 and 147,539, respectively; Cincinnati and Chicago also topped 100,000. But New York, traditionally one of the most popular teams in baseball, drew a pathetic 60,667; Cleveland played at home before 44,478; and on the thirty-nine occasions when the Alleghenies were at home, they charged a twenty-five-cent base admission but still attracted a grand total of 16,064.

Figures for the Players' League are suspect. The partisan *Boston Globe* gave 980,887 as the league's aggregate attendance. Boston supposedly led with 197,346 and may have showed a small profit above $60,000 in expenses. One also has to be skeptical of 170,000 for Philadelphia, 149,000 for Chicago, and 140,000 for New York, although 58,440 for Cleveland and 61,156 for Buffalo are probably close to reality. Pittsburgh topped the 100,000 mark by a few thousand, but Ella Black called the claim of local investors that the club made money or at least broke even "absurd."[35] Perhaps the biggest disappointment was that John Ward's strong Brooklyn team drew fewer than 80,000 people to Eastern Park. If the Players' League offered the public the best brand of baseball, vast numbers of people didn't watch it—and it wasn't as much superior to the National League as the Brotherhood intended.

In any case, given the payrolls all the National League and Players' League clubs carried, the losses were heavy. Al Spalding lost an estimated $65,000 in Chicago. When Tim Murnane interviewed William H. Conant near the end of the season, Conant estimated total National League losses at $250,000 and put his own Boston club's losses at about $25,000. "I am tired of putting out the money to pay the bills," Conant told Murnane. But he said the Boston club had about five years worth of reserve money and vowed "no quarter" and "no compromise. Soden, Billings and I will continue to fight until one of the leagues is dead."[36]

Of course none of the Players' League clubs had that kind of money to fall back on. Losing $10,000 to $15,000, Buffalo had gone broke; Tim Keefe and W. H. Behannon sued the club for $450 in unpaid bills for balls and other equipment. Losses to Deacon White, Jack Rowe, and Connie Mack amounted, respectively, to $2,500, $2,500, and $500, although they got a little of their money back when another group of Buffalo men bought out the Players' League investors for $10,500 and entered the franchise in the former International League, reorganized as the Eastern Association. Frank Brunell reported that John Ward, Fred Pfeffer, and Ned Hanlon lost $4,000 apiece. Five members of the New York Players' League team said they hadn't been paid since September 1. The club's gate receipts totaled $59,000, but expenses totaled $67,000, leaving nothing in the way of dividends for either financial backers or player-investors. Brunell put overall league losses at $50,000 to $60,000, which had to be absurdly off the mark. They were probably closer to what Conant estimated his own league had lost.

Yet even as the losses mounted, a syndicate of Players' League investors made a bold move. As early as September 19, at the Southern Hotel in St. Louis, Brunell and Cleveland's Al Johnson met with Cincinnati president Aaron Stern. Two weeks later, at the Bennett House in Cincinnati, Brunell announced to reporters that after day-long negotiations, Stern had agreed to sell his National League franchise to the Players' League for $40,000. Initially Stern was invited to join the Players' League. He wasn't interested in doing that, but he was ready to sell, having, he revealed, lost $15,000 in the current season. "I had no idea the Brotherhood people would raise that money," remarked Harry Sterne, the club's secretary and Aaron Stern's junior partner.[37]

In fact, Brotherhood members had nothing to do with the purchase. The money came from Johnson, New York's Edward McAlpin and Edwin Talcott, Brooklyn's George W. Chauncey and Wendell Goodwin, Boston's Julian Hart and John C. Haynes, Philadelphia's Wagner brothers, and Chicago's John Addison and P. L. Austin. Those eleven men put up an average of $3,600 each. Stern was to receive $20,000 in cash, the rest in five notes paid every six months. Nobody from Pittsburgh or bankrupt Buffalo was involved in the purchase.

The deal was initially held up by the refusal of Bid McPhee, John Reilly, and Tony Mullane of the Reds to sign Players' League contracts. (Apparently Arlie Latham didn't object to returning to the Players' League, perhaps because he was busy getting married—for the fourth time.) Entreated by Brunell, Johnson, Goodwin, Stern, and Sterne, the trio finally signed for substantial bonuses. The final papers were affixed in the Cincinnati office of Louis Kramer, attorney for the Reds. Within a few days the three recalcitrant players and the rest of the Reds began a home-and-home postseason series with the Cleveland Infants that later moved to St. Louis and Louisville.

Although the sale of the Reds wasn't a complete surprise—word of the negotiations had leaked out—it was still a sensational event, especially since the Players' League season hadn't quite ended. Stern was ready to get out of the baseball business, but the motivation for the deal on the Players' League side wasn't clear at the time and is even less so now. Why would presumably savvy businessmen, nearly all of whom had already lost money on their Players' League investments, enter into still another risky venture? Cincinnati was supposed to be rich baseball territory, but it hadn't proven so for Aaron Stern in his first and only season as a National League owner.

Perhaps Al Johnson and his confederates sought to wound the National League by pilfering one of its prize franchises, as the League had pilfered the Association's

Cleveland, Pittsburgh, Brooklyn, and Cincinnati clubs. Or perhaps the idea was to acquire a stronger replacement for the misbegotten Buffalo franchise. The men behind the purchase said publicly that they intended the Reds to be locally owned, and they chose John Ward to be one of the trustees overseeing the club's assets in the transition period. But was that really the plan? Still another possibility is that the members of the syndicate, soured on their losses in the Players' League, intended to be part of the National League in 1891—although the postseason games between Cincinnati and Cleveland were bound to anger Al Spalding and associates. In any case, Ward said he was pleased with the Cincinnati purchase, which "will bring into our league one of the best ball teams. It will give us an ideal circuit."[38]

Whatever its motivation, ultimately the Cincinnati project produced little beyond long-running litigation having to do with Al Johnson's investment. By the time the deal was made, the Players' League's "money men" were already looking to cut their losses. A sharp late-summer downturn in financial activity—invariably called a "panic" in the nineteenth century—added to the anxieties of investors, who in a number of instances made their living as stockbrokers and bankers.

With the 1890 season finally at an end, John Ward declared he was for a peace settlement with the other two leagues. Asked about his earlier harsh words for men who had gone back on the Brotherhood, Ward now seemed ready to forgive—if not to forget. "This talk of refusing to play with Glasscock, Denny, Clarkson, or any of the other deserters from our ranks is all bosh," he told reporters in New York. "Of course it is a bitter pill, but for the sake of peace and harmony, we will swallow it!"[39] Ward was going to get his peace settlement, but it wouldn't be the one he expected—or the one he wanted.

1. *New York Times*, July 14, 1890, p. 2.
2. *Cleveland Plain Dealer*, August 6, 1890, p. 5; *New York Clipper*, August 16, 1890, p. 361.
3. *Cleveland Plain Dealer*, July 14, 1890, p. 5
4. *Sporting News*, August 2, 1890, p. 2.
5. *Sporting Life*, August 2, 1890, p. 8.
6. *St. Louis Post-Dispatch*, June 17, 1890, p. 8.
7. *Cleveland Plain Dealer*, August 7, 1890, p. 5.
8. *Sporting Life*, August 2, 1890, p. 9; *Chicago Tribune*, August 17, 1890, p. 3; *Boston Globe*, August 31, 1890, p. 16.
9. *Sporting News*, August 9, 1890, p. 1.
10. *New York Times*, August 6, 1890, p. 2.

11. David Nemec, *The Beer and Whiskey League: The Illustrated History of the American Association—Baseball's Renegade Major League* (Guildford, Conn.: Lyons Press, 2004), 195.

12. *Chicago Tribune*, August 15, 1890, p. 6.

13. *Sporting News*, August 16, 1890, p. 2; *Sporting Life*, September 6, 1890, p. 1.

14. *Cleveland Plain Dealer*, July 22, 1890, p. 5.

15. *New York Times*, August 21, 1890, p. 2; *Boston Globe*, August 23, 1890, p. 5.

16. *Sporting News*, September 13, 1890, p. 2.

17. *Chicago Tribune*, September 3, 1890, p. 6; September 6, 1890, p. 6.

18. Ibid., September 6, 1890, p. 6.

19. *St. Louis Post-Dispatch*, September 14, 1890, p. 6.

20. *Sporting Life*, September 13, 1890, p. 4; September 20, 1890, p. 1.

21. Ibid., October 11, 1890, p. 5.

22. As Cy Young's biographer has noted, although working both games of doubleheaders was fairly common in the 1890s, the doubleheader Young pitched to end the 1890 season was his first and his last over his twenty-three National League and American League seasons. Reed Browning, *Cy Young: A Baseball Life* (Amherst: University of Massachusetts Press, 2000), 14.

23. *Sporting Life*, September 20, 1890, p. 2.

24. Earned-run averages didn't become an official statistical category until the third decade of the twentieth century; baseball researchers have worked retrospectively to establish statistics for the period before that.

25. Dewald won one other game for Cleveland and never pitched in the major leagues again.

26. *Boston Globe*, September 27, 1890, p. 5.

27. Although nothing about it appeared in the baseball press at the time, Kelly probably left the club to attend the funeral of his mother-in-law, Mary Henifen, who committed suicide on September 25 by jumping into the Passaic River in New Jersey. See Alfred P. Cappio, *"Slide, Kelly, Slide": The Story of Michael J. Kelly, the "King" of Baseball* (Paterson, N.J.: Passaic County Historical Society, 1962), nineteen-page booklet in Michael J. Kelly File, National Baseball Hall of Fame Library. Marty Appel, Kelly's chief biographer, makes no mention of the suicide.

28. *Sporting Life*, October 4, 1890, p. 9.

29. *Boston Globe*, December 21, 1890, p. 9.

30. *Sporting News*, October 11, 1890, p. 3.

31. Different sources give different 1890 batting averages for Browning and Orr. The averages given here are from John Thorn et al., eds., *Total Baseball*, 7th ed. (Kingston, N.Y.: Total Sports Publishing, 2001).

32. *Sporting Life*, October 25, 1890, p. 2; Larry G. Bowman, *Before the World Series: Pride, Profits, and Baseball's First Championships* (DeKalb: Northern Illinois University Press, 2003), 186.

33. Bowman, *Before the World Series*, 189.

34. Ibid., 190.

35. *Sporting Life*, October 4, 1890, p. 9.

36. *Boston Globe*, September 29, 1890, p. 5.

37. *Sporting Life*, October 4, 1890, p. 1.

38. David Stevens, *Baseball's Radical for All Seasons: A Biography of John Montgomery Ward* (Lanham, Md.: Scarecrow Press, 1998), 133.

39. *New York Times*, October 10, 1890, p. 3.

CHAPTER 5

1890–91: "Lunkheads of the First Water"

I n August of the 1890 season, Cap Anson echoed the prediction the Cleveland
reporter R. W. Wright had made back in May. "The moneyed men [in the Players'
League] are wild for a compromise," Anson told the *Sporting News*. "They do not
care a rap for the players. What they want is to get back as much of the money they have
lost as they possibly can."[1] Anson was a bigoted man and often a martinet with his players, but he knew the baseball of his time inside out, and he knew whereof he spoke.

By season's end "compromise" was in the air. In Indianapolis to sign Amos Rusie
for 1891, John B. Day talked compromise, because "things must change." Wrote a New
York reporter, "It is apparent that the National League men have stepped down from
their uncompromising perch and now see the necessity for action."[2] When John Ward
said he favored a peace settlement, he had in mind some kind of agreement with the
National League and the Association whereby the Players' League would continue to
operate. But for all the talk of compromise, by October 1890 events were in motion that
would doom the Players' League.

On October 8 the most powerful man in the National League returned home. Al
Spalding arrived on the liner *City of New York*, having spent two months touring Europe.
Interviewed dockside by reporters, he let it be known that his views on the League's conflict with the Brotherhood and the Players' League hadn't changed a bit. He still vowed
no compromise and readied himself to resume the fight, although now he intended to
pursue a new strategy.

The very next day, Spalding and Day met at the Fifth Avenue Hotel with Al
Johnson, Wendell Goodwin, and Edward B. Talcott. The meeting was arranged by
Allan W. Thurman, a Columbus attorney and stockholder in that city's American
Association franchise, whose role as the go-between in dealings between club own-

ers and Players' League investors moved the baseball press to dub him the "White-Winged Angel of Peace." To Spalding's and Day's surprise, Johnson, Goodwin, and Talcott "bubbled over with details of their financial woes and begged for mercy," as Spalding's biographer has put it.[3]

Although nothing decisive came out of the October 9 meeting, it marked the beginning of a process stretching over the next four months whereby the Players' League went out of business. When Spalding returned to Chicago, he described his and Day's get-together with the three Players' League financiers as "undoubtedly a splendid thing for the game." Johnson, Goodwin, and Talcott were "perfect gentlemen, while they, I think, did not go away with the impression that we have horns." On October 14, Day and other local National League stockholders met with the New York Players' League investors in the office of Cornelius Van Cott. Aware that the National Leaguers now had the upper hand, Day denounced those who said they wouldn't play with Jack Glasscock and others on his 1890 team. He added that he didn't want Jim O'Rourke back anyway, because "We want ball players on the New York team, not orators."[4] Meanwhile Spalding was traveling from city to city, talking to local club owners and Players' League financiers. Suspicious of all the National League-Players' League contacts, the Wagner brothers, owners of the Philadelphia Players, wired league president Edwin A. McAlpin to protest what had gone on in New York.

The next week the National League club owners voted to expel the Cincinnati franchise, basing their action on the postseason games the Reds had played with the Cleveland Players' Leaguers. They then voted to approve the operation of a new National League franchise in Cincinnati by John T. Brush, who had sold his Indianapolis club the previous spring and bided his time, in anticipation of gaining another one in the National League. Mike Kelly, hanging around the Fifth Avenue Hotel while the magnates met, acknowledged his doubts about whether the Players' League would operate in 1891.

Spalding's travels and meetings with people around the National League and the Association bore fruit on October 22. At the Fifth Avenue Hotel in Manhattan, Spalding, Day, and Brooklyn's Charles Byrne sat down to talk peace with Thurman, recently elected Association president; Bill Barnie, Baltimore manager and stockholder; and Chris von der Ahe; plus Johnson, Talcott, and Goodwin. John Ward, Arthur Irwin, and Ned Hanlon were on hand to represent the interests of the player-investors. In that day's *Boston Globe*, Tim Murnane naively put it down as "a telling victory" that three players served on the Players' League's six-man committee to meet with "the long-headed magnates of the National League."[5]

But "White-Winged" Thurman, elected to chair the meeting, ruled that the players couldn't participate in the discussions, on the grounds that to do so would violate the agreement made when the conference was arranged: the committees representing the three leagues would consist solely of what Spalding characterized as "the moneyed men . . . on a purely business basis." Ward, realizing he and his peers were being outgeneraled, protested that Spalding had been a player (as had Barnie), and that the players all had investments in their clubs. "Do [you] gentlemen," he asked, "wish to go on record as saying that the occupation of a ball player bars him from business associations with respectable men?" Getting no response, Ward turned to sarcasm: "I suppose if I were to retire from the field you would look upon me as a proper person."[6] Thurman ruled the players had to leave the room while a vote was taken. Predictably, the vote went 6–3 to exclude the players, the National League and Association representatives voting together and the Players' League investors resignedly accepting the outcome.

Barred from the meeting, Ward was angry, denouncing the Players' League investors for "not treating the players in good faith." Keefe seemed bewildered: "I don't know what to think about it all. The capitalists have all along professed to have our interest at heart, yet it seems as though they were doing something underhanded." Thurman averred the players' only purpose in being present was "to watch Messrs. Goodwin, Talcott, and Johnson," adding that in any future meeting "you can put it down that . . . there will be no members of the Brotherhood of Base Ball Players present." Spalding argued that "the Players' League had no more right to introduce them into the meeting than the National League would have to bring forward its players."[7]

Henry Chadwick agreed the players had no place trying to intrude on the affairs of the baseball businessmen. Both Chadwick and *Sporting Life* also credited Buck Ewing—who repeatedly professed his friendship for John B. Day—with helping to bring Day together with the Association and Players' League people. That may or may not have been accurate; in any case, it only lengthened the trail of suspicion that had followed Ewing since the previous spring.

From that point on, the watchword in baseball circles ceased to be "compromise" and became "consolidation"—not consolidation of leagues but of individual franchises. As Harold Seymour and Dorothy Seymour Mills observed, "Instead of standing together as a unit on a common policy," the Players' League investors "were preparing the way for piecemeal surrender." The report from Chicago was that the local Players' League club was way behind on its payroll and "a wreck financially."[8] Chief stockholder John Addison, ready to sell control of the club to Spalding, traveled to McAlpin's home at Ossining, New York, to talk with the Players' League president. Of course McAlpin, with Talcott, was in negotiations for a merger of the New York club with Day and associates.

Within another week it was announced that both the New York and Brooklyn Players' League organizations had merged with their National League counterparts. It turned out that although the New York deal was complete, Edward Linton, one of the major stockholders in the Brooklyn Players, didn't like the terms of the deal. His refusal to merge his stock with that of Charles Byrne and associates and that of Wendell Goodwin and George W. Chauncey blocked the deal—at least for the time being. The merger of the Pittsburgh clubs was in the works; with the Buffalo Players' League franchise defunct, that city had gained admission to the reorganized Eastern Association. So by the beginning of November, the Players' League had lost four of its original member clubs, with Chicago on the way out and the status of the Cincinnati acquisition uncertain.

What of the players themselves? New York Brotherhood members met to talk about what they should do. Jim O'Rourke, Danny Richardson, Roger Connor, and Tim Keefe strongly opposed any settlement with Day and associates, but it was already too late for that. The fate of the "real Giants" of 1890 was already decided. Tim Murnane stated the obvious: "The actions of Talcott, McAlpin and other stockholders of the New York club have shown . . . that these men have no idea of protecting the players."[9]

Early in November, Ward, Hanlon, Irwin, Al Johnson, and the remaining nonplayer investors from Boston, Philadelphia, and Chicago came together at the Continental Hotel in Chicago. Although Johnson was on hand to represent both Cleveland and Cincinnati, the others knew he had also been talking with National League people, and they no longer fully trusted him. After electing Boston's Charles Prince to succeed McAlpin as Players' League president, the conference adjourned without taking any further action. Prince, though, was talking about forming a reorganized, six-member Players' League with backing from Johnson, the Wagner brothers, and Brooklyn hold-out Linton.

Interviewed by the *New York Clipper*, Ward spoke bitterly of the defecting investors: "When they started in with the fight they knew very well what to expect, and they have no right to squeal now. There are lots of players who have put their all into the Players' League who are willing to play for nothing next season to continue the fight. No, I am not in favor of consolidation." Yet a few days later Ward told Tim Murnane he wasn't opposed to consolidation, although it had to be accomplished on the principles of the Players' League: no player sales, profit-sharing with the players, equal distribution of receipts among clubs, and no reserve clause.[10] Surely by then Ward must have realized whatever he or anybody else in the Brotherhood said or did was of little consequence.

Meanwhile, Al Spalding was in negotiations with John Addison to acquire the Chicago Players' League club. Their dealings were complicated and drawn out, but both men remained determined on a settlement whereby Addison could rid himself of the Players' League. Still, Addison was present in Pittsburgh on November 10, when president Prince convened the first—and last—annual meeting of the Players' League. "I found our league in a badly disrupted condition," Addison later related. The representatives of the various clubs "were watching each other as though suspicious of every move." Because Buffalo was no longer considered a member, Deacon White and Jack Rowe were ignored and decided to go home. The next day the Pittsburgh investors, minus Ned Hanlon, officially withdrew the franchise from the league. With considerable understatement, Murnane described Ward, Prince, the Wagners, and Al Johnson "as feeling quite blue over the way matters had shaped themselves."[11]

Johnson admitted that his older brother Tom warned him against putting his money into the Players' League venture, but he had nurtured visions of big profits transporting big crowds to his new ballpark by his electric trolley lines. The lines and the ballpark had been built, but the anticipated multitudes hadn't come. Murnane put Johnson's investment in baseball at $27,500: $20,000 to build the Cleveland ballpark and $7,500 that went into the Cincinnati venture. Johnson's losses he estimated at $17,500. Johnson wanted $25,000 for his holdings and offered them to the Robisons, Cleveland National League owners. Frank Robison's response, which he made public, was that he wouldn't give Johnson one cent in a buyout.

Meanwhile players started scrambling to get back to their old clubs or to catch on with new ones. "Pete Browning . . . blew into town on Wednesday morning, and the price of whiskey has in consequence gone up," reported the *Sporting News*'s Louisville correspondent. Before leaving for Florida, Browning said he would play for Cincinnati next year, although he didn't make clear which Cincinnati he meant. During the National League's regular meeting in November, Mike Kelly spent a long time at the Hoffman House in the company of Spalding and Triumvir William H. Conant. Asked about what had transpired, Kelly denied having signed anything; he had only told Spalding and Conant he would rather play with Boston in the National League than Boston in the Association. Back at the Fifth Avenue Hotel, Spalding flashed telegrams from Ed Williamson and Jimmy Ryan, stating they wanted to get back with their old Chicago club. J. Palmer O'Neill, president of the newly merged Pittsburgh club, claimed he had offered Ward $10,000 per year to play for the Alleghenies. "Put it in writing," replied Ward. But when O'Neill did so, Ward backed off from signing a contract.[12]

The National League meeting adjourned early in the afternoon of November 15, following the appointment of a committee consisting of Spalding, Day, and Charles Byrne to try to bring the remaining Players' League investors into line. At 3:30 p.m. Spalding and Charles Prince met at the University Club; then Spalding talked with J. Earle Wagner at the Hoffman House. Then Wagner and Prince got together with Al Johnson at the St. James Hotel, followed by another meeting between Wagner and Spalding. "Tonight," wrote Murnane, "ends a week of the greatest diplomatic work ever known in baseball."[13] Nothing immediate came out of all that running around and parleying, but it was obvious that what was left of the Players' League was up for grabs.

In St. Louis, Charles Comiskey was asked about the future of the Players' League. "It is dead," he replied, "and today every man is looking out for himself." Having had nothing but bad things to say about Chris von der Ahe the previous winter, Comiskey now moved to reconcile with "der boss President." He called on von der Ahe at his residence, as did Tip O'Neill, Silver King, Joe Boyle, and William "Yank" Robinson, a little infielder who had played five years for the Browns and then spent an often-besotted season with the Pittsburgh Burghers. Figuratively if not literally, the players went to their former employer hat in hand. Subsequently, the Browns' owner and his onetime captain dined at Tony Russo's seafood restaurant and went hunting and fishing in the marshlands of Missouri's "boot heel" region, south of St. Louis. Comiskey told reporters he thought he would be back with the Browns in 1891. As for the Players' League investors, their surrender to the National League "was just the kind you would expect from lunkheads of the first water. . . . Talcott, of the New Yorks, was the first to weaken, and now all the rest of the capitalists who were in with the play are following in his foot steps." The main lesson Comiskey gained from his Brotherhood-Players' League experience (as his biographer stated it nearly thirty years later) was that "in the future only one vote would be cast in any club that he was financially interested in."[14]

In Chicago, Al Spalding finally concluded his negotiations with John Addison. Spalding was willing to pay $25,000 for the Chicago club, but Comiskey and several other players threatened to sue for what Addison owed them. "I do not propose to go down into my pockets to pay men as ungrateful as these ball players," declared Addison.[15] (How players who hadn't been paid what their contracts called for could be considered ungrateful, Addison didn't bother to explain.) So Spalding paid him $18,565 in cash. Of that, Addison distributed $11,000 among the nonplaying stockholders; the remaining $6,435 was parceled out in back salaries to twelve players, in amounts ranging from $1,398.58 for Comiskey to $256.90 for Dell Darling. Addison also bought the stock of five players at 50 percent of par, paying $2,800. Comiskey's contract also specified he was to receive $1,300 out of receipts, which Addison refused to pay, prompting Comiskey to file suit for breach of contract. Ed Pfeffer waived all claims to back pay and stock purchases and the next day went to Spalding's office to make up with his old boss. Addison took his own payment in the form of $15,000 in stock in the consolidated New York franchise, which McAlpin and Talcott transferred to him. At the end of December, Spalding took possession of the local Players' League club's books and offices, as well as its South Side ballpark.

Meanwhile, the Jenney and Graham Gun Company took over the Brotherhood's offices in Chicago for back rent. Frank Brunell had already moved out and taken a job as the *Chicago Tribune*'s racing editor. About 15,000 leftover Players' League guides, published early in 1890, were sold as scrap paper.

Freed of his Players' League obligations, Addison unburdened himself to writers for Chicago's seven daily newspapers. He revealed that although the Chicago club had taken in $57,000 in receipts, that figure didn't cover expenses after the players were paid $41,000. Addison went on to say that the Players' League's biggest mistake was in not planning for losses. The capital stock that went into the construction of ballparks—salaries, expenses, and anticipated profits—was to be paid out of receipts. The Brotherhood counted on people deserting the National League and Association and filling their ballparks, but "They counted without their host."[16]

With consummate hypocrisy, Edwin W. McAlpin now pointed his finger at "a few traitors in our camp [who] proceeded in undoing in a few hours what we had accomplished and succeeded in building up in an entire season."[17] He was correct in saying that as soon as Players' League investors started talking consolidation, the National Leaguers saw their weakness. But McAlpin described it all in the third person, whereas he, of course, had become a stockholder in the consolidated New York clubs and had advised Addison in his dealings with Spalding.

Late in November, in Columbus to confer with Allan Thurman, Spalding boasted that "The National League is doing all it could to get rid of the Players' League. . . . True, the tail is wiggling at Boston and Philadelphia, but the organization is dead beyond recognition." Apparently Spalding had a hand in Thurman's becoming Association president. Ralph Lazarus, co-owner of the Columbus club, related that Spalding had urged Thurman to take the job, "his idea being that the Association ought to have a President in whom the League people have confidence."[18] So at the Association's regular meeting in Louisville, Zach Phelps stepped down and Thurman was elected. Reporters on the scene noted that Comiskey accompanied von der Ahe to Louisville.

"The Players' League is as dead as the proverbial door nail," proclaimed Spalding when he got back to Chicago, "and no amount of hustling can revive it."[19] Spalding and Thurman—the millionaire ex-ballplayer and the successful attorney—had become downright chummy. The Association's new president traveled to Chicago to talk over the possibility of putting a franchise in that city. Spalding didn't object in principle, although he insisted the Association agree to no Sunday ball, no liquor at the ballpark, and a fifty-cent base admission. Apparently Thurman was willing to accept those terms. In the following months, getting the Association into Chicago remained a live option, even if the "beer and whiskey league" would have to forgo its distinctive identity to operate in the nation's second largest city.

A week later Spalding was back in New York, where he and Thurman had a meeting scheduled with Charles Prince during the Association's December confab. Having finally given up on organizing a four-team Players' League, Prince now sought a place in the baseball establishment, in the form of an Association franchise in Boston. Tim Murnane was invited to be present at the Albemarle Hotel for Prince's meeting with Spalding and Thurman. On behalf of Julian Hart and the other investors in the Boston Players' League club, Prince formally applied for entry into the Association.

The problem was that the Triumvirs, having endured one season of competition in the local baseball market, were determined not to endure another. The Association, on the other hand, intended to get rid of Toledo, Syracuse, and Rochester, and craved the rich Boston market.

All kinds of contacts between previously hostile parties were taking place. While the Association's proceedings were underway, Murnane located John Ward and escorted him to the newly opened Manhattan Athletic Club for lunch with, of all people, Al Spalding. Earlier a staunch Players' League partisan, Murnane now heaped extravagant praise on Spalding as "the man who has taken it upon himself the arduous task of settling up the present bad state of affairs." After a round of hand shakes, "the party sat down to wrestle with the bones of a few tender birds."[20] Spalding reminded Ward that today, December 13, was the second anniversary of the world baseball tourists' landing at Melbourne, Australia. No, corrected Ward, it was the fourteenth. They then exchanged reminiscences about the trip.

After lunch the trio talked for two hours in the club's reading room. Spalding wanted it understood that whatever he said wasn't official, to which Ward replied sarcastically, "Why certainly; the League can't meet a player, you know." When Spalding brought up the subject of a settlement of baseball's tangled circumstances, Ward spoke as if the realities of the past few months hadn't sunk in. He warned that any settlement had to seem to the public "fair and above board. The game of base ball would be very poor if stripped of its sentimental features."[21] He also reiterated his opposition to the "sales system" and the way the reserve had come to be used. Spalding disagreed, contending player sales had been the salvation of the minors, and citing the Des Moines Western Association club, which was kept going after 1888 with sales money, most notably the sale of Bill Hutchinson to Chicago for $3,500.

Worn down by his labors with the Brotherhood and the Players' League, Ward said he was thinking of "getting out of the business" and giving full time to his law practice, to which Spalding countered that Ward would play another ten years. He joked that if Ward had died the previous June, the Players' League would have died with him. "I was almost dead long before that," Ward sighed, "but struggled along, thinking the other fellow was in a hard way." Spalding replied, "You gave us a hard battle."[22]

As the sporting goods tycoon implied, the battle was all but over. Spalding continued to play a major role in getting matters tidied up. Later, at the Fifth Avenue Hotel, J.

Earle and George Wagner waited in the lobby until they were invited up to Thurman's room. Three weeks earlier the Wagners, having paid off the debts of the bankrupt Athletics, had assumed full ownership. They discussed with Thurman and Spalding the prospect of keeping an Athletics franchise in the Association. Nothing definite came out of that, but the situation looked promising.

In mid-January, while both the National League and the Association were in session at the Fifth Avenue Hotel, Spalding and Thurman met with Charles Prince at the Manhattan Athletic Club and assured him Boston would have a franchise in the Association. At midnight on January 18, after much wrangling, a joint confer-ence committee made up of Spalding, Thurman, John B. Day, Charles Byrne, Chris von der Ahe, and Bill Barnie voted unanimously to approve Boston's admission. The Boston Triumvirs had finally dropped their opposition to the Association's moving into Boston, but only after imposing tough conditions. All players would have to be put back under reserve, base admission at the Congress Street Grounds would be fifty cents, the Boston Beaneaters would have Decoration Day to themselves, and the Boston Association team could have Independence Day. Lastly, the Association team must have a distinctive nickname, so nobody could confuse it with the Beaneaters—as if that were likely to happen.

Shortly thereafter, papers were signed that made not only Boston but Philadelphia members of the Association. With the Boston and Philadelphia Players' League finan-ciers now among its "magnates," the Association had to get rid of Syracuse, Rochester, and Toledo. The Toledo owners wouldn't go quietly. They secured a temporary injunc-tion against the Association and held up a financial settlement for a few weeks, although they eventually came around and took their share of a three-way buyout totaling about $20,000. The Association brought its membership up to seven by awarding a franchise to Washington, a sometime member of both the Association and the League. So far the reconstructed Association consisted of holdovers St. Louis, Louisville, Columbus, and Baltimore, plus newcomers Washington, Philadelphia, and Boston. Would the eighth member be Chicago?

Meanwhile, Ward, Johnson, Fred Brunell, Dan Brouthers, Arthur Irwin, and Edward Linton gathered at the St. James Hotel for the purpose of disbanding the Players' League. As soon as the meeting started, a wire arrived from several minor Brooklyn stockholders protesting that Linton had no power to represent them, which

Albert G. Spalding, about the time of the Brotherhood War.
(National Baseball Hall of Fame Library, Cooperstown, N.Y.)

Chris von der Ahe, at the height of his power and influence.
(National Baseball Hall of Fame Library, Cooperstown, N.Y.)

John B. Day, some years after he lost his holdings in the New York Giants.
(National Baseball Hall of Fame Library, Cooperstown, N.Y.)

John Montgomery Ward, in his early years as a prosperous New York attorney.
(National Baseball Hall of Fame Library, Cooperstown, N.Y.)

Charles Comiskey, captain of the St. Louis Browns.
(National Baseball Hall of Fame Library, Cooperstown, N.Y.)

Arlie Latham as a St. Louis Brown.
(National Baseball Hall of Fame Library, Cooperstown, N.Y.)

Mike Kelly in his prime.
(National Baseball Hall of Fame Library, Cooperstown, N.Y.)

Buck Ewing, captain, New York Giants.
(National Baseball Hall of Fame Library, Cooperstown, N.Y.)

Adrian Anson, captain, Chicago National Leaguers.
(National Baseball Hall of Fame Library, Cooperstown, N.Y.)

Bill Hutchinson as a Chicago National Leaguer.
(National Baseball Hall of Fame Library, Cooperstown, N.Y.)

Kid Nichols in 1890, his first year as a Boston Beaneater.
(National Baseball Hall of Fame Library, Cooperstown, N.Y.)

Amos Rusie as a New York Giant.
(National Baseball Hall of Fame Library, Cooperstown, N.Y.)

Pete Browning as a Louisville player.
(National Baseball Hall of Fame Library, Cooperstown, N.Y.)

Brooklyn Bridegrooms, 1889 American Association champions.
Back row, left to right: George Smith, Pop Corkhill, Adonis Terry, Dave Foutz, Darby O'Brien, Doc Bushong, and Joe Visner. Middle row, left to right: George Pickney, Bob Caruthers, Hub Collins, manager Bill McGunnigle, Tom Burns, Bob Clark, and Tom Lovett. Seated in front: Mickey Hughes. With the exception of Bushong, Visner, and Hughes, the 1890 National League and World Series champion consisted of the same players.
(National Baseball Hall of Fame Library, Cooperstown, N.Y.)

Frank Selee, Boston Beaneaters manager.
(National Baseball Hall of Fame Library, Cooperstown, N.Y.)

Boston Reds, 1891 American Association champions: top row, left to right: Bill Joyce, Morgan Murphy, Bill Daley, manager Arthur Irwin, Hugh Duffy, Charlie Buffinton, and Tom Brown. Middle row, left to right: John Irwin, Hardie Richardson, Paul Radford, and Dan Brouthers. Bottom row, left to right: John O'Brien, George Haddock, Cub Stricker, and Duke Farrell. Club president Charles Prince sits in the middle of the team picture.

(National Baseball Hall of Fame Library, Cooperstown, N.Y.)

left the meeting without a quorum. In a bizarre twist, Jim Hart and Cap Anson were called in to represent Chicago, restore the quorum, and vote with the others for a permanent adjournment.

At that point Linton was still unwilling to sell his stock to Charles Byrne and the rest of the Brooklyn group and even filed for an injunction to block the merger of the Players' and National League clubs. Within another six weeks, though, Linton and Byrne agreed on $10,000 as the price of Linton's stock and signed papers legally effecting the merger.

In February 1890, Ward and other Players' Leaguers had gathered at Nick Engel's saloon to drink champagne in celebration of their legal victory over John B. Day and the National League. Now, at the same place, Ward, Al Johnson, Frank Brunell, and Francis Richter held something of a wake for the Players' League. Ward proposed a bitter toast to the "treachery, stupidity, and greed" that killed the organization. "Let the wine go 'round," he said, "the war is over. The [Players'] League is dead, long live the [National] League."[23]

In *Spalding's Official Base Ball Guide* for 1891, Henry Chadwick commemorated the impending return of the Brotherhood members to their old leagues and old teams (and to the reserve clause) by including a parody of a four-line poem by Elizabeth Akers Allen entitled "Rock Me to Sleep, Mother," originally published in 1860 in the *Saturday Evening Post*. Allen's verses epitomized mid-Victorian sentimentalism:

Backward, turn backward, O Time, in thy flight,
Make me a child again, just for to-night.
Mother, come back from the echoless shore,
Take me again to your heart of yore.

The parody, published in the *Cleveland Leader* and probably written by John B. Foster, went like this:

Backward, turn backward, O Time, in thy rush,
Make me a slave again, well dressed and flush!
Bondage, come back from the echoless shore,
And bring me the shackles I formerly wore.[24]

Al Johnson was in limbo. He was sole owner of the Cleveland franchise, which belonged to a league that no longer existed, and, after the Wagner brothers and Charles Prince gave him their Cincinnati shares (he thought), he became the majority owner of another franchise in the same nonexistent league. (Whether the Wagners and Prince actually gave him their shares would later be contested.) So far Johnson had gotten nowhere in his dealings with the Robisons, who advised him to take his business to John T. Brush, slated to be the National League's new operator in Cincinnati. At the beginning of the Players' League endeavor, the young Clevelander was the most enthusiastic of its financiers; at the end he was the only one with nothing to show for it.

The postmortems on the demise of the Players' League were numerous and varied. As far back as October, Ella Black wrote that she had favored the players "striking out for themselves, but I wanted them to do it alone. . . . The taking in of outside persons has been the ruin of the new body. . . . As it is now the players have little more to do with it than they had in the former seasons." The *Sporting News* editorialized that morally the Players' League had been a success in showing the evils of the owners' hold on them, and in teaching the owners that players had rights. But it had failed financially because "its fortunes have been guided by a lot of numbskulls who knew nothing about the business of the game." Moreover, the purchase of the Cincinnati club was "the biggest fool move in the history of base ball," for which the St. Louis weekly blamed Frank Brunell.[25]

Brunell himself argued that having acquired Cincinnati, the Players' League could have survived if not for "the treacherous eagerness of our New York and Brooklyn clubs to get in out of the wet." Otherwise, the league made three vital mistakes, according to Brunell. As John Addison also pointed out, the whole enterprise was undercapitalized; the league should have gone into the fight capitalized at $50,000, not $20,000. Each club, thought Brunell, should have employed a skilled business manager to look after its finances. Finally, the Players' League "should have fought the National League in its own way for its own men on the question of contracts." In other words, the Brotherhood should have encouraged contract jumping. Players who signed Players' League contracts and then went back to the National League "made it possible for the National League to go on."[26]

James D. Hardy, in his history of the pre-1900 New York Giants, lists a number of reasons for the Players' League's lack of success besides undercapitalization, betrayal, and failure to attract or hold onto a third of the players in the National League. Three competing leagues, head-to-head competition in seven cities, and three-way competition in two others confused and eventually alienated much of the baseball public. Players' League grounds and stands were poorly maintained, the double-umpire system wasn't popular, and the too-lively ball and lengthened pitching distance made for a kind of play that was unfamiliar to ticket buyers. But what Hardy emphasizes is the naiveté of both players and investors about baseball's profitability. The record crowds and profits of the 1889 season were deceiving. Then came the financial panic of the late summer and fall of 1890, which "sharply aggravated the fundamental economic miscalculation the Brotherhood leaders had made. . . . Most clubs never made much money, even in the best years, and some never made any."[27]

So what baseball old-timers would refer to as the "Brotherhood war" was over, fading into the game's history as an episode in a long-ago time, about which a dwindling number of people knew or cared.[28] Seventy-five years would pass before another potent players' union emerged, and when it did, it wouldn't form a separate league but would be similar to the craft unions of the American Federation of Labor, with which the Brotherhood had refused to affiliate.

The efforts primarily of Al Spalding and Allan W. Thurman accomplished the extinction of the Players' League and the restoration of something resembling the status quo ante bellum in professional baseball. It seemed the game's affairs would return to normality—however normality might be defined in a professional sport whose relatively short history, even before the advent of the Players' League, had been marked by chronic conflict and instability. The club owners in the National League and the Association convened at the Fifth Avenue Hotel in mid-January 1891, confident that they again held the upper hand in their dealings with the players. As Ralph Lazarus put it, "The days of high salaries are past. . . . We will pay living salaries and no more."[29]

In their joint meetings, the bigwigs from the two leagues, though still not working in full trust, reached accord on a new National Agreement to replace the 1883 arrangement whereby the League—officially at least—recognized the Association as an equal. The new pact also included the minor league Western Association and set up a three-man National Board, consisting of Thurman; John I. Rogers, representing the League; and Louis C. Krauthoff, president of the Western Association. Thurman was elected chairman.

The board's first order of business was to oversee the return to their 1889 clubs of the men who had been on Players' League rosters, if their former clubs still wanted them.

That turned out to be a complex, explosive issue, regarding which Thurman's actions precipitated the breakdown of the short-lived inter-league comity and brought on still another baseball war. For the American Association, the Angel of Peace turned out to be an Angel of Death.

1. *Sporting News*, August 23, 1890, p. 5.
2. *St. Louis Post-Dispatch*, September 28, 1890, p. 24.
3. Peter Levine, *A. G. Spalding and the Rise of Baseball* (New York: Oxford University Press, 1985), 64.
4. *New York Times*, October 14, 1890, p. 3; October 15, 1890, p. 4.
5. *Boston Globe*, October 22, 1890, p. 10.
6. Harold Seymour and Dorothy Seymour Mills, *Baseball: The Early Years* (1960; reprint, New York: Oxford University Press, 1989), 243; *Boston Globe*, October 23, 1890, p. 7. Until recently, Harold Seymour was credited with sole authorship of *Baseball: The Early Years* and the subsequent volumes in his trilogy: *Baseball: The Golden Age* (New York: Oxford University Press, 1971) and *Baseball: The People's Game* (New York: Oxford University Press, 1990). Now we know that his wife Dorothy Seymour Mills was in every sense of the word Seymour's coauthor, so in citations in this book, she is so indicated.
7. *Sporting Life*, October 25, 1890, p. 1; *New York Clipper*, November 8, 1890, p. 553.
8. Seymour and Mills, *Baseball: The Early Years*, 241; *Sporting News*, November 11, 1890, p. 1.
9. *Boston Globe*, October 27, 1890, p. 2.
10. *New York Clipper*, November 8, 1890, p. 553; *Boston Globe*, November 11, 1890, p. 2.
11. *Sporting News*, November 22, 1890, p. 1; *Boston Globe*, November 13, 1890, p. 10.
12. *Sporting News*, October 25, 1890, p. 1; *Boston Globe*, November 13, 1890, p. 10.
13. *Boston Globe*, November 16, 1890, p. 4.
14. *Sporting News*, November 22, 1890, p. 1; *Sporting Life*, November 8, 1890, p. 1; Gustave W. Axelson, *"COMMY": The Life Story of Charles Comiskey* (1919; reprint, Jefferson, N.C.: McFarland, 2003), 79.
15. *Sporting News*, November 22, 1890, p. 1.
16. Ibid.
17. Ibid., 2.
18. *New York Clipper*, November 22, 1890, p. 601; *Boston Globe*, November 20, 1890, p. 2; *Sporting News*, November 29, 1890, p. 2.
19. *Sporting News*, November 29, 1890, p. 1.
20. *Boston Globe*, December 14, 1890, p. 6.
21. Ibid.
22. Ibid.
23. David Stevens, *Baseball's Radical for All Seasons: A Biography of John Montgomery Ward* (Lanham, Md.: Scarecrow Press, 1998), 143; *Boston Globe*, January 17, 1890, p. 6.
24. *Spalding's Official Base Ball Guide, 1891* (Chicago: n p., 1891), 49.
25. *Sporting Life*, October 11, 1890, p. 6; *Sporting News*, November 1, 1890, p. 4; November 8, 1890, p. 4.
26. *Reach's Official American Association Base Ball Guide, 1891* (Philadelphia: A. J. Reach Company, 1891), 7.
27. James D. Hardy, *The New York Giants Base Ball Club: The Growth of a Team and Sport, 1870–1900* (Jefferson, N.C.: McFarland, 1996), 133.
28. Until, of course, a substantial percentage of the membership of the Society for American Baseball Research discovered the fascinations of pre-1900 baseball, its so-called pre-modern era.
29. *Sporting News*, November 22, 1890, p. 1.

CHAPTER 6

1891: "Mad Clean Through"

The first sign the new National Agreement had achieved something less than the peaceable kingdom was that National League clubs were putting under reserve as many as twenty-six players. That didn't sit well with the Association people, because the understanding at the recent joint meeting in New York was that none of the sixteen clubs in the two leagues would reserve more than fourteen. At the end of January, National League president Nick Young ruled that the Boston League club, which had twenty-three players under reserve, had to turn over nine to the National Board, so the new Boston Association club could have its pick. Yet whatever Young said or did on that issue quickly became moot in the face of something much more disruptive.

In his long career as a baseball journalist, Tim Murnane was usually a perceptive observer of what was going on. But it's unlikely anything he ever wrote landed farther from the mark than his judgment that the election of Allan W. Thurman rather than Young as chairman of the National Board was a victory for the Association and "likely to smooth over the troubled waters of the base ball sea."[1] Within a matter of days after the completion of the National Agreement, the Association was up in arms over the signing of players by National League clubs who were supposed to be returned to the Association. Pittsburgh signed Louis Bierbauer and Connie Mack, who had been, respectively, with the Brooklyn and Buffalo Players' League clubs; Harry Stovey, who was supposed to be assigned to the new Boston Association club, signed with the Boston Beaneaters. Mack had been Washington's first-string catcher in the National League in 1889; both Bierbauer and Stovey had been with the Athletics that season. Stovey took Arthur Soden's offer of $4,000 at least in part because, sharing his mother's staunch Methodism, he never liked playing on Sundays in the Association's western cities.[2]

Stovey, of course, was one of the great players of the era, a .308 batter with 136 stolen bases for the Boston Players. The slightly built Bierbauer—described in *Sporting Life* as "the bright, particular star of the Association"—had teamed with John Ward to form the Players' League's best second base-shortstop combination.[3] The string-bean Mack wasn't much of a hitter, but he played in a period when catchers were valued more for their savvy, their throwing arms, and their ability to take punishment than for their prowess at bat. Mack also gained a little managing experience when he took over the captaincy of the Buffalo team from Jay Faatz during the last month of the 1890 season. Ned Hanlon, Pittsburgh's newly named manager, signed him for $2,400 with a $500 advance.

Outraged, the Association people denounced Hanlon and president J. Palmer O'Neill as "pirates"—a tag that stuck to become the enduring nickname of the Pittsburgh team. The Wagners, Charles Prince, Chris von der Ahe, and others in the Association demanded a special meeting of the National Board, which convened in Chicago early in February. "You can be assured on it," predicted J. Earle Wagner, "they will be awarded to us by the National Board." Wagner proved as much a prophet as Tim Murnane. The board voted 2–1 to uphold the signing of Bierbauer, Stovey, and Mack by the National League clubs, Thurman voting with John I. Rogers, and Western Association president Krauthoff—a self-described "purely disinterested person"—casting the dissenting vote. That Thurman had sided against his own organization on such a fundamental issue was bad enough; worse still, before the Chicago meeting, Thurman had polled the Association's club owners on whether they would agree to leaving Bierbauer and Stovey in the National League and had received a unanimous "no." J. Earle Wagner declared he would go to court to get back Bierbauer; Bill Barnie, one of the negotiators of the National Agreement, returned to Baltimore from Chicago fuming that he was "mad clean through."[4]

As an attorney, Thurman considered the strict legalities of the situation more than its possible ethical aspects. James Shiffert, in his history of early Philadelphia baseball, has noted that turmoil in the Athletics' affairs after the 1890 season explains why Bierbauer and Stovey weren't reserved by October 10, the date specified in both League and Association bylaws. The Wagner brothers didn't assume ownership of the Athletics franchise until November 22. So neither player was properly reserved; if the fault lay with anybody, it lay with Zach Phelps, who, as Association president at the time, didn't attend to the proper paperwork. So Thurman believed he was on sound legal grounds in casting his vote with the League's representative on the board.

Mack was a special case. The National League franchise that employed him in 1889 no longer existed. The previous November, Mack had signed a personal-services contract with Charles Prince, who at that time was still entertaining ambitions to keep the Players' League going. Prince might have pressed his claim to Mack in court, but in the end he acquiesced in Thurman's ruling, based on the fact that when Mack signed with Prince, Boston had not yet been admitted to the Association.

No argument justifying the loss of Bierbauer and Stovey, legal or otherwise, was acceptable to the Association, several of whose club owners rightly believed they had been snubbed, cheated, and exploited by the National League for the past eight years. Chris von der Ahe, J. Earle Wagner, Larry Gatto of Louisville, and Harry von der Horst of Baltimore got together at the Grand Hotel in Cincinnati, then took a train over to Frankfort, Kentucky, to seek counsel from Zach Phelps, who happened to be serving as a delegate to the Kentucky constitutional convention. They all agreed the Association should hold an emergency meeting to discuss its relationship to the League.

They met at the Murray Hill Hotel in Manhattan on Tuesday, February 17, with National Leaguers Talcott, Byrne, and Frank Robison keeping tabs on the proceedings from the nearby St. James Hotel. On Prince's motion and von der Ahe's second, the Association owners voted unanimously to withdraw from the National Agreement, to fire Thurman, and to elect Louis Kramer of Cincinnati, the Association's attorney, as their new president. They also provided that 51 percent of each club's stock would be held by Kramer, a device intended to prevent any member club from selling out to the National League, and to split ticket receipts 45 percent–45 percent, with the remaining 10 percent to be deposited in the Association's general fund. Charlie Jones, Jimmy Macullar, Pop Snyder, and John Kelly—all ex-players except for Kelly—were hired to umpire the Association's games. The next day Barnie, as vice president, and George Munson, as secretary, officially notified Nick Young that the Association was no longer a party to the National Agreement.[5]

Charges and countercharges flew back and forth. Reelected to the National Board chairmanship by Rogers and Krauthoff, Thurman put out a statement contending that the real reason he was fired was his opposition to an Association club in Cincinnati, which, he argued, would have violated the National Agreement. He claimed he had it all arranged for the Association to move into Chicago (presumably on Al Spalding's terms), but Arthur Irwin, who was to manage its Boston team, arrived at the National Board's Chicago meeting to voice his opposition to an Association franchise in that city. Thurman's veracity was suspect. Shortly after he voted against the Association in Chicago, he wrote Ralph Lazarus proposing that Lazarus join him in a scheme to take Columbus into the National League. Lazarus made the letter public and would have nothing to do with Thurman's overture. A nonplussed Abraham B. Cohen, Lazarus's partner in the franchise, could only exclaim, "Talk about dealing!"[6]

Meanwhile, Brooklyn's Charles Byrne and Frederick A. Abell denounced their fellow-National Leaguers for the breakdown of relations with the Association, whose withdrawal from the National Agreement they felt was fully justified. Along with Philadelphia's Al Reach, they pledged not to sign anybody under contract in the Association. But Al Spalding insisted that the Association wanted to break the National Agreement all along so it could be free to move into Cincinnati. Rarely one to mince words, Spalding termed the Association's abrogation of the National Agreement "the work of a few irresponsible professional managers with anarchistic tendencies" who wanted the Cincinnati "jam pot."[7]

However that may be, at the Murray Hill Hotel conference the Association did give up on Chicago and vote to put a team in Cincinnati to compete with the Reds, now under the ownership of John T. Brush. Al Johnson, who supposedly held a majority interest in the franchise wrested from the League the previous September, was to head up the Association's Cincinnati operation. "When we saw how our president treated us," said Bill Barnie, "we lost no time in taking in Cincinnati."[8]

Johnson—up to now a man without a baseball team—had lingered in Association councils and even been elected to the organization's board of directors, at the same time that he continued his contacts with National League owners. With a straight face, he could tell a *Washington Post* reporter, "The League treated me shabbily, while the Association has set me in gold and thrown a halo around the frame." Although rumors persisted that Johnson had his eye on a deal with the National League, J. Earle Wagner, for one, dismissed such talk. "I do not believe," he said, "that Johnson would sell out the [Association] for $100,000 or twice that much."[9]

That was Wagner's second prophecy to misfire. Within less than three weeks after the Association voted to add Cincinnati, Johnson met with J. Palmer O'Neill in

Cleveland and sold out to the National League for $30,000, with each League club contributing in varying amounts. From the Association's standpoint, Johnson's action was the second betrayal inflicted upon it within two months.

Johnson may have thought he had made a nice deal and rid himself of his baseball misadventures, but his troubles were just beginning. In common pleas court in Cincinnati, the Association club owners filed a petition to stop the sale. J. Earle Wagner and Charles Prince testified that the previous fall they hadn't actually given their shares in the Cincinnati club to Johnson, only permitted him to hold them in trust. If so, Johnson lacked a majority interest and couldn't sell his holdings to the League. The court accepted that argument and issued an injunction prohibiting the League from paying anything to Johnson. With the $30,000 held in escrow, the next ten years saw dreary, fitful litigation over the money. Finally, in 1901, a settlement was reached whereby the $30,000 was divided among Johnson, Prince, Wagner, and various League owners and former owners. Al Johnson died that year at the age of thirty-seven.

Meanwhile, the Association hurriedly put together its Cincinnati entry, with George Munson, who had returned to his old job as St. Louis Browns secretary, handling most of the work. Although Ed Renau, a local man, was its president, the Association club owners collectively financed the franchise. Despite his losses in 1890, Chris von der Ahe was willing to purchase about three-quarters of the stock. The fact that one of their peers now held controlling interests in two of their teams didn't seem to bother the other Association owners. After all, since the previous summer, ownership of the New York Giants had been split between five League clubs.

The Association's withdrawal from the National Agreement meant that neither League nor Association was obliged to honor the reserve lists of the other organization. For a time in the fall of 1890, Mike Kelly talked with Arthur Soden about returning to the Boston League club, but as the *Boston Herald*'s Jacob C. Morse noted, Kelly had gotten used to running things as captain of the Boston Players' League champions; and he didn't like the idea of taking orders from Frank Selee, a relative newcomer he didn't know. Kelly bided his time through the winter, to the increasing irritation of the new Boston club's Charles Prince and Julian Hart. On the same day Barnie and Munson notified Nick Young that the Association no longer recognized the National Agreement, Hart gave Kelly an ultimatum to make up his mind about which league he intended to sign with. At the end of February, the *Boston Globe* published a petition signed by nearly seven hundred people—including seventy-two members of the Massachusetts legislature—calling on Kelly to play with the local Association club.

On March 18, Kelly finally signed a personal services contract with Prince for a reported $4,700, and told a local newspaper he would probably captain the Cincinnati team. To boost the new club's chances against the League's Reds, the Boston owners agreed to "loan" Kelly to Cincinnati. Frank Bancroft, who over the past thirteen years had managed various minor and major league clubs, became the club's business manager. Byron Bancroft "Ban" Johnson, the twenty-seven-year-old sports editor of the *Cincinnati Commercial-Gazette*, would serve as its secretary. The local press quickly foisted the singular nickname "Kelly's Killers" on the team.

It's a measure of Kelly's magnetism that his very presence in Cincinnati was supposed to make the Association franchise a success. "Outside of his playing strength," wrote one columnist, "Mike Kelly is a valuable adjunct to any club owing to his advertising propensities."[10] But if Kelly in Cincinnati seemed like a good idea at the time, the whole undertaking faced difficulties that ultimately would prove insurmountable. Like the Players' League clubs a year earlier, the Cincinnati project started out with no playing grounds. Whereas the National League ballpark was easily accessible by various streetcar and rail lines, the property Munson obtained was situated in the outlying city limits at Ridgely and Watson streets, in a sparsely settled section called Pendleton—a good four miles from downtown. Around the beginning of March, construction of the ballpark got underway in a low-lying area close by the Ohio River, which meant that from time to time the grounds would be flooded. Only one rail line extended as far as Pendleton, so most customers would have to reach the site as best they could, often traveling by river boats they boarded at the foot of downtown.

The Association intended to offer Sunday baseball in Cincinnati, as it had done during the city's seven-year membership in the circuit. But in the face of vocal opposition to Sunday ball from the city's mayor and organized protests by local Methodist ministers, it seemed likely the Association would run into trouble on that score. In large part it was his fear of a crackdown on Sunday ball that had made Aaron Stern decide to take his franchise out of the Association following the 1889 season, and if anything, Sabbatarianism was stronger than ever in the Queen City.

For the second year in a row, the players had the advantage in their dealings with the club owners. The Association voted not to sign anybody already under contract in the

National League, but the League observed no such scruples. The previous fall, Ralph Lazarus had boasted that the days of big salaries were over. Now he as well as all the other club owners found themselves again in hot competition for playing talent. A year earlier it had been the Players' League wooing players from the National League and the Association, and the two older leagues doing everything they could to woo players back. Now the League and Association were locked in baseball's fourth war since 1882.[11]

Most former Players' Leaguers signed with Association clubs, presumably because of continuing antagonism toward the National League's owners and the players who had deserted the Brotherhood. Of the 127 men who had appeared in the Players' League, only 33 were on National League rosters at the beginning of the season. The New York Giants were an exception. Despite their contempt for Jack Glasscock and other "turncoats," most of the 1889 Giants mainstays returned to their old club, including Buck Ewing, Roger Connor, Tim Keefe, George Gore, and Jim O'Rourke. John B. Day re-signed the forty-year-old O'Rourke (a .360 batter in the Players' League), despite proclaiming the previous fall that he wanted no "orators." The combination of those veteran performers with Glasscock, Mickey Welch, Amos Rusie, and John Ewing (who followed his brother from the Players' League) looked to make the 1891 Giants an especially potent entry. The previous December, Day and Edward B. Talcott looked over the Brotherhood Park at 157th Street and Eighth Avenue, decided it was a better facility than Manhattan Field, and leased it from the Lynch estate. Thus the Giants would occupy still another playing site (the fourth) to be called the Polo Grounds.

On April 2, John Ward and Helen Dauvray arrived from Europe aboard the *Teutonic*, beamingly reconciled. Although in September, Ward told reporters he would be willing to swallow the "bitter pill" of playing with men who had betrayed the Brotherhood, it turned out he wouldn't have to play alongside Jack Glasscock after all. Before leaving the country, he obtained his release from John B. Day and signed to captain the Brooklyn Bridegrooms. Having directed Brooklyn to two pennants in two years, Bill McGunnigle wanted more money than Charles Byrne was willing to pay, whereupon Byrne unceremoniously fired him. McGunnigle was left to wonder what he had to do to keep his job. (He quickly signed to manage Providence in the Eastern Association.)

Washington Park in the Red Hook section of Brooklyn, site of the Bridegrooms' home games since 1884, was far more accessible to Brooklyn's kranks than Eastern Park in East New York, where Ward's Wonders had played well but drawn poorly in the

Players' League. But George W. Chauncey—who had been as big an investor in the Wonders as Wendell Goodwin and Edward Linton—insisted, as a condition of joining the amalgamated Brooklyn franchise, that the team play its home games at Eastern Park, which was owned by Chauncey's Ridgewood Land and Improvement Company. (Presumably Chauncey had written off the $7,500 in back rent on Eastern Park.)

It wasn't a good decision to move the Bridegrooms, and it wouldn't be a good team. Ward had available Dave Foutz, Tom Burns, Bob Caruthers, Darby O'Brien, Adonis Terry, Tom Lovett, and nearly all the others from the two-time pennant winners. When he arrived home from Europe, Ward condemned "the atrocious action of certain League clubs in trying to induce Association players to break their contracts."[12] Yet he was quite willing to take on outfielder Mike Griffin, late of the Philadelphia Players, who had first signed with the Athletics. Although Ward's roster looked good on paper, he had never played in the same league with most of his men, several of whom had seen their best years, and the National League was going to be a lot stronger than in 1890.

Except for Harry Stovey, Billy Nash was the only member of the Boston Players' League team to go over to the National League. After signing with Arthur Soden, Stovey wrote Nash, who was playing in California, urging him to join him on the League team. The highly regarded third baseman did so for a three-year contract reputed to be $5,000 a year. Frank Selee still had John Clarkson, Kid Nichols, Herman Long, Tommy Tucker, Charlie Bennett, and others from his 1890 club. The addition of Stovey and Nash made the Beaneaters a formidable outfit, although Charlie Getzein would prove ineffective in the box and get his release early in the season.

Rejoining Cap Anson's Chicago club (still called the Colts) were infielders Fred Pfeffer, outfielder Jimmy Ryan, and pitcher Ad Gumbert. Ed Williamson retired at age thirty-three, having never fully recovered from the leg injury he suffered in Paris on Spalding's world tour. Gumbert was Anson's number-two starter, although Bill Hutchinson continued to carry most of the pitching load. Outfielders Walt Wilmot and Cliff Carroll and third baseman Tommy Burns were other holdovers from the team that had come close to a pennant last season, while twenty-year-old Bill Dahlen, a slick infielder with a potent bat, had starred in the New York State League. Al Spalding now owned both West Side and South Side parks, so he directed that the Colts play Mondays, Wednesdays, and Fridays on the west side, Tuesdays, Thursdays, and Saturdays on the south side.

On April 14, Spalding resigned the presidency of the Chicago club after nine years in the position, naming Jim Hart to succeed him. As Spalding and his wife sailed for Europe, some may have assumed he had withdrawn from active involvement in baseball affairs. But he would continue to control one of the National League's most consistently profitable franchises, and he would continue to be a major influence in the game.

At Philadelphia, John I. Rogers refused to take back anybody who had gone over to the Players' League except Ed Delahanty and Jim Fogarty. With ninety-two errors to his discredit in his Players' League season, Delahanty proved to himself and everybody else he was no infielder; but in 1891, settling into center field, he was an improved player, on the verge of becoming one of the game's best. A native San Franciscan, Fogarty came east in late winter already having contracted tuberculosis. On May 10, in Philadelphia, he died of that era's most dreaded contagious disease.

Otherwise Harry Wright—whom Rogers and Al Reach retained with considerable reluctance—had among his holdovers pitcher Kid Gleason, catcher Jack Clements, infielders Al Myers and Bob Allen, plus slugging Sam Thompson and the brilliant Billy Hamilton. With Hamilton in left, Delahanty in center, and Thompson in right, the Phillies had the makings of one of the strongest outfields in the game's history.

Wright might have had the services of another outfielder, but that young man made a life-changing decision to pursue a higher calling than baseball. Billy Sunday had been in the major leagues since 1883 and was the substitute outfielder on Cap Anson's powerhouse teams of the mid-1880s. He put in two full seasons with the Alleghenies, then was traded to the Phillies late in the 1890 season. By that time Sunday was a born-again Christian, actively involved as a lecturer for the Young Men's Christian Association. Never much of a batter, Sunday was known for his speed in the outfield and on the bases. Offered a $2,200 contract for 1891, he asked John I. Rogers for his release and, at twenty-eight, gave up baseball for full-time YMCA work. Within a decade or so, Billy Sunday had become one of the foremost itinerant evangelists in the nation's history.

John T. Brush's Cincinnati franchise was a wholly new one, the old one having been expelled from the National League after it was bought by Al Johnson and company. After that fiasco, nearly all of the 1890 Reds signed contracts with Brush, including Arlie Latham, who continued in his dubious role as captain while Tom Loftus occupied the bench as manager. The Reds also signed Charles Radbourn, but after winning twenty-seven games to help Boston to the Players' League title, the Ol' Hoss's right arm was about played out. Second baseman Bid McPhee, first baseman John Reilly, pitcher-outfielder Tony Mullane, outfielders Charles "Lefty" Marr and John "Bug" Holiday; and pitchers Billy Rynes and Jim Duryea were all back. But like Brooklyn, the Reds were going to find it tougher going in a much-improved National League.

Not so Cy Young, who became the unchallenged ace of Cleveland's pitching staff. Although manager Bob Leadley's everyday lineup looked pretty strong, after Young, the pitching talent quickly thinned. Leadley's holdovers included outfielder George Davis, shortstop Ed McKean, and catcher Chief Zimmer. Outfielder Jimmy McAleer and infielder Oliver "Patsy" Tebeau had spent 1890 with the Cleveland Players; McAleer jumped St. Louis's reserve list, while Tebeau had remained on Cleveland's National League list. At second base was Clarence "Cupid" Childs, a .345 batter with Syracuse in the 1890 Association. Sold to Cleveland at season's end, Childs then signed to play for Bill Barnie at Baltimore. Although he returned his $200 advance, Baltimore sought an injunction to keep him from playing for Cleveland. The Robisons' lawyers successfully argued in a Baltimore court that the termination of the National Agreement released Childs from any obligation to Baltimore. Besides regaining Childs, Cleveland raided Columbus for pitcher Frank Knauss, outfielder Ralph Johnson, and utility man Jack Doyle. More litigation ensued, but the Childs judgment provided a legal precedent for the National League's continuing forays into the Association.

Pittsburgh moved from Recreation Park, sometime home of the awful Alleghenies, to Exposition Park, the Players' League grounds. In addition to manager and center fielder Ned Hanlon, the team consisted mostly of former Players' League Burghers. (The *Sporting News* predicted Hanlon would "prove an ignominious failure as a manager." As for his center-field play, "Hanlon could not throw out a cow.")[13] Besides the "pirated" Louis Bierbauer, former Players' Leaguers included first baseman Jake Beckley, shortstop Fred Shugart, outfielders Fred Carroll and John "Jocko" Fields, catcher Connie Mack, and pitchers Pud Galvin and Al Maul. Catcher-infielder George Miller was the lone holdover from the Alleghenies.

The actions of Pittsburgh owner J. Palmer O'Neill ensured that his ball club would live up to its new nickname. Hanlon's roster also included Mark Baldwin and Charles Reilly. Baldwin had pitched well for the Chicago Players, while Reilly had been Columbus's regular third baseman; both signed contracts with Columbus. Late in February, amid rumors he planned to jump to Pittsburgh, Baldwin wired Ralph Lazarus from his residence at Homestead, Pennsylvania: "Depend on me; will not go back on my contract; we are in it."[14] A few days later he signed with Pittsburgh, as did Reilly.

O'Neill not only obtained Baldwin's services to pitch; he also quickly dispatched him as well as Guy Hecker, the Alleghenies' 1890 manager, to work on other Association players. Baldwin's nickname was "Fido," although it might well have been "Blood Hound." Early in March, he traveled to St. Louis to track down local residents Silver King, whom von der Ahe had already signed, and Jack O'Connor, a twenty-one year old catcher-outfielder under contract to Columbus. When von der Ahe heard about Baldwin's activities, he swore out a warrant for his arrest. Found in a local pool hall, Baldwin was hauled off to jail. The pitcher hired an attorney who secured his release, whereupon von der Ahe had him jailed again. Released again, Baldwin filed suit against the Browns' owner for $20,000, charging false arrest and malicious prosecution. (The suit dragged on until 1895, when a court awarded Baldwin $2,500.)

On that mission into St. Louis, Baldwin was unsuccessful in getting King to jump his contract, although he signed O'Connor and gave him $750 of O'Neill's money as an advance. But then O'Connor changed his mind and, without returning the advance, reported for spring practice in Columbus at Recreation Park, in the city's German Village district. He explained his behavior with consummate cheek: "It was bribe money, and they can't recover it. I didn't intend to play with the Pittsburg [*sic*] club of the National League, but as long as it was throwing money around so freely, I thought I might as well get some. I consider that the loss of the money serves the National League right for trying to lower base ball by trying to induce players to jump contracts."[15]

Meanwhile Guy Hecker went to Columbus, where he failed to sign Hank Gastright, then made a difficult trip into eastern Kentucky to convince Scott Stratton to desert Louisville. In Louisville, Pete Browning, who had vowed never again to play for the local club, also signed with Hecker.

Louisville's *Sporting News* correspondent provided a cruel valedictory for the Louisville native, who had been the foremost player in the city's history. After charging that Browning had "disappointed the Louisville base ball public thousands of times," the pseudonymous "Arsun" went on to give a description of how with the bases loaded, Browning "dragged his old whiskey-soaked carcass up to the bat and struck out. . . . There are cranks in this city who have gray hairs in their heads as the result of Browning's dissipation."[16]

It's interesting to speculate on the bidding the man Browning edged for the Players' League batting title might have occasioned if he had chosen to jump Columbus's reserve list. The previous fall, Dave Orr suffered a stroke during a postseason exhibition game. At thirty-one, his baseball career was over.

The Association's Boston Reds were made up largely of the Players' League champions, including Dan Brouthers, Duke Farrell, Tom Brown, Hardie Richardson, Morgan Murphy, and Bill Daley. Little Hugh Duffy, who batted .320 for Comiskey's Chicago team and led all three leagues in runs scored, resisted the Beaneaters' blandishments and signed with Prince and Hart for $5,000. They also signed Charlie Buffinton, who had pitched for the Philadelphia Players and managed the team after Jim Fogarty quit, as well as George Haddock, who had toiled for Buffalo, mostly in vain. John O'Brien (like Brooklyn's William O'Brien, called "Darby") pitched for Cleveland in the Association, National League, and Players' League. Outfielder Paul Raymond, 5' 6", and infielder John "Cub" Stricker, 5' 3", were O'Brien's teammates at Cleveland; Bill "Scrappy" Joyce was the regular third baseman for Ward's Wonders. Manager Arthur Irwin, regular shortstop on the 1890 team, remained on the playing roster but appeared in only six games.

Although he had vowed never to rehire any of "mein Prowns" who went with the Players' League, Chris von der Ahe was pleased to take back Comiskey, Tip O'Neill, Jack Boyle, and (he thought) Silver King. He didn't want Yank Robinson, who ended up with Kelly's Cincinnati club. Von der Ahe also signed hard-hitting Denny Lyons, who had accepted his release from the Athletics the previous September, and Dummy Hoy, who said (or signed) that he lost a month's pay at Buffalo. Cap Anson, whom Hoy described as "quite expert in talking upon his fingers," offered him $2,500; with von der Ahe he was making $3,500.[17] With Tommy McCarthy (who resisted Cleveland's entreaties), Shorty Fuller, and Jack Stivetts back from last year's team, St. Louis kranks could entertain hopes of a return to past glories.

Baltimore finished the 1890 American Association season with a team that had been playing in the Atlantic Association, plus three valuable late-season signees who, along with Denny Lyons, received their releases from the bankrupt Athletics: outfielder Curt Welch, catcher Wilbert Robinson, and pitcher Sadie McMahon. For all his reputation as a tippler and carouser, Welch was still regarded as one of the game's premier center fielders; Robinson and McMahon still had years of stardom ahead of them. George Van

Haltren was on Chicago's reserve list, but he opted for Baltimore and a two-year contract at $3,500 before signing with Anson, thus technically conforming to Association policy. Asked why he hadn't stayed with Chicago, Van Haltren answered bluntly: "More money. I am not playing ball for pleasure."[18] Barnie also had Perry Werden, a massive first baseman who had been with Toledo in 1890, and veteran infielder Sam Wise, Connie Mack's good friend and his teammate at Buffalo. Besides loaning Mike Kelly to Cincinnati, Boston also loaned Baltimore left-hander Kid Madden, who had pitched sparingly for the Boston Players.

As opening day neared, having lost Mark Baldwin, Charles Reilly, Frank Knauss, Ralph Johnson, and Jack Doyle, Columbus manager Gus Schmelz was down to eight men. Schmelz had to hustle to sign enough minor leaguers and released major leaguers to fill out his roster. If the National League had targeted Columbus for its player raids, the suspicion among Association people was that Allan W. Thurman might have had something to do with it. But if so, it did Thurman little good in his relations with the National League. On March 20, John I. Rogers and Louis Krauthoff voted him off the National Board when he insisted that, in addition to his $1,000 chairman's allowance, the League owed him $1,500. Nick Young replaced the erstwhile White-Winged Angel of Peace in the board's chair.[19]

Two infielders, two outfielders, a catcher-outfielder (the prodigal O'Connor), and two pitchers remained from Columbus's 1890 team. Phil Knell, a smallish left-hander who had won twenty games for the Philadelphia Players, displaced Hank Gastright as the ace of the team variously called "Senators" or "Solons"; but with a mediocre cast otherwise, it wasn't going to be a happy season for Gus Schmelz.

The Athletics were a new ball club playing for new owners in a new playing site, although the site wasn't new to the owners. The Wagners leased Forepaugh Park, home of the Players' League Quakers. They kept Bill Sharsig as manager, although after only seventeen games, they replaced him with outfielder George Wood. Wood and ten other former Players' Leaguers, most of whom had been with the Philadelphia entry, were on the Athletics' roster. Gus Weyhing would be the staff ace, as he had been for the Brooklyn Players the previous season.

The Athletics also had Ice Box Chamberlain. Although Chamberlain had pitched well in Columbus, he hadn't liked Gus Schmelz any more than he had Chris von der Ahe. On one occasion, when Schmelz posted an order in the team's dressing room requiring daily practices, Chamberlain spat tobacco juice on it. Fined $50, he refused to pitch until the money was refunded. After the season he returned to his home in Buffalo, obtained his release, and signed with the Athletics, where he would win twenty-two games but lose twenty-three.

The Association champion Louisville team reverted to being called the Colonels and, to the dismay of the city that had turned out a record attendance in 1890, also reverted to its old losing ways. Jack Chapman's roster was made up almost wholly of holdovers, which didn't bode well in an Association that, for all the damage it suffered from the League's incursions, was still loaded with talented players who had been elsewhere a year earlier. By midseason, with the Louisville team struggling through a road trip, the *Louisville Commercial* suggested that "It would probably be a good thing if Manager Chapman and the club would lose themselves and never reach home again."[20]

And then there was the Association's new entry in the nation's capital. In one season in the Association (1884) and four in the National League (1886–89), Washington had finished at the bottom every year except 1887 (when it beat out Indianapolis for seventh place) and never attracted more than 80,000 to its home games. Already the city had gained the title, "First in war, first in peace, last in the league." Washington's population of about 230,000 exceeded only Louisville and Columbus in the Association. The 1891 edition of what was usually called the "Nationals" was owned by a syndicate that included August Mencken, a Baltimore cigar manufacturer. (August Mencken's eleven-year-old son Henry Louis Mencken would grow up to become a renowned—and often reviled—literary and social critic.)

Sam Trott, who had managed Newark in the International League in 1890, began the season in charge of the Washington club. Before the season opener in Baltimore, he gave his players an hour-long lecture in which he urged hustle, discipline, no late hours, and "no drinking, unless he knew what was being taken."[21] Trott lasted eleven games before Pop Snyder resigned from the Association's umpiring staff to replace him. Snyder was succeeded by two others before the season ended. Washington had a capable catcher with a strong bat in James "Deacon" McGuire but not much talent elsewhere. Washington native Paul Hines, who like Harry Stovey disliked Sunday ball (and was excused from it), had put in a notable career going back to the National League's inaugural season, but he was thirty-nine years old and painfully slow in the outfield. Fred Dunlap, once considered the king of second basemen, broke his leg sliding into a base early in the season and received his release in June. Washington's ace pitchers—if they could be called that—were nineteen-year-old Wilfred "Kid" Carsey, who led both leagues with thirty-seven losses, and thirty-three-year-old Frank Foreman, signed following his release by the Cincinnati Reds. Foreman had bounced around from team to team the past few years and, after losing twenty games in 1891, continued to bounce around.

As for the Association's team in Cincinnati, it might have been a competitive outfit if Mullane, McPhee, and John Reilly, who received bonuses to sign with the illusory Cincinnati Players' League franchise, hadn't opted to return to the National League with John T. Brush's Cincinnati Reds. As it was, Mike Kelly's Killers were made up mostly of has-beens, never-were's, and never-would-be's; Kelly himself was far and away the most notable player on his roster. Most of his everyday players had been around awhile, although none had particularly distinguished themselves. The strength of the team was in its pitchers—at least it seemed that way. The staff included Ed Crane, whom John B. Day didn't care to have back with the Giants. Cannonball Crane weighed over two hundred pounds and could be overpowering—when he was serious and sober. Frank Dwyer, who weighed only 145 pounds and was 5' 8" tall, had won sixteen games in 1889 for the former Cincinnati Association team and then pitched ineffectively in twelve starts for the Chicago Players. But Dwyer turned out to be Kelly's most reliable boxman; over a twelve-year career, he would record 176 victories. At season's start, Kelly also had Willie McGill, now all of seventeen. The little left-hander showed a lot of promise with the Cleveland Players, but things wouldn't work out for him in Cincinnati.

Given last year's financial losses, the continuing boost in players' salaries with the renewed baseball war, and the impossibility of playing lucrative inter-league exhibition games, only a few League and Association teams left their home cities for spring training. Cap Anson took his Colts to Denver, thinking the team could make money in games first with Denver and then with other Western Association teams, as Chicago played its way east. That was a mistake; in Denver and along the route home, the Colts endured mostly snow and cold. The Boston Reds' departure for Charleston, South Carolina, was delayed a day because of a storm in Norwich, Connecticut. A train wreck outside Danville, Virginia, held them up still more. They couldn't work out in Augusta, Georgia, because heavy rains had caused the Savannah River to flood the ballpark. They missed one train to Charleston, then were delayed by a stalled electric inter-urban train outside the city, finally arriving in Charleston for a few days of practice before they started back to New England.

The Cleveland team trained at Jacksonville, Florida, and played against Pittsburgh and various amateur and semipro clubs in the northern and central parts of the state. On March 26 the Spiders took the field at Gainesville against a group of young men recently back from Cuba, where they played a series of mostly losing games with top Cuban teams. Their leader was Al Lawson—the same Al Lawson who failed as a pitcher in the National League in 1890. The team included eighteen-year-old John McGraw, Lawson's teammate at Wellsville, New York, where Lawson had caught on after being released by Boston and the Alleghenies. Facing Leon "Lee" Viau, Cleveland's 5' 4" veteran left-hander, McGraw hit three doubles, scored three runs, and played an errorless shortstop. Reports of the game in the Cleveland newspapers and in *Sporting Life* and the *Sporting News* prompted inquiries and offers from various minor league clubs. The 5' 6 ½", 118-pound McGraw joined Cedar Rapids in the Illinois-Iowa League, although before the season was over, he would be in higher company.

En route to Jacksonville, the train carrying the newly christened Pittsburgh Pirates passed through Columbus. The sheriff of Franklin County and the Columbus club secretary were waiting to serve an injunction issued in common pleas court prohibiting Charles Reilly from playing in either Cleveland or Cincinnati. Reilly foiled the authorities by leaving the train at Zanesville and taking another to Washington Court House, where he rejoined his new teammates. As an indication of how ugly things were getting, the Columbus Order of Elks lodge expelled the wayward third baseman.

So in an atmosphere of lies, deception, litigation, and general confusion—not unlike the circumstances a year earlier—the 1891 major league season got underway. For all their antagonism, League and Association club owners remained in agreement on one rule change adopted by the joint rules committee before the breakup of the National Agreement: unlimited substitution of players, although as always, once a player left, he couldn't return. That, of course, opened the way for unrestricted pitching changes, pinch hitters, pinch runners, defensive switches, and other stratagems that, while managers were slow to employ them, would change the way baseball was played.

On April 2, Mike Kelley made his debut in the Association in a Fast Day exhibition game with Boston at the Congress Street Grounds, before a crowd of about 7,000.[22] John Ward, delayed in port by customs regulations, wired Charles Byrne an apology for being absent from the Brooklyn-Boston National League exhibition at the South End Grounds. Although the Association and League played in the same city on that date, and occasional conflicts occurred during the regular season, no deliberate competing dates were scheduled.

Not having had much in the way of an exhibition season, the Association began its regular season on Wednesday, April 8, two weeks ahead of the League and in generally unpleasant weather. Preceded by a parade and renditions by Eichorn's Orchestra of "Dixie" and "My Old Kentucky Home," the Louisville Colonels raised their championship pennant, then scored five times in the top of the ninth inning on Hank Gastright to defeat Columbus, 7–6, Ed Daily getting the win. Washington began its season encouragingly, defeating the Athletics at Forepaugh Park, 9–8, before 2,226 customers. Some 4,800 in Union Park, the day's biggest crowd, watched Baltimore's Sadie McMahon hold on for a win over Boston, 11–7. Arthur Irwin's choice was John O'Brien, who went the distance.

Cincinnati was supposed to open the season at home, but construction was still far from complete on what would be called either Pendleton Park or the East End Grounds. So Kelly's Killers traveled to St. Louis, where the King held court at the Lindell Hotel. Local scribe Joe Pritchard related that admirers "stood ten deep around Kel's chair. . . . He had the whole town on his staff." Kelly was his usual expansive self. "I have had enough of that League gang of monopolists," he declared, "and rather than to have played under them again I would have quit the business."[23]

Matters were less pleasant for Kelly when the Killers, in blue uniforms with "pea green" stockings, took the field on Wednesday, April 8, before about 3,000 shivering locals, plus Hi Hi Dixwell. Although Dixwell had given his heart to the Boston Reds, he traveled to St. Louis to watch his friend Kelly command his new team. Kelly sent Willie McGill to the box; Comiskey called on Jack Stivetts. With John Kelly having suddenly resigned from the umpiring staff, president Kramer hired Bill Gleason, a St. Louis native and former Browns shortstop, to replace him and to work the Cincinnati-St. Louis opener. The result was "everything but a riot," reported Pritchard. Gleason "set the crowd crazy by his decisions. He made Kelly wild. He had young McGill standing on his head."[24]

In the top of the fourth inning, Gleason called walks on six Browns batters. After five runs scored, Kelly took off his catcher's mitt, put on his coat, put Henry "Farmer"

Vaughn behind the bat, and left the field. Then in the bottom of the inning, the King of the Diamond played the part, reappearing to take his turn at bat despite Gleason's insistence that he couldn't. After Kelly reached base, the Killers scored four times to take the lead. Once the Killers were retired, the harried umpire finally got Kelly to leave. At the end of nine innings, with the score 7–7 and dark closing in, Kelly demanded that Gleason call the game. When he refused, the King ordered his men to stall and clown around, until the exasperated umpire declared a forfeit to St. Louis.

So began Mike Kelly's career in the American Association. Supported by Chris von der Ahe, who was also taken aback by his former shortstop's incompetence, Kelly wired a protest about Gleason to Louis Kramer in Cincinnati. Kramer polled the Association clubs on what to do. St. Louis, Baltimore, Columbus, Louisville, and of course Cincinnati wanted Gleason fired, which is what Kramer promptly did. Twenty-nine-year-old Jim Davis—who had spent six years as an infielder in the Union and American associations—was Gleason's replacement.

After a rainout, Davis took up his duties on Friday. Cincinnati won its first Association victory, Frank Dwyer prevailing over Joe Neale, 10–9. On Saturday, Willie McGill tried again for Cincinnati; Comiskey picked Clark Griffith, a twenty-one-year-old right-hander from a hamlet in Missouri. A half-inch taller than McGill but about twenty pounds lighter, Griffith had won twenty-seven games in the Western Association at Milwaukee. Although the American Association's policy was to refrain from signing National Leaguers under contract, it observed no such restriction where the minor leagues were concerned. Cincinnati first baseman Jack Carney had jumped from New Haven in the Eastern Association; Griffith did the same at Milwaukee. Griffith made a successful debut, limiting the Killers to five runs while the Browns piled up thirteen on McGill and a successor.

On Sunday an overflow crowd came to Sportsman's Park for a 10–2 Browns victory, Stivetts holding down the Killers while the Browns cuffed around Ed Crane. Commented Joe Pritchard, "The game showed conclusively how the game here has been enlivened by the American Association cutting loose from the National League and national agreement."[25] By Kramer's order, the forfeited game of the eighth was replayed on Monday the thirteenth. The Browns won again, 13–6, Neale coasting to a decision over Dwyer. With his pitchers having given up fifty-three runs in five games (counting the forfeit), Kelly must have begun to wonder why he agreed to leave his adoring followers in Boston.

Anybody who agreed to umpire in the Association must also have wondered why he did so. Although Columbus defeated the Browns on April 14 at Sportsman's Park, 9–8, the *Columbus Evening Dispatch*'s F. W. Arnold still panned forty-five-year-old Bob Ferguson, who was substituting for Jimmy Macullar: "Poor old blind Bob Ferguson, who is yet on earth and umpiring in St. Louis, gave additional evidence yesterday of his infirmity." From Boston, Jacob B. Morse indicted the Association's whole staff: "It is the greatest folly in the world to think of appointing old and stiff ball players to be umpires."[26] With his wife seriously ill in Baltimore, Macullar resigned and was replaced by the ubiquitous Jack Kerins. Shortly after Pop Snyder quit to take over from Sam Trott as Washington manager, Bobby Matthews, who had endured a rough time in the Players' League, took Snyder's place. By the beginning of May, only Charlie Jones remained from the four umpires the Association hired back in February.

On April 18, 1891, in the Association's first regular-season game in Boston, the talent-rich Reds downed the Athletics, 6–3. Hugh Duffy delighted the Congress Street assemblage of 4,000 with two home runs over the short left-field fence off Gus Weyhing. George Haddock, no doubt happy at last to be pitching for a good ball club, was the winner. In the early going, the Louisville Colonels looked as if they might be capable of defending their pennant, winning four of their first five games and twelve of their first fifteen. But on Sunday, April 20, before a capacity 7,500 at Eclipse Park, Jack Chapman's team lost to St. Louis and yielded first place to Boston. After that they were on their way to the Association's nether regions. As of May 15, despite losing veteran outfielder Hardie Richardson to a broken leg, Boston led the Association with a 20–8 record, followed by Baltimore (17–9) and St. Louis (18–13). Louisville had slumped to 16–16; the Athletics were at 12–14; Cincinnati had won 14, lost 18; and the Washington team had won only 7 times in 26 tries. "As at present constituted," commented a local reporter, "the Nationals are not fast enough for the company they are keeping."[27] On May 8, in what became an all-too-common display of incompetence, Washington made eighteen errors—eight of which were charged to second baseman Tommy Dowd—in a 20–4 loss to St. Louis, which scored only three earned runs.

On Friday, April 24, Kelly's Killers finally opened at home. Only 1,760 showed up at the still-unfinished park in Pendleton to watch the new ball club lose to Louisville on a muddy field, 10–9, McGill taking the defeat. Kelly singled and hit two doubles off John Doran, another undersized left-hander.

If the Killers were deficient at most positions, they soon learned that they were also deficient in the political clout necessary to prevent interference with their Sunday home dates. Mayor William Mosby and his Sabbatarian constituents proved more determined than the American Association on the subject of the Sabbath. On April 26 about 5,800 people—arriving by the one available streetcar line and by carriage, buggy, omnibus, and riverboat—were on hand for Cincinnati's first Sunday game since 1889. The authorities allowed the game to proceed to its conclusion, Louisville winning, 12–6. But then police came on the field, arrested both teams, and hauled them to the Fulton District Station, where they posted bonds, had their names registered, and were released. The same thing happened a week later, except that this time well-to-do local kranks had already signed for their bonds.

Then, on May 24, matters took an even more ridiculous turn. The Killers played in Philadelphia on Saturday, after which J. Earle Wagner paid $1,500 to charter a train to take the two teams to Cincinnati for a Sunday game. After a record run of eighteen and a half hours, the players arrived just before game time. The two thousand or so spectators were given refund tickets, to be used if the police stopped the game. The Athletics batted first and didn't score. After two Cincinnati batters went out, no less a personage than Phil Dietsch, the city's police superintendent, ordered his squad of sixty policemen onto the field in a show of overwhelming force. Placed under arrest, the players of the two teams changed into street clothes, while a mounted squad and three police wagons waited outside the park. At the Fulton District Station they were booked and released on bonds of $300 each, which Otto F. Betz, a wealthy baseball-minded local citizen, put up for them. Six days later a police court jury took all of ten minutes to acquit the Cincinnati and Athletics players.

That became the routine whenever the Killers tried to play a Sunday home date. On one occasion, Kelly stood trial in police court and was acquitted when the prosecution couldn't convince the jury that Sunday was truly the first day of the week. Ban Johnson, doubling as Killers secretary and *Commercial-Gazette* sports editor, was among the many who couldn't understand why Mayor Mosby objected to Sunday ball when Cincinnati's saloons and theaters stayed open on the Sabbath.

Besides harassment on Sundays, Kelly had to contend with several players who liked their liquor as much as the Killers' captain—maybe even more. Kelly announced he and his men had bet each other hats they wouldn't take a drink during the season. Yank Robinson, for one, acted as if he wanted a new hat. After watching him at second base in the Killers' opening series in St. Louis, Joe Pritchard commented, "It is said that he is not drinking a drop, and I believe it, as his head was clear as a bell, and he was in the pink of condition." Yet neither Kelly nor his players held fast. As the late Lee Allen wrote in his history of Cincinnati baseball (no doubt with some exaggeration), "After each game the King would hold court, sitting with his players at a long white table that groaned with food and drink. Far into the night the players would remain to talk over each game with their admirers."[28]

Kelly had particular trouble with the twenty-nine-year-old Crane and the seventeen-year-old McGill. In Louisville on the night of April 23, Cannonball took McGill out on the town. When they got into a fracas and ended up jailed at the police station house, Kelly paid their fines of $20 apiece plus costs and then assessed his own fines of $30 apiece. The next night, when they started out of the Galt House again, Kelly intercepted them, bawled out Crane for corrupting the teenage pitcher, and told him he was fined again. Crane slapped the King, whereupon Kelly floored him with one punch.

After farce came tragedy. When young McGill's father in Chicago read about what had happened, he headed for Louisville to straighten out his boy. Near Indianapolis his train derailed, and Thomas McGill suffered mortal injuries in the wreck. He lingered for nearly three weeks at St. Vincent's Hospital in Indianapolis. Informed in Baltimore his father was near death, McGill hurried to Indianapolis, arriving just before the elder McGill died.

In eight starts, McGill had won just twice and lost five times. Shortly after he rejoined the Killers, Kelly notified him his transfer to St. Louis had been arranged. With the Browns, the little left-hander would find life better. As for Ed Crane, he continued to pitch well at times as well as to drink and carouse. A few weeks after the Louisville episode, he went on another spree in Boston. When the Killers returned to Cincinnati, Association president Kramer called the pitcher to his office, gave him a stern lecture, and fined him $50.

If Kelly had regrets about coming to Cincinnati, he also had his bright moments. Baseball was always fun for the King. On April 28, at Pendleton Park, McGill got

Columbus's Charlie Duffee, who had hit three singles and a home run, to ground out to end the game, 9–8. Out in right field, as the scene was rendered by the Cincinnati reporter Harry Weldon, Kelly "fell on his knees and, removing his cap, remained for several moments in the attitude of earnest supplication. Springing up and dusting off his pants, he emitted a shriek of joy, and, after executing a jig, capered gayly to the club house."[29]

On May 6, Kelly's Killers made their first regular-season appearance in Boston. With a good Wednesday crowd of 3,100 on hand, Kelly's friends presented him with the customary floral horseshoe, plus a new trap and still another horse, an iron-gray trotter. Boston won 6–1 behind Haddock. The next day Kelly rewarded his friends in dubious fashion, when, with two out in the bottom of the fourteenth inning, he hit Charlie Daley's first pitch over the left-field fence, scoring Emmet Seery ahead of him to win it, 10–9. As the faithful Dixwell and most of the otherwise partisan Boston kranks cheered him, Kelly did handsprings around the bases. That capped a splendid day for the Killers' captain, who had also hit a single and double and thrown out seven runners on eight steal attempts.[30]

Given the municipal administration's implacable stance on Sunday ball and the difficulty most people encountered reaching the ballpark, rumors began to circulate that the Association would relocate its Cincinnati franchise. It didn't help that the grounds flooded before a late-May game with Boston, making for conditions under which the teams combined for sixteen errors (seven by Yank Robinson alone). Boston won 21–16, ending the game with a triple play.

A group of Indianapolis businessmen sought to meet with president Kramer to discuss moving the Killers to the Indiana capital. Kramer replied, "The Association club will never move from Cincinnati." If the Indianapolis group wanted a major league franchise, he advised, they should talk to the League and John T. Brush. Added Chris von der Ahe, "The Association don't want Indianapolis, nor will it ever move its club away from Cincinnati."[31] That seemed to settle that—at least for the time being.

The National League season had its own comic-opera moments. The season was to begin on Wednesday, April 22. Returning from Florida for its home opener with Chicago, the Pittsburgh team had to pass through Columbus, where, as he had a few weeks earlier, the Franklin County sheriff waited to serve his injunction, this time on Mark Baldwin as well as Charles Reilly. Rustically disguised as farmers in overalls and fake beards, the two contract jumpers left their teammates in Cincinnati and proceeded to Columbus on the Panhandle Railroad. They got away with the ruse and went on to Pittsburgh.[32]

A few days later, fellow contract jumper Silver King arrived in the city, met with J. Palmer O'Neill, and finally signed a Pittsburgh contract for a reported $5,000. King admitted he had earlier signed with von der Ahe, but the contract wasn't legal because (1) Eddie von der Ahe had signed for him, and (2) the name recorded for the franchise was wrong. Or so the pitcher claimed.

The League's umpiring staff consisted of returnees Phil Powers, Jack McQuaid, and Tom Lynch, plus newcomer Tim Hurst, a 5' 5" former coal miner and prizefight referee who would prove sufficiently rugged and combative to weather eighteen years in the major leagues. (Once asked why he withstood the rigors of umpiring, Hurst replied, "You can't beat the hours," thus coining one of baseball's most enduring maxims.) The coming season would offer about as much rugged going for that quartet as for their frequently changing counterparts in the Association.

With phony attendance figures no longer necessary, the New York Giants accurately reported that a record 17,335 people bought tickets at the former Brotherhood Park for the Giants' home opener with Boston. Jim Mutrie had even put a new motto on the front of the Giants' clubhouse: "United, Greater and Stronger Than Ever." In a matchup of distinguished veteran versus rising youngster, John Clarkson outdueled Amos Rusie, 4–3. At Philadelphia, nearly 10,000 watched the Phillies lose a sloppy game to John Ward's Brooklyns, 14–8, Kid Gleason outlasting George Hemming. In Cincinnati, Cy Young pitched Cleveland to a 6–3 victory over Tony Mullane. And at Pittsburgh, 5,263 came to Exposition Park for the reconstituted locals' ten-inning 7–6 loss to Chicago. Bill Hutchinson relieved newcomer Pat Luby to get the win; the venerable Pud Galvin, whose career stretched back to the National Association, took the loss. Mark Baldwin, reported the *Tribune*'s Joe Murphy, "has been too busy keeping out of jail to get into condition, and has a lame arm."[33]

On April 30, Anson's Colts won the finale of their first series in Cincinnati, 7–4, with Bill Dahlen homering off Mullane. Mullane continually spatted with Phil Powers, who called ten walks on him. Finally the umpire began assessing fines on the pitcher. Although Mullane was Irish-born, his dark features and short temper occasioned the widespread belief that his ancestry was Italian. "The denizen of Mafia land subsided until the game was over," related the *Sporting News*'s Cincinnati correspondent; then Mullane followed Powers across the field and either hit the umpire on the jaw or kicked him (accounts vary). Powers fended him off with his chest protector and, in the safety of the clubhouse, upped Mullane's fine to $250. Although League president Young reduced the fine to a token $5, he sent "T. J. Mullane, Esq." a letter "to express my displeasure in writing" and to admonish him "never again, by any unmanly act, tarnish the reputation of the club you represent or our grand National Game." The *Cincinnati Times-Star* had no sympathy for Powers, described as standing "so far away from the plate that he needs field glasses to see it in the first place. That is the secret of his bad work."[34]

Chicago opened at home on Friday, May 1, before 6,500 enthusiastic kranks at the West Side Park. Joe Murphy contrasted the scene with the 1890 National League opener, with its "empty benches and a crowd which for coldness and stoical indifference outrivaled a gathering of Indian chiefs." Pittsburgh won, 5–2, Galvin taking the measure of Luby. Apparently missing the free-hitting Players' League, Murphy thought "the contest was a rather stupid one, as all pitchers' battles invariably are."[35] Four days later the Colts played for the first time on the South Side—a game Murphy must have found even more "stupid." In chilling temperatures, Ed Stein held Pittsburgh scoreless while Chicago scratched one run off Galvin.

For 1891, unfortunately, *Sporting Life* publisher Francis Richter didn't have Ella Black reporting on Pittsburgh baseball, so readers of Richter's Philadelphia weekly were deprived of the young woman's lively, perceptive, and often acerbic commentaries. Why Ms. Black didn't continue as a contributor isn't known, nor is anything known of her life after 1890. Her columns, written thirty years before women gained voting rights, were remarkable in the male-dominated times in which she lived.

Cy Young made his fourth start in Cleveland's home opener, again gaining a victory over Cincinnati. A capacity crowd of 8,600 came to new League Park at Lexington Avenue and Dunham (later East Sixty-sixth) Street, served by the Robisons' trolley line. After watching Young pitch in Brooklyn later in the season, the New York reporter Joe Donnelly described how he did it: "Before pitching the ball he holds it in his left hand, while he swings his right tree. Then he brings the latter around with a circular sweep, grabs the ball from the left, turns a half back hand spring and lets her go. When in form he is a puzzler."[36]

Later on it became conventional baseball wisdom that winning teams had to be "strong up the middle." With Young in the box, the 1891 Cleveland Spiders so qualified, with Zimmer behind the plate, Childs at second base, McKean at shortstop, and George Davis in center field. It should have been a better team, but with Henry Gruber or Len Viau following Young to the box, the Spiders gave up more runs than any other team in the League. They played above .500 for a while before faltering on an eastern trip and never recovered.

By the end of May, the League's strongest teams appeared to be New York, followed by Chicago and Philadelphia. On May 28, with Chicago in first place at 18–10, Boston's record was only 15–15. Tim Murnane, traveling with the Beaneaters on their first western trip, didn't think much of their pennant chances. For Chicago, Bill Hutchinson still carried most of the pitching load, usually spelled by Ad Gumbert and occasionally by Pat Luby and Ed Stein. Amos Rusie started most of the Giants' games, and although Mickey Welch was all but finished and Tim Keefe was still troubled by the finger broken the previous August, John Ewing had become a reliable second starter. Buck Ewing, however, wasn't a factor on the playing field. Unable to get over a lame throwing arm, he appeared in only fourteen games; otherwise he sat on the bench alongside Jim Mutrie. (An example of the period's sports medicine: Ewing sought treatment from a veterinarian, who put a plaster on his arm, then applied a hot iron, then put on heavy bandages. That was supposed to expand and loosen the muscles. It didn't work.)

All-out competitor that he was, Cap Anson expected his players to be ready whenever he needed them. On Saturday, May 16, with Brooklyn ahead by 8–5 at South Side Park, Hutchinson and catcher Malachi Kittredge went to the dressing room, thinking the game lost. When Chicago rallied in the eighth and ninth innings for six runs to go ahead, 11–8, Anson wanted Hutchinson and Kittredge to replace Luby and Tom Nagle, but they were nowhere in sight. Discovering them in the dressing room already in street clothes, he fined them $25 each and sent Stein to the box to preserve the game, which he did. The next day Hutchinson and Kittredge threatened to quit the team and didn't show up for Monday's morning practice. Although he was furious, Anson knew he couldn't win without Hutchinson, so when the pitcher and his favorite batterymate appeared at West Side Park for that afternoon's game, all was forgiven.

The Colts swept the four-game series from John Ward's Bridegrooms, who were turning out to be a major disappointment. Ward's reputation as a field leader was rivaled only by that of Anson and Charles Comiskey, but Ward wasn't able to do much to inspire his aging ball club. Tom Lovett and Bob Caruthers were still generally reliable, but George Hemming wasn't much help, and Adonis Terry had trouble getting anybody out. Ward's .277 batting average—eighty-three points below his Players' League mark—was still second-best on the team. He missed a third of the season with one injury or another; rumors resurfaced of renewed troubles in his marriage.

After the first two months of the 1891 season, even with all of their "pirated" players, Pittsburgh couldn't put a contending team on the field. Ned Hanlon continued to have trouble with various men who had been with him in the Players' League, especially Fred Carroll, who nourished managerial ambitions of his own, and pitcher Harry Staley, who enjoyed the ambience of saloons far too much. Mark Baldwin became Carroll's confederate in efforts to undermine Hanlon. Scott Stratton developed a sore arm, was released in June, and re-signed with Louisville. A few days later Pete Browning, having batted only .291 in fifty games, also drew his release, supposedly because he refused to take sides between the Hanlon and Carroll factions and thus played indifferently. Browning signed with Cincinnati, where he became his old self at bat, averaging .343 over the remainder of the season.

Baldwin and Silver Flint, an outstanding brace of boxmen for Chicago in 1890, often pitched well but got little support from a team that collectively averaged only .239 and finished last in fielding average. Baldwin's and Flint's combined record was 36–57; Flint's 29 defeats were the most in the League. Of Flint's woes at Pittsburgh, the *St. Louis Post-Dispatch* quipped, "Verily, the way of the transgressor is hard."[37] Although he was on the downside of a long and distinguished career, Pud Galvin still worked in 33 games, winning 14.

Cincinnati scored only 646 runs with a team average of .242, which improved only a little after Browning's arrival. As team captain, Arlie Latham continued to provide less leadership than irritation for his teammates and manager Jim Loftus. After a 9–2 defeat early in June in New York, both the *Cincinnati Enquirer* and the *Herald* blamed Latham for the Reds' floundering play. Latham played to the grandstand, charged the *Enquirer*'s Harry Weldon, and his "continual prattle" had upset loser Tony Mullane, who "several times asked his captain to keep still, but if anything these requests induced him to talk more." According to Weldon, Mullane was also unhappy because Ol' Hoss Radbourn was getting more pay. "The long and short of the matter is Tricky Tony is pitching for his release."[38]

Whatever it was bothering Mullane—it may have been the illness of his young son, who died the next month in Chicago—he struggled to a final 22–24 record. Billy Rhines, who had been superb in much of his first season, lost 24 of 41 decisions. At thirty-seven, Radbourn finally reached the end of the road. In his first start on April 26, he endured the worst defeat of his storied career, Cleveland bombarding him for twenty-six hits and twenty-seven runs, including home runs by Davis, McKean, and Jake Virtue. Until he asked for his release in August, he lost twelve more games, winning eleven. When he left for his home in Bloomington, Illinois, he had pitched 4,543 major league innings in 517 games, winning 309 and losing 194.

With the caliber of play substantially improved in both leagues, attendance continued to run far ahead of 1890. And with the 45–45 percent split of gate receipts in the Association, Baltimore's membership proved a distinct asset, especially in the early going when the Orioles stayed near the top. Even Washington, playing in a ramshackle facility on Georgia Avenue with trees scattered around the outfield, was drawing reasonably well. On Ladies Day, Thursday, May 21, close to 2,000 saw the usually deplorable Nationals defeat Louisville, 7–6, although a local scribe lamented that left fielder Harry Beecher and second baseman Charles "Pop" Smith "put up a game of which a schoolboy would be ashamed."[39]

The National League outdrew the Association for the morning-afternoon Decoration Day doubleheaders, 65,056 to 17,883. That was misleading; all the League games were played in the bigger cities of the East, while Association teams played in the West, and rain prevented the morning game in Louisville. In St. Louis, the Browns beat up on the Athletics, 17–3 and 15–3, to keep the Association's race closely bunched between Boston (27–14), Baltimore (25–14), and St. Louis (27–17).

St. Louis moved ahead of Baltimore on June 1 and 2 with 6–4 and 11–0 wins, in the first of which the Orioles' big Perry Werden stirred the crowd's wrath by pushing Browns second baseman Bill Eagan on a steal attempt. Werden and other St. Louis natives, commented the *Post-Dispatch*'s reporter, proved no place exceeded that city in producing tough ballplayers. "In Welch and Werden," he wrote, "the Baltimores have a beautiful team when it comes to playing 'dirty ball.'" The next day Willie McGill, "the boy wonder," shut out Baltimore, 11–0, on five hits.[40]

On Saturday, June 6, in the first appearance by any Boston team in St. Louis, the Browns won in ten innings, 11–10, before a crowd of 7,500 to move into first place. John

O'Brien was the loser in relief of George Haddock; Clark Griffith got the win in relief of Jack Stivetts. The *Post-Dispatch* was hard on Bob Ferguson, whose "eyesight was bleared and his judgment was the rankest of the rank."[41] On Sunday, 17,439 Browns rooters overflowed Sportsman's Park, as Boston regained the lead with a 6–5 victory, despite Denny Lyons's three-run homer in the top of the ninth inning. During that rally, captain Comiskey took advantage of the new substitution rule by sending Stivetts to bat for McGill (although it would be another twenty years or so before the term "pinch hitter" entered baseball usage).

Almost from the beginning, it had been a three-team race in the Association. Yet as of June 11, after winning two of three from Boston, Kelly's nondescript and booze-loving Killers had surprised most people—perhaps including themselves—by climbing into fourth place with 22 wins, 24 losses. The next day the Killers beat Columbus at Pendleton, 5–3, in a game characterized as "a potpourri of kicks, chewing matches, repartee, brilliant plays, exciting situations and cross-grained, off-colored umpiring."[42] After the game Kelly had to be held back from going into the Columbus omnibus after Jack O'Connor, who was fast making a reputation as the Association's dirtiest player. After another two weeks, though still in fourth place, the Killers were at the pinnacle of their season with a 31–28 record. From that point, however, it was all downhill for Kelly's team, which lost 12 of its next 19 and tumbled to sixth place.

In the League, Hutchinson pitched both Decoration Day games in Philadelphia, losing in the morning, 4–3, winning in the afternoon, 16–12. At that point everybody but Brooklyn and Cincinnati was playing above .500, with New York only a game behind Chicago and Philadelphia three back. The Colts split with the Phillies, lost two of three games in Brooklyn, and opened a series in Boston with Hutchinson pitted against John Clarkson in what the *Chicago Tribune* headlined "Battle of the Kings." A disappointing Saturday turnout of only about 2,500 saw Hutchinson come out the victor, 5–3, on two home runs by Walt Wilmot and one by Bill Dahlen. Phil Powers received rough treatment from Boston's players and kranks, especially after he changed two decisions in favor of Chicago.

In sweltering heat, Chicago dropped three of the four games in Boston, losing the finale 14–3, with Harry Staley, recently purchased from Pittsburgh, getting his first Beaneaters win. Nick Young had received so many complaints about Powers's umpiring that he reassigned him to work the New York-Pittsburgh game and sent Tim Hurst to

Boston. The Colts' losses left them tied for first place with New York, whose ten-game winning streak Galvin stopped, 14–3.

Chicago then went to New York and lost all four games in the new-edition Polo Grounds. On Saturday, June 13, a throng of 22,289—thought to be the biggest ever for a professional baseball game—filled the grandstand and bleachers, sat and stood in front of the outfield fences and the roped-off carriage park in center field, and watched from closely parked horse-drawn conveyances beyond the ropes. Mike Tiernan, Roger Connor, and Jim O'Rourke homered for the Giants, Anson for Chicago, in an 8–7 New York win. Rusie, who pitched two complete-game wins in the series, saved the game for Welch; Stein was the battered loser. Chicago left town trailing New York by two games, although the Giants were playing without Jack Glasscock, recuperating from a knee injury at his home in Wheeling. Boston, after a strong home stand, had taken over third place.

The Colts proceeded home by way of Cleveland and lost again, the diminutive Viau topping Hutchinson, 4–2, while Boston swept a Bunker Hill Day doubleheader from Brooklyn and moved into second place. After the defeat in Cleveland—the Colts' seventh loss in a row and eighth in their last nine games—Joe Murphy depicted Anson as "a ruin; a magnificent ruin. The dark shadow of defeat has settled on him."[43] That was both melodramatic and premature. The Colts won the remaining three games from the Spiders, including Luby's 3–2 victory over Cy Young on June 19. They arrived in Chicago again in second place.

Baseball writers around the National League seemed fascinated by Young's size and pitching style. "He is big enough to travel as a museum freak," marveled Murphy, "and his arms have the length of an ordinary man's leg. . . . The narrow confines of the box seem to hamper him some, and he has a step which is enough to frighten all the batting ability out of a batsman. When the foot rises in the air it looks as though it might land somewhere near the plate. . . . The ball is brought from away over the head and swoops down over the plate with speed enough to crack a safe."[44]

Meanwhile, in Brooklyn, Tom Lovett pitched the first no-hit game ever against the Giants, walking three, striking out four, and, thanks to errorless fielding, yielding no runs. New York erred five times behind John Ewing, who gave up four runs. Three days later, though, the Giants battered Lovett for nine runs on fourteen hits, including five by George Gore, while Rusie limited the Bridegrooms to two runs. At twenty years old, Rusie was pitching gilt-edged ball, despite having to cope with a horrible injury to his father, who fell under a moving train in Indianapolis and had to have his crushed leg amputated above the knee.

At home, Anson's Colts continued to play winning ball, sweeping four games from Cincinnati and three from Cleveland to run their streak to ten games. "Long John" (6' 3") Reilly was usually at first base for Cincinnati, but in the Chicago series he played center field. Joe Murphy described his play mercilessly: "John is not an outfielder. He need never be vaccinated while he is in center, for he wouldn't catch anything—not even the smallpox—if it brushed against him." Reilly homered in the series finale, an 11–7 decision for Hutchinson over Rhines, but Murphy didn't let up: "Long John Reilly's antics in center field . . . must be seen to be believed. . . . When he has to run any distance it is twenty to one on the ball with no takers."[45]

The Colts' winning streak pulled them back into the lead with a record of 36–22 to New York's 33–22 and Boston's 32–27. But then Ward's inconsistent Brooklyn team came into Chicago and swept an Independence Day doubleheader, Hemming shutting out the Colts, 8–0, in the morning, Lovett outpitching Hutchinson, 6–5, in the afternoon. Meanwhile, Boston won two close games from Pittsburgh, 2–1 (Staley) and 5–4 (Nichols); while New York swept two more close ones from Cincinnati, 3–2 (Rusie) and 5–4 (John Ewing). So at the mythical halfway point of the season, the Giants were back in first, at 35–23. Chicago's record was 36–26, Boston's 35–27. The rest of the League had faded: Brooklyn, 31–32, Cleveland, 32–33, Philadelphia, 30–31, Pittsburgh, 23–36, Cincinnati, 24–39.

Rumblings of discontent continued to emanate from Pittsburgh. Mark Baldwin, drawing a $4,000 salary, complained of a sore arm and didn't want to pitch. Ned Hanlon was said to be also on the outs with Pud Galvin, George Miller, and Louis Bierbauer, not to mention the dissident Fred Carroll. As Hanlon's unhappy contingent continued its spiritless play, he and J. Palmer O'Neill made a show of denying there was anything amiss in their relations. Yet shortly thereafter, O'Neill took the bizarre step of ordering Hanlon to remain at his residence in Pittsburgh for the next two weeks.

In the Association, the Columbus and Cincinnati teams were also less than happy families. After a late-season surge into second place in 1890, Columbus's prospects for 1891 looked good—that is, until defections to Cleveland and Pittsburgh gutted

Gus Schmelz's roster. F. W. Arnold, covering the Columbus outfit for the *Evening Dispatch*, seemed perpetually in a foul mood, upbraiding both players and umpires. "It's getting to be an open secret," he wrote late in June following still another loss, "that several of the best players on the team are hitting the lush rather hard." Then, "It's not true that Umpire [Charlie] Jones has the jaundice. His yellowness is from other causes. . . . Jones [is] decidedly the rankest umpire, bar none, that ever disgraced a Columbus diamond."[46]

A few weeks later, the word was his players didn't like Schmelz's "peculiar methods of team work" (although those methods served quite well after Schmelz took over midway through the 1890 season), in particular his fondness for the sacrifice bunt. Hank Gastright was sent home to Newport, Kentucky, without pay, "until he gets himself in condition to work," although he was quickly reinstated. Not so Jack O'Connor, a chronic malcontent. First Ralph Lazarus, Abraham Cohen, and the rest of the club's directors voted to suspend O'Connor indefinitely. Then Louis Kramer, without consulting the Columbus club, took the unprecedented step of expelling O'Connor from the Association for what Kramer termed "habitual drunkenness, disorderly conduct and insubordination." He also threatened actions against other "notorious toughs and drunkards in the American Association ranks." F. W. Arnold, who was also *Sporting Life*'s Columbus correspondent, suggested if Kramer wanted to go after other misbehaving players, he would "come very near to de-populating the Association before a week expires." But O'Connor got no sympathy in his hometown. "He long ago made himself very unpopular in this city by his ungentlemanly conduct on the ball field," was the verdict of the *St. Louis Post-Dispatch*.[47]

Out from under the baleful influence of Ed Crane, Willie McGill was pitching well for St. Louis. Left behind in Cincinnati, McGill's former saloon companion remained incorrigible. Scheduled to pitch in St. Louis, the Cannonball showed up "in a state of beastly intoxication," which cost him another $25 fine.[48] Kelly also hit Yank Robinson—who had failed to live up to Joe Pritchard's early season praise for his sobriety—with a like fine.

The King may have been losing heart; after dropping an Independence Day doubleheader to Baltimore, Cincinnati had won only once in its last ten games. On Sunday, July 12, the Killers defeated the Cuban Giants, 11–5, at Wallace's Ridgewood Park on

Long Island. Ed Crane was plainly drunk, while Kelly, appearing to be tight himself, performed some silly antics, as did Yank Robinson and substitute catcher Jerry Hurley.[49]

Shortly thereafter, explaining he had a lacerated hip, Kelly put outfielder Ed Andrews in charge of the team and left for his home in South Hingham, Massachusetts. His absence seemed plausible enough, but it also prompted rumors he was in touch with the Boston Triumvirs about jumping to the Beaneaters. To which the King replied stoutly, "I have no intention of leaving my team. I shall fulfill my contract to the letter. I'm with the Association, and I'm there to stay."[50] As for the Triumvirs, John B. Billings denied making Kelly an offer; Arthur Soden said he wouldn't consent to it anyway; William H. Conant added that if his two partners were opposed, there would be no offer.

And then there was the boys-will-be-boys episode involving the Browns' Jack Stivetts and roommate Joe Neale. On St. Louis's steamy mid-summer nights, the pair took to sitting naked in their boarding house room before an open window. A druggist named Layton, who lived with his family across the street, understandably found that offensive and, at 10:30 one night, started throwing stones at the two pitchers. The commotion brought a policeman, who arrested all three men. In police court they were released on bond, with the case to be continued because the Browns were about to leave town.

The Browns split their Independence Day doubleheader in Philadelphia, while Boston won both games from Columbus at the Congress Street Grounds. That left Boston and St. Louis in a virtual tie: Reds at 44–22, Browns at 47–26. It was now a two-team race; Baltimore had slumped to 36–27, followed by Cincinnati (32–37), Columbus (33–38), the Athletics (30–36), Louisville (28–41), and Washington (21–43).

The one thing the owners of all sixteen major league teams agreed upon was that their payrolls were too big. Yet on the whole, they ought to have been pleased with the way the season had gone so far. Tight races in both leagues were keeping attendance at levels comparable to those of 1889. Independence Day crowds in the National League totaled 42,193; in the Association, 37,695. For the rest of the 1891 season, the Association proceeded in its customary rowdy, rollicking way, employing eleven different umpires by season's end. At least its campaign ended without controversy over who won—or who should have won. The League's season, on the other hand, concluded in a bitter dispute over the honesty of the outcome.

1. *Boston Globe*, February 14, 1891, p. 2.
2. A copy of Stovey's 1891 contract, signed by Soden, is in the Harry Stovey File, National Baseball Hall of Fame Library, Cooperstown, New York. The contract stipulated that Stovey would be paid on the first day of each month, beginning April 1 and extending through October 31. So he would be contractually obligated to appear in whatever postseason games the Beaneaters played.
3. *Sporting Life*, January 31, 1891, p. 6.
4. *New York Clipper*, February 14, 1891, p. 777; February 21, 1891, p. 703; *Washington Post*, February 16, 1891, p. 1.
5. The Association also continued to use the Reach baseball, manufactured by a company founded by Al Reach, co-owner of the Philadelphia National League club, but subsequently brought under the control of A. J. Spalding and Brothers. The irony of that seems to have escaped the Association bigwigs.
6. *New York Clipper*, February 28, 1891, p. 809.
7. Harold Seymour and Dorothy Seymour Mills, *Baseball: The Early Years* (1960; reprint, New York: Oxford University Press, 1989), 254.
8. *Washington Post*, February 20, 1891, p. 6.
9. Ibid., February 28, 1891, p. 6; *Sporting News*, March 14, 1891, p. 4.
10. *Sporting News*, July 26, 1890, p. 3.
11. First war: National League vs. American Association, 1882; second war: National League and Association vs. Union Association, 1884; and of course third war: National League and Association vs. Players' League, 1890.
12. *Sporting Life*, April 4, 1891, p. 1.
13. *Sporting News*, April 11, 1891, p. 4.
14. Ibid., February 28, 1891, p. 1.
15. Ibid., March 21, 1891, p. 1; *New York Clipper*, March 28, 1891, p. 47.
16. *Sporting News*, April 11, 1891, p. 2.
17. *Washington Post*, May 11, 1891, p. 6. I assume Denny Lyons kept the $500 advance Comiskey gave him in September 1890 to sign with the Players' League for 1891.
18. *Sporting Life*, April 4, 1891, p. 6.
19. Thurman returned to his successful legal practice in Columbus and took an active role in local and state Democratic Party affairs. In July 1891 he gave the keynote address to the Ohio Democratic convention, subsequently held appointive positions in the state government, and became a leading proponent of eugenics.
20. Quoted in *Cincinnati Evening Post*, July 24, 1891, p. 4.
21. Ibid., April 11, 1891, p. 3.
22. Fast Day, originally a religious holiday of fasting and meditation, originated in Boston in 1670 and was observed in Massachusetts, New Hampshire, and Maine into the nineteenth century. By the last part of the century it had become essentially a secular holiday. In 1894 the Massachusetts legislature changed Fast Day to Patriots' Day.
23. *Sporting Life*, April 18, 1891, p. 4; *St. Louis Post-Dispatch*, April 8, 1891, p. 8.
24. *Sporting News*, April 11, 1891, p. 1.
25. *St. Louis Post-Dispatch*, April 13, 1891, p. 8.
26. *Columbus Evening Dispatch*, April 15, 1891, p. 2; *Sporting News*, May 2, 1891, p. 1. If Morse was justified in his criticism of the Association's umpires, he made little sense with his argument against publishing players' batting averages each week. "I do not know of anything more demoralizing," he wrote. "It does no good to flaunt figures in the face of players at the end of each week, indeed it is provocative of considerable harm." If the averages had to be printed, Morse thought sacrifice bunts and sacrifice flies should be as well. That would indicate a player's full value to his team, as opposed to "the player who works for himself and feasts upon the public presentation of his selfish work" (*Sporting Life*, May 2, 1891, p. 1.). Later, the regularly published statistics included sacrifices along with batting averages and runs scored.
27. *Washington Post*, May 11, 1891, p. 6.
28. *Sporting Life*, April 18, 1891, p. 4; Lee Allen, *The Cincinnati Reds* (1948; reprint, Kent, Ohio: Kent State University Press, 2006), 43.

29. *Columbus Evening Dispatch*, April 29, 1891, p. 2.
30. Under the scoring rules then current, Kelly was credited only with a triple.
31. *Columbus Evening Dispatch*, May 28, 1891, p. 2; *Washington Post*, May 29, 1891, p. 6.
32. The decision in the Cupid Childs case, announced at nearly the same time, rendered moot the Columbus club's efforts to enjoin Reilly and Baldwin from playing in Ohio. In June the judge in common pleas court in Columbus refused to make permanent the injunction against the two players.
33. *Chicago Tribune*, April 24, 1891, p. 6.
34. *Sporting Life*, May 9, 1891, p. 1; *Sporting News*, May 9, 1891, p. 1; May 30, 1891, p. 2.
35. *Chicago Tribune*, May 2, 1891, p. 6.
36. *Sporting Life*, June 13, 1891, p. 9.
37. *St. Louis Post-Dispatch*, June 27, 1891, p. 8.
38. Ibid., June 6, 1891, p. 8.
39. *Washington Post*, May 22, 1891, p. 6.
40. *St. Louis Post-Dispatch*, June 2, 1891, p. 8; June 3, 1891, p. 8.
41. Ibid., June 7, 1891, p. 3.
42. *Columbus Evening Dispatch*, June 12, 1891, p. 2.
43. *Chicago Tribune*, June 18, 1891, p. 6.
44. Ibid.
45. Ibid., June 24, 1891, p. 6.
46. *Columbus Evening Dispatch*, June 29, 1891, p. 2.
47. *New York Clipper*, July 11, 1891, p. 303; *Cleveland Plain Dealer*, July 2, 1891, p. 2; *Sporting Life*, July 11, 1891, p. 5; *St. Louis Post-Dispatch*, July 4, 1891, p. 8.
48. *Sporting Life*, July 4, 1891, p. 8.
49. Obviously Kelly and his players didn't share Cap Anson's and the St. Louis Browns' qualms about taking the field against black ballplayers.
50. *St. Louis Post-Dispatch*, July 20, 1891, p. 8; *Cincinnati Evening Post*, July 21, 1891, p. 3.

CHAPTER 7

1891: "I Should Expect to Be Hanged"

Unconstrained by the National Agreement, the American Association found the Western Association, most of whose members were losing money, to be a ready target for player raids of its own. Baltimore signed three Minneapolis players; St. Louis and Columbus plucked several from that club and from Omaha; Washington, after releasing six players in July, replenished its roster from Omaha; and Louisville took a husky right-hander named Jouett Meekin from St. Paul. Undoubtedly outfielder Jesse Burkett, batting .349 in August when Lincoln folded, would already have been playing in the American Association if Frank Robison hadn't purchased his contract for Cleveland the previous year, after he failed as a left-handed pitcher with the New York National Leaguers. Burkett joined Cleveland at the beginning of a sixteen-year career that put him in the Hall of Fame. By mid-August, with the Western Association down to four franchises, the National League was also adding players from that circuit, but unlike the Association, the League's clubs were buying them under the terms of the National Agreement.

But the traffic moved both ways. The Western Association's Denver club remained solvent, and that's where the banished Jack O'Connor landed. Pittsburgh insisted that because O'Connor had signed a contract and taken a $750 advance (which he wouldn't return), it had rights to his services. J. Palmer O'Neill appealed to League president Nick Young, but there really was nothing Young could do. O'Connor tried to get himself reinstated by the Columbus club, even sending his priest to plead his case before the club's directors—to no avail.

Meanwhile, pitcher Red Ehret and third baseman Harry Raymond jumped from Louisville to Lincoln (joining Sioux City when Lincoln shut down). Reportedly angry because Louisville had released catcher and close friend Paul Cook, Erhret went on a three-day bender before leaving town. He and Raymond may have known something was up. In mid-July the Falls City Bank failed. It held a $6,000 mortgage on the Louisville club, along with Scott Stratton's $2,000 in savings, Jack Chapman's $1,500, and $200 to $350 for four other Colonels. Two Philadelphia bank failures followed shortly. The Athletics' George Wood lost $750 when the Keystone Bank went under; Wood's team-mate Bill Hallman saw his $400 in the Spring Garden Bank disappear. Forty-three years before the creation of the Federal Deposit Insurance Corporation, that's what happened when banks failed.

Although the war between the League and the Association continued unabated, there were a few signs the organizations might be moving toward peace. As early as May, John T. Brush approached Frank Bancroft, business manager of Brush's Association rival in Cincinnati, about the possibility of a settlement. Brush also talked with Association president Louis Kramer and subsequently, when the St. Louis Browns visited Cincinnati, with Chris von der Ahe. Brush wanted the local baseball market to himself, and he offered to compensate the Association for the $12,000 cost of the Pendleton ballpark if the Association moved its franchise to Indianapolis. Nothing came of those contacts, but at least one League club owner had indicated a willingness to deal with the other side.

Yet League clubs, particularly Pittsburgh, continued to try to pry players out of the Association. Although so far Pittsburgh's high-powered pitching duo of Silver King and Mark Baldwin hadn't lived up to their promise, J. Palmer O'Neill was still using Baldwin as his agent in nefarious dealings with the other league's personnel. Baldwin made a trip to Philadelphia, where he first tried without success to get Athletics infielders Joe Mulvey and Tommy Corcoran to jump to Pittsburgh; then he sought out the Browns' Denny Lyons and Jack Boyle. That pair took advantage of an idle Sunday to go on a binge in Atlantic City, leaving themselves in no condition to play against the Athletics on Monday. They spent much of that evening in the company of Baldwin, who plied them with drink and promises of more money. Finding that the Browns' train had already left for Boston, Baldwin tried to get them to accompany him to Pittsburgh. Lyons backed out; Boyle wouldn't jump without Lyons. While Baldwin returned to Pittsburgh, the two Browns finally caught a train for Boston, arriving on Wednesday. Von der Ahe was waiting to tell them they were each fined two weeks' pay. Lyons was penitent; Boyle said he was still thinking about Baldwin's offer (although he stayed with the Browns).

On Wednesday, July 8, the Browns took the field at the Congress Street Grounds, where Boston owners Charles Prince and Julian Hart had gone back on their agreement to charge the League's fifty-cent admission price and, like the rest of the Association's clubs, sold tickets for twenty-five cents. Lacking their star third baseman and regular catcher, the Browns were still able to beat Boston two straight games and take over first place.

On Friday the tenth, an off day, Prince and Hart treated the two teams to lunch at Chebacco Lake and the Hamilton Polo Club, where the Browns and Reds entertained a number of prominent citizens, including Congressman Henry Cabot Lodge, with a seven-inning exhibition. Then the players—for the first time for most or all of them—watched a polo match by club members, followed by a lavish dinner at the Chebacco House. William E. Russell, Massachusetts's thirty-four-year-old governor, arrived during dinner to add his remarks to those of von der Ahe, Hart, and others. After a round of toasts and songs, the party rode in carriages by moonlight to the local train station and back into Boston. The next day, before 9,000 kranks at the Congress Street Grounds, Duke Farrell hit a three-run homer off Jack Stivetts to win Charlie Buffinton's game, 4–3. St. Louis left town with a 51–27 record to Boston's 46–25.

At the other extreme in the Association were the hapless Washington Nationals, who played their home games in a ballpark that not only had trees in the outfield, but a playing surface littered with lumps and holes. After the locals' 3–2 loss at home to Kelly's Killers on July 16, with Kid Carsey unable to overcome his teammates' eight errors, the *Washington Post*'s reporter wrote sourly, "of all the games played this season at National Park that of yesterday was the worst." Various Nationals "made such plays as should cause them to go home and weep for forgiveness."[1]

Three days later nearly 4,000 people came to the Washington ballpark, expecting to see the new players from the Omaha club. None appeared, which put the crowd in a surly mood. When Jack Kerins threatened to have a spectator ejected, bleacher-seat occupants came on the field to yell at the umpire. Eventually the game proceeded to another Cincinnati win, Frank Dwyer besting the unfortunate Carsey, 5–2.

The National League race continued to be a seesaw contest between Chicago and New York. After taking two of three games at home from Philadelphia, Anson's Colts opened a series with the Giants on Friday, July 10, at West Side Park before an audience of 4,200. They jumped on Amos Rusie for eight runs in four innings in what ended as an 8–6 win for Bill Hutchinson. On Saturday, on the south side, about 10,000 Chicagoans suffered through a 15–6 drubbing, Rusie coasting to victory. On Monday, Rusie went to the box for the third time in four days and topped Hutchinson, 7–3, as Jim O'Rourke and Roger Connor sent balls over the fences. New York left town in first place by thirty percentage points.

Boston opened its series in Chicago by losing a 4–0 shutout to Ad Gumbert, Clarkson taking the loss. The next day Anson's tenth-inning sacrifice fly off Harry Staley scored Hutchinson to win it, 6–5. The series finale was another extra-inning battle, won by Chicago in twelve innings, 8–7, when shortstop Jimmy Cooney blooped a single to right field; Anson, Cliff Carroll, and Cooney all scored on Harry Stovey's very wild throw over home plate. That put the Colts back in first, 42–29 to New York's 39–27. Frank Selee's third-running Beaneaters had slumped to 34–32.

For some time both Tim Keefe and Jack Glasscock, the latter fined for lingering too long with a leg injury in Wheeling, had been on the outs with Giants captain Buck Ewing. In Keefe's case, some of it was continuing suspicion about Ewing's dealings with John B. Day during and after the 1890 season, whereas Keefe had remained a Players' League loyalist to the end. Moreover, over the first half of the present season, Ewing had seen fit to send Keefe to the box only eight times, despite Keefe's insistence that the index finger on his pitching hand had fully healed. Keefe also believed that Al and J. Walter Spalding, part-owners of the Giants since the previous summer, still resented the competition in 1890 with his and Behannon's sporting goods store.[2] On July 21 the man who had won 252 games for John B. Day in the Association and the League received his release, proving again (if further proof were needed) that although professional baseball has always has been long on sentimentalism, it's never had much room for genuine sentiment. Keefe's departure didn't sit well with Connor, Danny Richardson, and other Giants who had been fellow Brotherhood members. Three weeks later Keefe signed with Harry Wright's Phillies, although in eleven games he could do no better than a 3–6 record.

If the Giants had their discontents, Pittsburgh's were bad enough to affect the play of an ostensibly talented team. After Cleveland administered back-to-back poundings to Baldwin and King, a Cleveland scribe writing as "Drucalion" remarked of the Pittsburgh outfit, "Not a man knows what teamwork is [and] but two on the team have life enough in them to keep them awake." The *Pittsburgh Chronicle-Telegraph* waxed sarcastic regarding the local team's misfortunes: "In spite of the efforts of the brand of heavy hitters who have their home grounds in Allegheny to reach the bottom, Cincinnati holds the place and seems determined to keep it. Whenever Hanlon's famed men try hard to lose a game . . . the Cincinnati club blasts the hopes of the seekers after the bottom place by losing."[3]

They weren't "Hanlon's famed men" much longer. Late in July, J. Palmer O'Neill caught two of the Pittsburgh club's directors out of town, unilaterally fired Hanlon, and quickly signed Bill McGunnigle, who had been managing Providence in the Eastern Association. When the directors backed Hanlon, McGunnigle temporarily yielded the job. After a few more days of confusion, the directors grudgingly agreed to McGunnigle's hiring. Hanlon refused to continue as captain, so Louis Bierbauer assumed that responsibility. When McGunnigle finally took over the team, it had slipped back into last place with a 31–47 record.

Circumstances at Brooklyn weren't that bad, but John Ward was experiencing what must have been his most frustrating season thus far in professional baseball. Ward had played on four pennant winners at Providence and New York, and he was used to winning—if not finishing first, then at least contending. Yet he couldn't get the Brooklyn team out of the bottom half of the League. Bill McGunnigle suggested that much of Brooklyn's trouble stemmed from the players' resentment that Charles Byrne had hired Ward to direct the team instead of giving the job to Hub Collins. Whatever truth there was in that, it didn't help Ward that on July 30, at Eastern Park, Collins and outfielder Tom Burns had a horrible collision chasing Roger Connor's soft fly. Burns got up all right, but Collins suffered a deep gash on his forehead, had to be carried from the field, and remained unconscious through the night. Disabled for most of the rest of the season, Collins never fully recovered and died the following spring.

If Byrne was having doubts about leaving the Association (as was widely rumored), he was also doubting the wisdom of hiring the illustrious Ward to lead his Bridegrooms. On July 24, after Tim Hurst ejected Ward in the opener of a doubleheader in Pittsburgh, the Brooklyn captain came to the Exposition Park press section to seek Byrne's approval for arguing with the umpire. He didn't get it. Asked if Ward would play in the second game, Byrne snapped, "If I had my way, he wouldn't play at all."[4]

Ward was in no better mood than the club president. He said Brooklyn wouldn't sign a petition being circulated by Chicago president Jim Hart to allow nonplayers on the coaching lines. That, thought Ward, "would permit a club to go out and hire a cheap man with a fog horn voice to get up and make a terrible din for no other purpose than to rattle the opposing team." Ward complained about the coaching-line behavior of Boston's Herman Long and Tommy Tucker: "You should hear their noisy coaching this season. It is something awful."[5] The petition got nowhere; it would be nearly two decades before teams employed managers' assistants—or "coaches"—who would station themselves off third or first base during games.

After defeating Cincinnati to end their home stand in first place, Anson's Colts started a road trip on July 25 with a slipshod 15–14 win over the Cleveland Spiders, now led by third baseman Patsy Tebeau. In what Joe Murphy, traveling with the Colts, exaggerated as "the most awful game ever played in Cleveland," Chicago committed eleven errors, Cleveland six.[6] Only two Spiders runs were earned. Cy Young had one of the sorriest days of his career, taking his punishment until George Davis came in from the outfield to relieve him.

Chicago won two of three games in Cleveland, the last a 6–3 victory for Gumbert over Len Viau. At one point in that game, Tim Hurst climbed into the grandstand and pointed out a heckler to a park policeman, who removed one Merton Yondall of Garrettsville, Ohio, from the park, while spectators gathered in front of the grandstand in protest. The *Cleveland Plain Dealer* thought Hurst had "made a pale jackass of himself," but Joe Murphy depicted Cleveland's crowds as "made up of about as narrow-minded and prejudiced a set of people as I have ever seen at a ball game. . . . The crowd abused Hurst as if he were a pick pocket." Murphy blamed the Cleveland players, who "have certain ways of putting the crowd on an umpire that are cowardly and reprehensible."[7]

Tim Hurst followed the Chicago team to Cincinnati, where Anson's men swept three games. During Gumbert's 8–4 decision over Tony Mullane, the fiery Reds pitcher repeatedly accused Anson of having paid Hurst to favor Chicago. He kept it up until Anson shouted, "Oh shut up, you bloody Italian; go on and pitch your game." Noted Murphy, "The bloody Italian shut up."[8] The next day the Colts jumped on the fading Radbourn for a 7–4 win, their sixth in a row. Amos Rusie pitched a no-hit game against Brooklyn in New York on July 31, but the Giants' loss to the Bridegrooms the next day dropped them to third place at 43–33. Boston had surged to 46–34 and moved into second, but at that point Chicago enjoyed a comfortable lead with 51 wins, 32 losses.

Then Chicago lost all three games in Philadelphia before traveling to Boston. With Hutchinson and Kid Nichols both in top form, the Colts edged the Beaneaters in ten innings. The game turned on a maneuver by Anson. With the score 2–2 in the top of the tenth, Walt Wilmot and Bill Dahlen singled. Anson came to bat and started jumping back and forth across the plate, which wasn't against the rules then. Not knowing what to do, Nichols just held the ball until the umpire awarded Anson first base. Rattled, the young pitcher hit Cliff Carroll on the foot to bring in Wilmot with the go-ahead run. In the bottom of the inning, Hutchinson barely escaped with the win.

Meanwhile, New York beat Pittsburgh and reoccupied second place. The next day, Friday, August 7, Silver King shut out the Giants; while in Boston, with about three hundred fellow citizens of Norwich, Connecticut, cheering him on, Hutchinson outlasted Clarkson, 6–5. Hutchinson took a rest on Saturday, as Harry Staley held the Colts to three runs; Boston reached Pat Luby for four. In New York, Rusie and Pud Galvin struggled for twelve innings before the Giants scored three times in the top of the thirteenth for a 10–7 Giants win. Rusie gave up fifteen hits, Galvin seventeen. Buck Ewing, who had taken a lot of criticism for his protracted absence from the lineup, played second base and got a key hit in the Giants' winning rally.

The following Monday, in the Polo Grounds, Chicago won 4–3, scoring the winning run when Fred Pfeffer trotted home on Rusie's wild pitch in the top of the ninth inning. Hutchinson notched still another victory. What followed, though, were three consecutive losses to John Ewing and Rusie, while Boston swept three games from Pittsburgh. The Colts won two of three from Brooklyn; New York did the same in its series with Cincinnati; and Boston took two from Cleveland before a rainout. Chicago won both of its games in Pittsburgh, where Bill McGunnigle's arrival had effected no turnaround in the fortunes of an underachieving team. In New York, Nichols and Rusie hooked up in another classic. Rusie struck out ten Beaneaters but gave up three runs; Nichols had eight strikeouts and allowed one hit and no runs. The Giants won on Tuesday the eighteenth to make their record 51–38. Boston was in second place at 55–39, having won 21 of its last 28 games. After their 12–9 road trip, the Colts went home still holding the lead, at 59–39.

Cincinnati kept swapping last place with Pittsburgh, amid growing unhappiness with captain Arlie Latham on the part of manager Tom Loftus and Reds players in general. In Boston, the quadruply married Latham sat in the grandstand with a group of female admirers, then donned his uniform, came on the field late, and grabbed a ball catcher Jerry Harrington was tossing with Bid McPhee. Harrington barked at Latham, who replied, "I am the captain of the team and will do as I please." Livid, Harrington refused to play that day or in the other two games in Boston. Loftus fined him $100 and sent him home when he still wouldn't play in Philadelphia. In *Sporting Life*, Ban Johnson wrote that all the Reds disliked Latham, and that naming him captain had been Loftus's biggest mistake.[9]

Then there was *l'affaire* McAleer. On August 18 the Reds opened a series at home with Cleveland. At one point in the game, Jimmy McAleer rounded third base on his way home, only to be blocked by Latham. Whereupon the Cleveland outfielder responded by kicking Latham in the rear, to which the Reds' captain responded with a blow to the mouth that sent McAleer sprawling. McAleer grabbed a bat and started after Latham, who took off for the clubhouse. As McAleer ran after him and threw the bat (and missed), several other Spiders joined the chase, along with a few policemen and some of the small crowd on hand. The police were successful in heading off McAleer and, waving their billy clubs, in herding the spectators back to their seats. Finally everybody cooled down and the game resumed, but through no effort on the part of umpire Phil Powers, who just stood at home plate and observed the goings-on. Cleveland won the game, 6–2, after which Latham blamed Powers for the loss—not that the outcome made much difference for either of the run-of-the-mill ball teams. "Phil Powers," said the Reds' embattled leader, "is the worst excuse for an umpire that ever faced a pitcher."[10] That night Powers wired Nick Young his resignation.

At the beginning of August, Boston and St. Louis remained in a tight battle for the Association pennant. Arthur Irwin's Reds came into St. Louis holding a 58–27 to 57–31 lead over Comiskey's Browns. On Saturday, August 1, Duke Farrell hit two home runs and sent the overflow crowd home unhappy after a 7–3 defeat, John O'Brien topping Jake Stivetts. Another overflow on Sunday cheered Denny Lyons's two doubles and two singles as the Browns hit Charlie Buffinton for eight runs, while John Easton, recently signed after being released by Columbus, held Boston to three. Monday's game was another 8–3 St. Louis victory, Willie McGill limiting the Reds to three hits. Clark Griffith—promptly signed by Boston after being released by the Browns, even though he had won eleven games for them—took the loss. In the Tuesday finale, the Reds could manage only three hits again and were shut out by Stivetts, 8–o. Boston left town only 11 percentage points ahead of St. Louis, 59–30 to 60–32.

Then McGill, the bothersome teenager, got into trouble again. Shortly after the Boston series, he "took French leave" (the nineteenth-century's version of AWOL). According to the *Cincinnati Evening Post*, his mother—"who since the death of her husband, has suffered for the constant presence of the little pitcher lad"—came down from Chicago and persuaded him to quit baseball.[11] Yet a few days later, the same Cincinnati paper had McGill in Chicago dickering with Anson about jumping to the Colts. McGill was quoted as claiming Chris von der Ahe, using "insubordination" as an excuse, had been docking his semi-monthly checks $25 and $50. Whatever McGill was doing in Chicago, he wasn't gone for long. Accompanied by his brother, he returned to St. Louis and resumed taking his regular turns in the box, although von der Ahe fined him another $50 for leaving the team.

At the end of July, Louis Kramer once again affirmed the Association's commitment to Cincinnati: "Cincinnati will never be abandoned by us and next season will be represented by a much stronger club." Although rumors persisted that Mike Kelly would jump to the National League, the King trumpeted, "I'm with the Association and I'm here to stay. I have no idea of leaving my team. I shall fulfill my contract to the letter."[12] But with a sixth-place team playing at home at an inconvenient site, where arrests of players happened during or after every Sunday game, the Association's prospects in Cincinnati looked increasingly bleak. The team just got worse. Late in July, in losing a three-game home series to St. Louis, Kelly's pitchers gave up forty-three runs, including all twenty scored on Frank Dwyer in a 20–12 carnage. After releasing the bibulous Yank Robinson, Kelly signed two local amateurs to play second base, while Robinson returned to his hometown to play out the season with the Browns. Meanwhile Ed Crane took French leave of his own, then showed up on the Cincinnati League staff. With the Killers, Crane's record was 14–14, although he gave up fewer earned runs per nine innings than any pitcher in either league. With the League's Reds, he won four, lost eight.

John T. Brush's visit to St. Louis early in August to meet secretly at the Southern Hotel with von der Ahe and Chicago president Jim Hart fed speculation von der Ahe and the other Cincinnati stockholders were about to make a deal with Brush. Again, the rumor was that the Cincinnati franchise would move to Indianapolis, with the Killers' home games in September and October transferred to the Association's eastern cities. Kramer dismissed such speculation as "the veriest nonsense. Pay no attention to any National League canards."[13]

Meanwhile, the Louisville club, vying with Washington for last place, was reorganized under a local group that bought 742 shares in the franchise and elected T. Hunt Stuckey as its new president. But Louisville had a history of chronic financial difficulties, and H. E. Gillette, owner of the Western Association's Milwaukee franchise, was maneuvering to buy the Colonels and move them to the "Cream City." On August 14, Gillette traveled to Louisville and, with von der Ahe, Billy Barnie (acting as Gillette's agent), and Zach Phelps (now the Association's attorney), met with the club's new directors. They rebuffed Gillette's offer, after which he began dickering with von der Ahe for the purchase of Cincinnati.

So despite Kramer's and Kelly's protestations, neither Kelly nor the Killers were in the Association to stay. On Thursday, August 13, the Killers met Boston in what, as events played out, would be the American Association's final game in Cincinnati. A decent weekday crowd of 1,250 watched the home team take another defeat, Buffinton holding the Killers to one run while Boston scored seven times on Dwyer, with Kelly behind the plate. Dan Brouthers whacked a single, double, and triple.

The next day, as the team arrived in St. Louis for a series with the Browns, Kelly and his players and business manager Bancroft had already learned the club was to be sold. Late that night Gillette received a telegram confirming that St. Louis, Boston, Washington, and Baltimore had agreed to the transfer of Cincinnati to Milwaukee. Queried as to whether he intended to join Cincinnati's League team, Kelly responded by telegram to various newspapers: "I will not break my contract with the American Association. I will be the last to leave."[14]

The Killers lost two games to the Browns, with Kelly pitching three innings of the 7–3 defeat on the fifteenth after Willard "Grasshopper" Mains was disabled by a drive off his ankle. But the Browns had already damaged their pennant chances by losing two of three games to the Athletics and then dropping three games to Baltimore, while Boston was beating up on Louisville, Columbus, and Cincinnati. On Sunday evening, August 16, Boston's record was 67–31 to the Browns' 66–37.

The Browns and Killers didn't play on Monday the seventeenth, presumably because the final details of the purchase were being worked out at the Lindell Hotel.

Although von der Ahe held out until he got his price, by the end of the day the sale was completed. The price was $12,000—half in cash, half in notes—of which von der Ahe was to receive $6,000.[15] Milwaukee already had a strong club and had been leading the Western Association by a comfortable margin, so manager Charlie Cushman took only pitchers Dwyer and Mains plus infielders Jack Carney and Jimmy Canavan and catcher Farmer Vaughan from the Killers' roster. The rest were left to catch on wherever they could, while Ban Johnson lost his $75-per-month salary as the Killers' secretary.

The Association's hastily put together Cincinnati enterprise proved an all-around mistake. Ending with a 43–57 record, the sixth-place Killers had drawn about 63,000 people to Pendleton Park. In eighty-two games with the Killers, Kelly batted .297. He also pitched in three games with one decision, a loss.

On the morning of Tuesday the eighteenth, the Milwaukee Brewers arrived in St. Louis. That afternoon they made a successful debut in the Association, knocking around Stivetts and defeating the Browns, 7–2. Headlined the *Cincinnati Evening Post*, "The Agony Over," followed by the comment, "This city did not go into mourning over the loss of the Association club."[16]

With the Cincinnati-Milwaukee matter resolved, Kramer announced he would resign from the Association's presidency effective at the end of the month. Citing the amount of time the office took away from his Cincinnati legal practice, Kramer also complained about being called to St. Louis twice during the negotiations over the sale of the Killers. He denied any "rupture with the Association."[17] The club owners agreed to bring back Zach Phelps to fill the president's chair, as of September 1.

What of Kelly, "whose zany five months in Cincinnati," as Marty Appel puts it, "were history."[18] Kelly's repeatedly proclaimed fealty to the Association held—at least for a time. Being under a personal-services contract to Charles Prince, Kelly had no contractual obligation to either Cincinnati or Milwaukee, so he wasn't being disingenuous when he said, "I will not break my contract with the Association." What he did was board a train for the East to join the Boston Reds, leaving St. Louis on the night of the seventeenth. When he missed connections at Albany, New York, he hired a special train and gave the engineer $50 to get him to Boston in time for Wednesday's game with Baltimore. At Pittsfield, Massachusetts, he caught up with the Boston-bound train he missed in Albany, just as it was pulling out of the station. Dropping his bags, he raced to catch up with it and, as onlookers sang "Slide, Kelly, Slide," jumped onto the last car.

The exploit got front-page coverage in the *Sporting News*.[19] He wasn't called the King of the Diamond for nothing.

Kelly's appearance in the Boston lineup in left field on the afternoon of Tuesday the eighteenth produced a remarkable weekday turnout of some 11,000 people at the Congress Street Grounds. Probably at his insistence, Arthur Irwin made him team captain in place of Hugh Duffy. The Reds defeated Baltimore three straight times, while St. Louis lost another game to Milwaukee and two games out of three to Columbus. By August 26, Boston enjoyed a solid lead over the Browns, 75–32 to 68–40.

The Browns' situation wasn't hopeless, although various players behaved as if it was. Besides McGill's sojourn in Chicago, the incorrigible Denny Lyons went on another binge just before the Cincinnati-Milwaukee switch. Fed up with Lyons, von der Ahe announced that he was suspended for the rest of the season. "Lyons is still missing," reported the *St. Louis Post-Dispatch* on August 20, "and is supposed to be devouring all the red liquor in town."[20] Jack Stivetts (he of the naked window-sitting episode) showed up drunk at a "lawn party" von der Ahe staged at Sportsman's Park the night of August 19, following a rainout that afternoon. Stivetts became so unruly the Browns' owner called the police, who took him to a precinct station, held him briefly, then released him. Stivetts cursed out Von der Ahe, who announced his suspension as well, although that lasted only two days. The next day von der Ahe also lifted the suspension on Lyons, who was his customary contrite self.

While the Association was ridding itself of Cincinnati and adding Milwaukee, Chicago continued to hold first place in the National League. Boston was making it a close race, while preseason favorite New York had stalled in third. Pitcher Tom Vickery, acquired from Omaha, made his Chicago debut in the opener of the Colts' home stand, a 14–2 slaughter of Cleveland that was mercifully stopped by rain after six innings. Two more wins from Cleveland followed, then three in a row from Brooklyn, where John Ward was finding life increasingly unpleasant. After one of the games in Chicago, four Bridegrooms sat up all night playing cards. The next morning Ward found eighteen empty beer bottles in the room. He fined each player $10 and sat down Darby O'Brien, said to be the ringleader of the group. The next day Brooklyn committed ten errors; the Colts made twenty-eight hits, including two home runs each by Walt Wilmot and Jimmy Ryan. Final score: Chicago 28, Brooklyn 5, with Luby easing to victory. George

Hemming, whose foremost achievement so far in the season had been striking out Harry Stovey nine consecutive times, pitched all the way.

The Colts made it eleven wins in a row when Hutchinson decisioned Philadelphia's Kid Gleason, 6–1. The streak ended on August 29. Vickery was thumped for eight runs, while Phillies newcomer Bill Kling held Chicago to five.²¹ The next day Gleason came back to gain a 6–2 victory. Chicago's record was now 66 wins, 40 losses. Boston took three of four games in Cleveland, which put its record at 60–42. "It now begins to dawn on even the most stupid," asserted Joe Murphy, "that the League pennant is slowly but surely floating Chicagowards."²²

Meanwhile, the League and Association club owners—at least some of them—had become sufficiently weary of their war to talk peace. John T. Brush had taken it upon himself to initiate a peace movement; the real purpose of the early August meeting in St. Louis between Brush, von der Ahe, and Jim Hart was to lay the groundwork for a full-fledged peace conference. The Association chose a peace delegation consisting of Kramer, von der Ahe, and Phelps; the League's delegates were Brush, Jim Hart, and Charles Byrne. The conference was to begin on Tuesday, August 25, at the Arlington Hotel in Washington. The *Washington Post* credited "the indefatigable efforts of John T. Brush, the little Napoleon of base ball," with bringing together the two organizations.²³

The Association's committee held an informal meeting in the morning, with the formal session with Brush, Hart, and Byrne scheduled for 3:00. Their train was late getting into Washington, delaying the start until late afternoon. Several other club officials from both leagues were also present to observe the proceedings. The delegates met until 7:00, adjourned for dinner, and reconvened at midnight. Kramer, chosen to chair the meeting, put the question to the joint committee that all players on the payrolls of their present clubs would remain so "despite any previous contracts."²⁴ In other words, the two leagues would respect each others' reserves. The question carried unanimously.

So far, so good. Then somebody interrupted the proceedings with a telegram from Boston: Mike Kelly had jumped from the Association back to the National League and signed with the Beaneaters. With that bombshell, the meeting adjourned. The next morning the Association's peace committee, plus J. Earle Wagner and Billy Barnie, met at the Hotel Randell and drafted a letter demanding that Kelly be returned to the Boston Reds. When the National Leaguers responded with a noncommittal statement, the

Association formally withdrew from the conference. Peace had seemed almost within grasp, only to have everything blow up because the National League had finally recaptured the most popular player of his time.

Charles Byrne and Frank Robison were both disgusted by the turn of events. "If we keep up this childish bickering," Byrne said a couple of days later, "the public will leave us severely alone, and club owners and players alike will suffer." Exclaimed Robison, "The idea of allowing Kelly to break up the peace conference! Why, I would give up a hundred Kellys before I would let him stand in the way of my money interests."[25]

The Boston Triumvirs' justification for signing Kelly—explained George B. Billings, John B. Billings's son and the Beaneaters' assistant secretary—was that when the Cincinnati franchise was transferred, the Association's Boston club no longer had a claim on him. Which, of course, wasn't the case, inasmuch as Kelly had been under a personal-services contract to Charles Prince. On August 25, William H. Conant, club secretary George Floyd, and the Billings met with Kelly at the Adams House and signed him. Regardless of what the Triumvirs had said earlier in the summer, they were so eager to have Kelly back in the National League they were willing to pay him a stunning amount of money: a two-year contract for a total of $25,000 with a $13,000 advance, plus an all-expenses-paid postseason European trip for Kelly and his wife Agnes (who surely fit the definition of "long-suffering").

Frank Selee, who knew nothing beforehand about the move to sign Kelly, received the news by telegram in Cleveland. Accompanied by George Floyd, Kelly took a 10:00 p.m. train, arriving in time for the game scheduled with the Spiders on Thursday, August 27. If, as the *Boston Herald*'s Jacob Morse had written the previous fall, Kelly didn't want to play for Selee, then now he would be doing just that, and he would no longer captain the team. Billy Nash retained that title.

That afternoon the King stepped on a National League ball field for the first time in nearly two years. He caught Clarkson, who was pitching with a 12–2 lead when rain stopped the game after eight innings. Kelly hit a double off Ed Beatin, scored twice, and drew censure in the local *Plain Dealer* for trying to trip Cupid Childs to prevent him from scoring. "Kelly plays the same dirty ball as of yore," scolded the paper. "It isn't truly ball but dirty."[26] The next day he occupied right field, started in on Tim Hurst as soon as Cy Young threw his first pitch, and even argued the umpire into reversing himself when he initially called out Nichols on Zimmer's pick-off throw. Boston got to Young for nine runs; Cleveland made four on Nichols.

Kelly's great leap from Boston to Boston occasioned considerable press commentary, nearly all of it unfavorable. "Mike Kelly has done some pretty bad things in his life," editorialized the *Sporting News*, "but all agree that the latest in jumping the Association is the worst of all." Julian B. Hart told the *St. Louis Post-Dispatch*, "If you had said to me last Tuesday, 'I have received positive information that M. J. Kelly has been killed or has jumped, but I can't find out which,' I should have said, 'The man has been killed. That can happen to anyone; but Kelly jump—never.'" Asked if he would be willing to take Kelly back, Hart said, "In the language of Othello, 'Never more be officer of mine.'"[27]

Tim Murnane was convinced that "this will kill Kel," because he owed his success to favorable press coverage, and now the writers would be down on him. "He will be dead to the world before another year." Murnane also suggested wryly that Kelly would have to play with his left arm if, as he reportedly said in St. Louis, he would cut off his right arm before deserting the Association. Jacob Morse suspected George Floyd and other League people had worked on Kelly until "in a condition where he did not know whether school kept or not, he signed the contract with the League."[28] (It's not clear if Morse meant Kelly's suitors got him drunk or just wore down his willpower. His contemporaries would have found the first possibility more likely.)

Ignoring the reality that the two leagues were still very much in conflict, Cap Anson was talking about a postseason series with the Boston Association team. "The Chicago club can defeat any club on the face of the earth," boasted the Colts' leader.[29] It looked that way at the end of a three-game series at home with New York. On August 31, before some 4,000 Monday kranks on the west side, Rusie and Hutchinson both pitched eleven scoreless innings, until it was too dark to continue. The next day's game was another pitchers' duel, Vickery overcoming John Ewing, 4–1, before about 8,000 on the south side. Coming back on one day's rest, Rusie left after giving up eight runs in three innings in a comfortable 14–2 win for Gumbert. Lowly Cincinnati, getting fine performances from Billy Rhines and the unpredictable Cannonball Crane, beat Boston for the second day in a row.

Boston arrived in Chicago for a three-game series with a 62–45 record to the Colts' 68–41. On a cold Thursday, September 3, on the south side, Kelly was in right field as Clarkson yielded ten hits and a like number of runs, while Hutchinson held the

Beaneaters to one run. Joe Murphy complained about the coaching antics of Tommy Tucker, who emitted "a series of yells like that of a driver trying to start a balky team." The next day the thirty-nine-year-old Anson decided to have some fun with the local baseball writers, who liked to characterize him as aged (which, relative to most players of his time, he was). On another cold day, with about 3,500 in the West Side stands, he came on the field wearing a white wig under his cap and a phony white beard that reached almost to his belt buckle. He played the entire game in that costume, making three hits and trying to get umpire Tom Lynch to award him first base when Kid Nichols's pitch grazed his whiskers. Lynch demurred, saying, "they aren't really yours and you couldn't take first base just because somebody else's whiskers got hit."[30] It was another Chicago win, 5–3, Vickery benefiting from Wilmot's three-run homer over the right-field fence. Kelly sat that one out with a sore hand, but late in the Saturday game, the last of the home stand, he came in to relieve Charlie Gamzel and catch Harry Staley. Boston won a tightly pitched contest, 3–2, Gumbert taking the tough loss. After that Anson took his team on the road with a seemingly safe lead over Boston, 70–42 to 63–47.

John Clarkson generally lived an orderly life, but he was also given to moods and sulks when he pitched poorly. According to Anson, for whom Clarkson worked four seasons, he needed frequent praise and reassurance. After being hit hard in Thursday's game, he went on what was described as "a three-cornered jag." The usually mild-mannered Selee was furious when he saw the pitcher's condition and tried to send him home, only to have Clarkson claim to have missed the train. He was still drunk when he showed up on Saturday at South Side Park, where Selee told him he was fined and suspended. Clarkson was left behind when the team entrained for the East that night; when he sobered up, he had to pay his own fare back to Boston. Commented Jacob Morse, "It is said that Clarkson never thought of getting drunk until Kelly joined the team."[31]

In the Association, Boston continued to extend its lead over St. Louis; at the same time the National League stepped up its efforts to get players to jump to the League. According to Harold Seymour and Dorothy Seymour Mills, the League "added a new technique to player-stealing by introducing division of labor. Instead of all its clubs competing with each other hit-or-miss for Association players, each club was assigned to go after certain ones."[32] Having abandoned the Association and broken up the peace conference, Mike Kelly continued his confounding ways by persuading Jack Stivetts and

Tommy McCarthy to sign to play for the Beaneaters in 1892. Billy Nash worked on the Boston Reds' Dan Brouthers, Hardie Richardson, Bill Joyce, and Tom Brown, although all except Brouthers had already signed for 1892 with Charles Prince. Out of the lineup with an injury, Cleveland's Patsy Tebeau traveled to Columbus and took Baltimore's Curt Welch, Sadie McMahon, and George Van Haltren on a tour of the city's saloons. Although Tebeau left town claiming to have all three under contract, in fact his principal accomplishment was to get Welch so drunk he stayed behind when the Orioles left for the East.

"Under existing conditions," lamented the *Washington Post*, "it is almost impossible to keep players in a proper state of discipline. From all quarters come reports of star players getting drunk, and when they are suspended declare their indifference as they are determined to sign elsewhere next season."[33] The Washington directors beseeched Association president Phelps to do something toward peace, but peace was nowhere in sight. On September 16 the League's club owners convened in New York, voted to disband their peace committee, and listened for an hour as John I. Rogers exhorted them to continue the fight with the Association. Declared John B. Day, "It is war." Added Arthur Soden, "I am in for fighting it out to the end and will put up as much money as anyone to keep it going."[34]

So as the war continued, so did the pennant races. At least it was still a race in the National League. In the Association, Boston kept on winning, while Comiskey's St. Louis team was in increasing disarray. Boston's pitching may have been a little better, but otherwise the Browns put about as much talent on the field, maybe more. Comiskey supposedly was unexcelled as both a first baseman and field leader. Jack Boyle was a first-rate catcher and strong batter; the outfield of Tip O'Neill, Dummy Hoy, and Tommy McCarthy was the finest in the Association; and when sober, Denny Lyons rivaled Duke Farrell as the hardest-hitting third baseman in the game.

Of course "when sober" was the necessary qualifier where Lyons was concerned. In mid-September, he went on his third binge of the season, this time accompanied by Jack Stivetts and Willie McGill, whose age was no constraint at a time when underage drinking was yet to be defined in state laws and local ordinances. Stivetts, already having signed to play in the League next season, was visibly under the influence when he pitched at Sportsman's Park against Columbus on the eighteenth, although he gave up only two runs before leaving after six innings. Utility man John Munyan took over and gave up eight runs in a 10–6 loss. Stivetts got off with a few days' suspension, but von der Ahe, blaming Lyons for the loss of the pennant, suspended the wayward third baseman for the rest of the season. Whereupon Zach Phelps went a step further and, following Louis Kramer's precedent in the O'Connor case, officially expelled Lyons from the Association.

Von der Ahe forgave McGill for his latest transgression, but when Comiskey bawled out McGill in the Sportsman's Park clubhouse, the pitcher bridled and wanted to fight. That was a mistake—Comiskey was six inches taller and about twenty pounds heavier. He settled the issue by simply picking McGill up and throwing him against the wall. A few days later the diminutive lefty pitched a 6–3 win over Washington, which moved the *Post-Dispatch* to comment, "McGill, after his contact with Barleycorn and Comiskey, was in surprisingly good form."[35]

While all that was going on, Boston came into St. Louis and split two games before losing the series closer, George Rettger, another refugee from the Western Association (which had disbanded), topping Buffinton, 4–2. That ended the season's series between the two teams. Boston left for Louisville leading the Browns 81–35 to 74–45, but Comiskey's team had won ten games to Boston's eight. Jack Chapman's Colonels were still in seventh place, but they made it tough on the pennant-bound Bostons. The Reds lost two out of three in Eclipse Park, while the Browns swept a three-game series from Baltimore. On September 25, however, Boston clinched the pennant by completing a three-game sweep in Baltimore. That evening, Hi Hi Dixwell, the Reds' much-traveled rooter, treated them to a multicourse champagne dinner at the Eutaw House.

On October 1, 1891, the city of Boston celebrated the Reds' championship with a big parade from the intersection of Boylston and Charles streets to the Congress Street Grounds. Buffinton and Washington's Kid Carsey both pitched well in a game that meant nothing but was surprisingly well played. The Reds won 2–1, the sixteenth-consecutive time they had beaten the downtrodden Nationals. For little Carsey, who yielded only five hits, the game pretty much typified his season. Four days later Boston finished its schedule, dividing a doubleheader with the Athletics. The next day, while the Reds and Athletics played an exhibition in Trenton, New Jersey, Washington closed its season at home with two messy losses to Baltimore, 15–3 and 15–11. With rain falling, the second game was called after five innings. Kid Madden, who had begun the season with the Reds, was the winning pitcher. "It may be added," grumbled the local *Post's* reporter, "that Washington has had a surfeit of the class of baseball that has been presented here."[36] Although nobody could have known it at the time, that was the last game ever played in the American Association.

By winning the doubleheader, Baltimore edged the Athletics for fourth place, 71–64 to 73–66. As in 1890, the Association's final standings had an odd look, with nine teams again listed. Milwaukee, strengthened by additions in the Cincinnati transfer, won 21 of 36 games in the six weeks after it entered the Association and technically finished in third place. Cincinnati was listed where it was on August 16, sixth at 43–57. Columbus finished in what was actually sixth place (61–76). Louisville won twelve games in a row and the battle for seventh place, 54–83 to 44–91 for Washington, which over the season used eleven pitchers, four catchers, two first basemen, two second basemen, three third basemen, four shortstops, and ten outfielders. At the end, only Kid Carsey, Frank Foreman, and Deacon McGuire remained from the opening-day roster.

After August 4, St. Louis's record was a respectable 25–19, but Boston won 34 of its last 46 games and finished 93–42 to St. Louis's 85–51. Except for the St. Louis Maroons in the lopsided Union Association, the Reds won more games than any major league team had won up to then. Von der Ahe, however, attributed the Browns' failure not to Boston's superior play "but to a genuine up-and-down fight between Lyons, Stivetts and a couple of other players with John Barleycorn. That's the curse of base ball—the drunkard."[37]

Arthur Irwin's Boston team led the Association in team batting average (.274), runs (1,028), stolen bases (447), home runs (57), doubles (182), and triples (123). Dan Brouthers was the Association's batting leader (.350), while Duke Farrell led in home runs (12) and, as later computed, 112 runs driven in (one more than Brouthers). Of center fielder Tom Brown's season, David Nemec has written, "If there had been a Most Valuable Player Award in 1891, Brown would surely have won it."[38] Besides batting .321, the native of Liverpool, England, led both leagues in total bases, triples, runs, and, as the Reds' lead-off man, times at bat.

Baltimore's Sadie McMahon again led the Association in wins (35) and innings pitched (502). But if one discounted Milwaukee, Boston had the stingiest pitchers, allowing batters slightly more than three runs per nine innings. George Haddock, a 26-game loser with Buffalo in the Players' League, compiled a sparkling 34–11 record; Charlie Buffinton won 29; John O'Brien 18. For all his lapses from Victorian civility,

Jack Stivetts earned his money (minus von der Ahe's fines), pitching in 64 games and winning 33, while Willie McGill stayed out of trouble enough of the time to post an 18–9 mark for St. Louis, which made his season's record 20–14. In the first game of the season-closing doubleheader at Sportsman's Park, Ted Breitenstein, a young left-hander signed out of St. Louis amateur ball, pitched a no-hitter versus Louisville.

If the Browns fell short in the pennant race, they led the Association in attendance by a big margin, attracting some 220,000 to Sportsman's Park. Boston's home attendance was about 170,000; the Athletics drew a couple of thousand less. Crowds in Baltimore declined in the last part of the season, although the Orioles still drew 150,000 or so. Louisville's attendance fell by about 60,000 from 1890, but that was still the second highest in the franchise's history. Washington's total of 112,000 was the largest in the Capital's history and exceeded Columbus by about 7,000. Overall attendance in the Association increased by nearly 400,000 from the previous season.

Amid charges of chicanery, betrayal, and spitefulness, and in an atmosphere of general disgust, the National League's season ended a day earlier than the Association's.[39] On September 7, Chicago opened its last extended road trip with a Labor Day doubleheader in Brooklyn. Anson wasn't awakened at his hotel until 11:00 a.m. By the time he reached Eastern Park, his team was far behind. It ended 21–3, with the Bridegrooms battering Tom Vickery and Jimmy Ryan, who went to the box when the game was out of reach. Bob Caruthers was the beneficiary of the onslaught. Things went better in the afternoon. Although Brooklyn scored eight runs on Hutchinson, a three-run homer off Tom Lovett by catcher William "Pop" Schriver (a veteran major leaguer obtained from the Western Association) won it, 9–8. Both Boston teams were at home for Labor Day, but the Beaneaters' games with Cleveland were rained out, as was the Boston-St. Louis doubleheader. (The rainouts provided Mike Kelly with the occasion to corral Jack Stivetts and Tommy McCarthy for the National League.)

After an off day, on which Boston and Cleveland split two games, Hutchinson won a 4–2 decision from newcomer Bert Inks. In the midst of a tough pennant race, Anson had a couple of discontented players on his hands. Tommy Burns sulked in the Eastern Park grandstand during both Labor Day games, angry with Anson about something. He reconciled with the Colts' leader on Wednesday and played third base. Malachi Kittredge, sore because Anson was using Schriver most of the time, disappeared in Chicago and received a $50 fine. He showed up in Brooklyn, ready to rejoin the team.

The Colts took a Thursday morning train to Philadelphia and arrived in time to defeat the Phillies 6–1 behind Ad Gumbert. The next day John Thornton throttled Chicago by the same score, but on Saturday, Anson's men won a game in which both Gumbert and Tim Keefe pitched well, 3–2. Boston won all three of its encounters with Cincinnati, but after Chicago had played two series in the East, the Beaneaters had still gained only one game.

The big series with Boston began on Wednesday, the sixteenth, with 5,391 people on hand at the South End Grounds. Nick Young assigned two umpires to work the three games: Tim Hurst on the bases; the well-regarded Jim Gaffney, late of the Western Association, behind the plate. The Beaneaters erred repeatedly as Chicago scored seven runs on Harry Staley, while the sturdy Hutchinson limited Boston to one. Kelly started in right field but left the game, still complaining of an injured hand. Nearly 4,000 paid to watch Thursday's game, another Chicago victory, 8–4, with the usually weak-hitting Kittredge homering and doubling off Clarkson, whose record against Chicago for the season fell to 2–6. Gumbert got the win.

Joe Murphy trumpeted, "Boston's chances are as dead as the Greenback party." The *Cleveland Plain Dealer* believed the Beaneaters "might as well give up hope of flying the flag," and the *Cincinnati Evening Post* announced, "Chicago defeated the Bostons today and clinched the pennant." Boston salvaged the series finale on Wednesday before another big crowd. Hutchinson gave up seven runs, including a home run by Charlie Bennett, and Chicago made seven errors. Nichols held the Colts to two, defeating them for the first time after four tries. Even after that loss, *Sporting Life* was convinced that "Boston has been tried and found wanting. Chicago now has the pennant safely."[40] The Colts left for New York with a seemingly secure 76–45 to 68–50 cushion.

Then they lost three straight games in the Polo Grounds. On the seventeenth, Rusie struck out eight, gave up six hits, and held Chicago to a single run, as the Giants got to Vickery for six scores. On Friday, they jumped on Gumbert for eight runs en route to a 9–3 win. George Gore and Roger Connor had three hits apiece in support of John Ewing. On Saturday, Rusie did it again, squelching the Colts on three hits and no runs. Only three of the Giants' eight tallies on Hutchinson were earned; Chicago committed six errors. Anson went hitless in the series, which drew Tim Murnane's subsequent comment that "the king of base ball captains was of no more account than a two-legged table."⁴¹ The three games ended the Chicago-New York schedule, with the Giants having won thirteen of the eighteen games.

Meanwhile, Boston and Pittsburgh played to a 7–7 tie, followed by three one-sided Beaneaters victories. With Chicago's and Boston's records now, respectively, 76–48 and 71–50, Murphy thought the Colts needed help from above: "Let Chicagoans, when they put their heads on their soft pillows tonight, pray softly and earnestly that brighter days may be evolved from the womb of the future."⁴²

Well might the partisan scribe hope for divine intervention. By winning the last game of the series with the Colts and taking three games from Pittsburgh, the Beaneaters were on their way to eighteen consecutive victories. Mike Kelly was in only sixteen of the thirty-nine games Boston played after he joined the team, and the *Columbus Evening Dispatch* jeered, "If ever a ball player was guilty of drawing a salary on suspicion, Mike Kelly is the player." Yet as Marty Appel has suggested, "Perhaps his presence had the effect of a magic potion."⁴³

After the trouncing in New York, Chicago opened a three-game set in Cincinnati before a Monday turnout of about five hundred by beating the languishing Reds, 5–4. Hutchinson and Tony Mullane both pitched well, but the Colts won it in the bottom of the ninth inning. Hutchinson led off with a walk, following which umpire Bob Emslie, another recent addition from the Western Association, called Schriver's pop-up bunt fair when it landed inside the base line and rolled into foul ground. Under the rules of the time, that was the correct call. Mullane went into a rage—which reminded Murphy "of an unfortunate canine who has swallowed a bunch of lighted fire crackers by mistake"—and stalked off to the clubhouse.⁴⁴ John Reilly, dispatched to bring him back, found the pitcher already undressed, so Arlie Latham gave up and called in Billy Rhines. Ryan bunted his first pitch toward third base; Latham bobbled the ball, loading the bases. Wilmot and Dahlen hit sacrifice flies, scoring the fourth and fifth runs to end the game.

On Tuesday, Vickery slow-curved Chicago to a 4–1 win, allowing only four hits. Ban Johnson—who had been writing critically about Latham for weeks, even suggesting the League should investigate Latham's lackadaisical play—sat on the Cincinnati bench at the start of the game. When the Reds came in from the field for the bottom of the first inning, Latham protested Johnson's presence to Emslie, who refused to order the reporter to leave. After considerable wrangling, Johnson quietly retired to the press box, with Latham vowing to whip him when he got the chance. After Hutchinson blanked the Reds on Thursday, 9–0, with Anson homering off newcomer Clarence Stevens, they returned home for three games with Pittsburgh. In Boston, the Beaneaters swept four games from Brooklyn and gained a half game on Chicago.

On Friday the twenty-fifth, at West Side Park, the Colts won again, beating Pittsburgh 7–4, while Boston won in Philadelphia, 5–2. Saturday's game on the south side ended in acrimony and confusion. Pittsburgh catcher George Miller berated umpire Jack McQuaid for calling Tommy Burns safe in the eighth inning to tie the game, 4–4. McQuaid ordered him to the bench, but Bill McGunnigle ordered him to go back in, whereupon the umpire declared a forfeit, as McGunnigle yelled that McQuaid was crooked. The trouble continued on Monday. McQuaid tossed Charles Reilly for interfering with Cliff Carroll's efforts to reach third base and Miller again, this time for throwing his mitt in Anson's face as Anson tried to catch a pop-up. After eight innings, with the score 6–6, McQuaid called the game because of darkness. Boston won its third in a row in Philadelphia and gained another half-game on Chicago. The difference was now 81–48 to 80–50.

Then the Colts went over to Cleveland for three games. At breakfast in the Hollenden Hotel on the morning of the series opener, Anson, his pennant in peril, sat down in a black mood. "If I had my way about it," he said to the others at the table, "every leader in the Brotherhood movement would have been forever barred from base-ball."[45] Looking at Fred Pfeffer, he accused him of being manipulated by John Ward, whereupon Pfeffer left the table without eating. Pfeffer's relations with Anson, never the best even before the Brotherhood war, were permanently poisoned.

That afternoon, September 28, Cy Young outpitched Hutchinson before a credit-able Monday turnout of 1,500. Working without Zimmer, his usual battery mate, Young allowed two runs in the sixth inning; Cleveland scored single runs on Hutchinson in the first, fourth, sixth, and seventh. Chicago won a wild one the next day, 14–13, Hutchinson getting the win in relief of Vickery. In the top of the ninth Ed McKean was thrown out trying for a bases-loaded home run that would have put Cleveland ahead. In the bottom of the inning, Dahlen doubled, went to third on Anson's single, and scored the winning run when Burns pushed a hit through shortstop, which McKean had vacated as Anson ran toward second. On Wednesday, however, Young again overcame the Colts, holding them to five runs while Chicago made six errors. Only four of the twelve runs scored on Vickery and Gumbert were earned. "It was almost pitiful to see Anson," reported *Sporting Life*'s Cleveland correspondent. "How the old man did run the bases and coach and urge his men, all to no avail."[46]

The five games played at Boston's South End Grounds from September 28 to September 30 would live in infamy for a generation of Chicago's baseball enthusiasts. Two of the five were makeup games that were supposed to be played in New York, but Nick Young polled six of the League's clubs, *not* including Chicago, and announced he had their approval to transfer the New York games to Boston. Jim Mutrie later said he wanted the two games moved on the assumption that "it would increase the receipts of the company."[47]

When the New York team came on the field on Monday the twenty-eighth, pitchers Amos Rusie and John Ewing and first baseman Roger Connor were nowhere to be seen. (Mike Kelly was present, but for whatever reason—sore hand or something else—he sat out all five games.) Buck Ewing sent to the box Roscoe Coughlin, who had pitched only six times all season, winning three, losing the same number. Regular catcher Dick Buckley was behind the plate for part of the game but left, pleading a dislocated finger. He was replaced by Frank "Buster" Burrell, late of New England semipro ball. Selee went with Kid Nichols. The Giants made eight errors; Coughlin gave up eleven runs; Nichols held New York to three tallies. *Sporting Life*'s correspondent remarked, "The Giants beat all records for indifferent and rocky playing in Boston this season."[48]

On the twenty-ninth the Beaneaters and Giants played two games, one of which was a makeup. Boston battered Mickey Welch, who had pitched infrequently up to then, for thirteen runs. The Giants scored six runs on Clarkson but made eight errors. In the second game, Mike Sullivan, released early in the season by the Beaneaters and then by Columbus, was in the box for New York. Catcher Burrell made all but one of New York's five errors in another easy Boston win, 11–3, for Harry Staley.

On the thirtieth, Boston swept another doubleheader, a regularly scheduled game and another makeup. In the opener, the Giants erred six more times, as Coughlin and Welch yielded sixteen runs to five given up by Nichols. The closing game of the series was a respectable display of baseball—at last. With but one error committed behind him, Sullivan held Boston to five runs, but the Giants could score only once on Staley. After Mike Tiernan's drive hit Staley on the cheek in the sixth inning, Clarkson relieved him and gave up two runs in the bottom of the eighth before Bobby Lowe threw out Tiernan at the plate to end the inning. Tom Lynch then decided it was too dark for the game to continue. Those two victories, together with Chicago's second loss to Cleveland and Cy Young, put Boston in first place.

In the five games, the Giants committed 26 errors, 25 in the first four. Boston scored 56 runs, 51 in the first four games. Amos Rusie and John Ewing remained in New York throughout the series; second baseman Danny Richardson played the first two games and sat out the rest; Dick Buckley was behind the plate for only a part of the opening game; Roger Connor missed the first three games, then showed up to play in the series-ending doubleheader; and Buck Ewing didn't play at all.

After Chicago's three games in Cleveland and the five-game fiasco in Boston, the Beaneaters' record was 85–50 to the Colts' 82–50—a difference of only about nine percentage points. Each team had three games remaining, so Chicago's pennant chances were still alive. Yet headlines in the October 1 edition of the *Chicago Tribune* screamed: "PLOT AGAINST CHICAGO." "Eastern Clubs Leagued to Defeat the Grand Old Man." "ROBBED OF THE PENNANT." "Unnerved by the Unequal Struggle[,] the Colts Lose to Cleveland While the Alleged Giants Throw Two More Games to Boston."[49]

The *Tribune* included a dispatch from New York that asked if the Giants had been "playing for a position," would Buck Ewing have held back Rusie and John Ewing and used the unknown Sullivan and Burrell, "the weakest catcher in the league." Another commentator from Philadelphia tactfully offered, "In one sense of the word it looks as though the Eastern cities are helping Boston to win, while it is the reverse in the West." Others were less tactful. The *Milwaukee Sentinel* called the New York-Boston games "a disgrace to the National Baseball League and a blow to baseball." The *Kansas City Star* declared, "Baseball has degenerated to the level of pool-room exhibitions," and the *Cleveland Leader* considered it "a sorry thing for the national game that Eastern jealousy of Chicago has made such contemptible work possible." From Boston: "The recent games between the New York and Boston league teams have been but a series of farces. Indignant spectators have gone to the box-office and demanded their money back, and the grand stand and bleachers have alike hissed their condemnation of the apparent crooked work." One krank was quoted as saying, "I have never seen such wretched playing as that put up against the Boston club by the New York 'Giants.'" For *Sporting Life* editor Francis Richter, it was "one of the most pitiable chapters of base ball history," something that gave "the cavillers [*sic*] and enemies of the game an opportunity, such as has not been offered itself since the '70s to question the integrity of professional base ball. Taken altogether, it is a bad mess."[50]

It seemed nearly everybody had a notion why the New York-Boston games went the way they did. Some said the eastern clubs had ganged up on Chicago, fearing if the Colts won the pennant with a team of mostly low-salaried players, the owners would be influenced to cut veterans' pay. Others saw it as persistent animosity toward Anson on the part of former Brotherhood members, especially among the Giants. Recalling the Anson-Pfeffer episode at breakfast in Cleveland, Joe Murphy observed, "The Brotherhood is dead, but its ghost is holding high revel in the National League at the moment." E. M. Guenther, of the Associated Press in Chicago, was convinced that not only had the Giants deliberately lost the five games in Boston, but that Brooklyn, whose captain's integrity had never been questioned, threw four games to the Beaneaters. "Is it not singular," asked Guenther, "that the Bridegrooms can lose so easily to Boston and win with such little effort from New York?"[51]

Yet Tim Murnane, ever a partisan when it came to Boston baseball, could find "no ground for supposing the teams of Brooklyn, Philadelphia and New York did any more than take things easy." He went on to insist that, "The last five New York games at the South End grounds were played about as well as any of the games in this city by the Giants." Besides, he said, "Men will not play hard ball after their position in the race is settled"—which remark may have said a lot about the baseball of Murnane's day.[52]

As for Anson, after the opening game in Boston on September 28, he was surprisingly uncritical. When a team had nothing to gain, he said, it was "always the case that the players are not exerting themselves." Although that might be "exasperating," he couldn't complain, "as my own men might do the same thing. Do I think there is any crooked playing in Boston? No sir, not a bit of it." At that point he was still confident. "Next Saturday might well see the pennant possessed by Chicago." The next day's doubleheader changed Anson's mind. Now he said he believed "there was crooked work in the East." And in his autobiography, published nine years later, he left no doubt about his feelings. New York played badly "for the express purpose of throwing us down and keeping the pennant in the East."[53]

Chicago's three remaining games were at home versus Cincinnati. On Thursday, October 1, before about 900 people at South Side Park, the mercurial Mullane limited the Colts to two hits and a single run, while the Reds scored six times on Hutchinson. Three costly Chicago errors led to three Reds runs, and Jim Keenan finished things off with a two-run, eighth-inning homer. By the same score, Boston clinched the pennant in Philadelphia, Clarkson topping Charles "Duke" Esper. At West Side Park on Friday, with nothing at stake, Vickery and Pat Luby pitched casually; Ed Crane and Billy Rhines did likewise; the Colts and Reds combined for eleven errors; and Tim Hurst called a halt to the proceedings after six innings, with Cincinnati ahead, 17–16. In disgust, Joe Murphy reported, "The Chicagos and the Cincinnatis are making a farce out of the national game these days and seem to have little regard for the public that pays its money to see a ball game." But Murphy also felt sorry for Anson: "Uncle, a melancholy yet magnificent ruin of the proud old man of three weeks ago, stood on the coaching lines in solitary grandeur."[54] Boston ran its winning streak to eighteen games, beating the Phillies 9–1.

Boston's streak and the season ended on Saturday. The Beaneaters arrived at the Huntingdon Grounds in barouches, wearing top hats manager Selee bought for them. A fine turnout of 3,500 saw a well-played game, Tim Keefe winning over Clarkson, 5–3. Mike Kelly caught Clarkson for four innings, in which he had three passed balls and made four wild throws before Ganzel relieved him.

On the South Side, about a thousand Chicago diehards witnessed another amateurish exhibition, marred by a total of twelve errors and highlighted by captains Latham and Anson doing the catching in the late innings. By winning 15–9, Cincinnati ceded the League's cellar to Pittsburgh, which lost to Cleveland. Murphy was even more disgusted with the Colts, reporting that "toward the end of the game they were roundly hissed, a reception not undeserved. When they play like they did yesterday they are obtaining money under false pretenses. . . . The crowd dispersed, wondering why it had gone to the game."[55] During the last week of the season, Chicago had lost five of six games.

Final National League standings: Boston, 87–51; Chicago, 82–53; New York, 71–61; Philadelphia, 68–69; Cleveland, 65–74; Brooklyn, 61–76; Cincinnati, 56–81; Pittsburgh, 55–80. Although the Giants topped the League with a .263 team batting average, Boston scored the most runs (847), allowed the fewest (638), and made the fewest errors (358). Philadelphia's Billy Hamilton led the League in batting (.340), as well as hits (179), runs (141), walks (102), and stolen bases (111). Mike Tiernan and Harry Stovey hit 16 home runs apiece; Stovey also led in triples and slugging average, while Anson drove in the most runs (120). Bill Hutchinson again led both major leagues with 44 wins, followed by Clarkson and Rusie with 33 each and Nichols with 30. Hutchinson also led everybody in games pitched (66), complete games (56), and innings (561). The fireballing Rusie led both leagues with 337 strikeouts. In his first full season in the big time, Cy Young pitched in 54 games, winning 27, losing 24 for a sixth-place team.

Clearly, Boston possessed the most overall talent and played the smoothest ball, but the outcome of the pennant race still left a foul odor hanging over the League. An interesting aspect of the whole controversy was that no allegations surfaced that gamblers had been involved in the games in Boston, although it had been only fourteen years since the bribery of several Louisville players decided the pennant. In an interview with Guenther, Chicago president Jim Hart (who had been Boston's manager two years earlier) did refer to the Louisville incident, "only that disgrace was brought about by monetary considerations, while this is personal animosity." Hart was unsparing in his vehemence. "Were I under indictment for murder," he declared, "with the circumstantial evidence against me as strong as it appears to be against the New York club, I should expect to be hanged. That somebody is guilty of treachery I am positive." Pointing to the absence of five Giants stalwarts from all or part of the series, Hart accused the New York management of either dishonesty or "gross incompetency." He intended to "probe the matter to its bottom" and "insist upon the expulsion of guilty parties, be they 'magnates,' managers, captains or players."[56]

Vigorous denials of "hippodroming" (the period's term for dishonest playing) issued from John B. Day and Jim Mutrie, as well as from Buck Ewing, John Ewing, and Danny Richardson. Day told the press, "I can state positively, as far as the New York officers and players are concerned, that there was no conspiracy to beat the Chicago team. Anson lost the pennant by being beaten in the West. The games between the New York and Boston teams were played as fairly as any games ever were." Frank Robison came to the defense of his friend Day, agreeing that it wasn't the games Boston won but the games Chicago lost to "the despised Clevelands whom the Chicago players and newspapers derided all the season."[57]

As for the absence of particular Giants, Day said Rusie was left in New York because he had earned a rest, although Mutrie claimed his arm was lame, and Rusie himself pleaded sickness, as did Richardson. John Ewing had supposedly been disabled after taking a batted ball on his foot in Philadelphia; Buckley's finger was dislocated by a foul tip in Boston. Mutrie revealed that he gave Connor permission to miss the opening game in Boston so he could look after personal business in Waterbury, Connecticut. Delayed by a train accident, Connor only arrived in Boston in time for the second doubleheader, on September 30. So much for explanations—or excuses. None of that accounted for the Giants' shoddy play in all but the final game of the series, or how on October 1 the supposedly sore-footed John Ewing could go to the box at the Polo Grounds and pitch a five-hit victory over Brooklyn.

Jim Hart got his "probe of the matter to the bottom"—sort of. On October 6 the directors of the New York club resolved to have its executive committee—consisting of Day, Edward B. Talcott, and J. Walter Spalding—investigate the games in Boston. The plot thickened. Since mid-summer 1890, Day had been only a minority stockholder in the New York club; most of its stock was in the hands of the Spalding brothers, Al Reach and John I. Rogers of Philadelphia, Ferdinand Abell, and Arthur Soden. Al Spalding even gave a small amount of New York stock to Cap Anson.

It was an absurd situation. The owners of the Giants were investigating their own team; J. Walter Spalding was the brother of the principal owner of Chicago; the principal owner of Chicago and its captain-manager were stockholders in the Giants. Arthur Soden, moreover, owned a third of the Boston club at the same time he held stock in the Giants. On the thirteenth, the three-man executive committee questioned Mutrie, the Ewing brothers, Rusie, Richardson, Connor, Jim O'Rourke, and utility man Archie Clarke. The players howled that their reputations had been damaged and talked about legal action against the newspapers or somebody.

The investigation was a total whitewash. John Ewing, it was found, remained in New York because he was injured, while Rusie was excused after he agreed to pitch a doubleheader versus Brooklyn on September 26, "although he was not in any wise disabled." Mutrie acknowledged that he excused Rusie and permitted Connor to go to Waterbury without consulting captain Ewing. Richardson played the first three games but then became "seriously ill . . . and has been ever since." Buckley, with injured finger, played part of the September 28 game "under protest" and couldn't play after that. Mutrie explained that he agreed to play the two makeup games and to transfer them to Boston only after being assured that six League clubs approved.[58]

Though acknowledging that with various players injured and Rusie unavailable, the two makeup games shouldn't have been transferred to Boston, Day, Talcott, and

Spalding concluded that all the players "assert that they played with as much desire and with as much effort to win the games from the Bostons as any other games they played." So, "any apparent indifference or carelessness on the part of the players was due entirely to the unfortunate circumstances above referred to, and not to any bad faith or intentional desire that Boston should win."[59]

On October 13 the Giants' full board of directors blithely endorsed the committee's report. The next month the National League's owners convened at the Fifth Avenue Hotel, where Jim Hart read a lengthy protest against awarding the pennant to Boston, on the grounds Chicago hadn't been consulted before the two games scheduled for New York were transferred to Boston. The League's board of directors—Nick Young, Al Reach, John T. Brush, J. Palmer O'Neill, and John B. Day (!)—went into session to consider the protest. Three hours later Young called in reporters, read the board's exoneration of the New York and Boston clubs, and announced the official awarding of the pennant to Boston. At the same time, the board acknowledged Chicago should have been consulted about the two makeup games.

It was, as Francis Richter put it, altogether a bad mess, the most bizarre aspect of which was the interlocking New York/Chicago/Boston ownership. What is one to make of it all? The most likely explanation for the Boston games is that the Giants—dissension-ridden and dispirited, their pennant chances dead—just didn't care if they won or lost. Moreover, some of them probably still harbored enough resentment of Anson that they were happy to help the Beaneaters beat him out of his pennant. Nine years later Anson rejected New York's and the League's official reasons for what happened in Boston: "I am free to confess right now that I do not believe it."[60] Yet John B. Day and Frank Robison were right in attributing the outcome of the pennant race to Chicago's two losses in Cleveland. It was Cy Young more than the alleged hippodroming in Boston that cost Anson, as it turned out, his last chance at a championship.

For all the controversy surrounding the way the pennant race ended, it was a generally successful season for the National League. The League's total attendance of 1,352,487 almost doubled that of 1890 and fell just short of the record set in 1889. Although Philadelphia wasn't in contention over the second half of the season, 217,282 people bought tickets at the Huntingdon Grounds. The Giants drew 210,568 at the Polo Grounds; 201,188 Chicagoans divided their patronage between the west side and south side ballparks. Up against tough local competition from the Association, the

Boston National Leaguers attracted 184,472. Brooklyn, a disappointing team whose home games took place at an out-of-the-way site, still played before 181,477. Cleveland's crowds totaled about 132,000, Pittsburgh's about 128,000. In his first year in Cincinnati, John T. Brush lost money with a bad team that could interest only 97,500 in coming to its west side ballpark. Although the League outdrew the Association by about 180,000, the nation's four largest cities—New York, Chicago, Philadelphia, and Brooklyn—were in the League, whereas the Association had only Philadelphia.

As soon as the season ended, both Anson's Colts and the Browns headed west to pick up some extra money playing exhibitions in Sioux City, Keokuk, and other towns, although they wouldn't play each other. Meanwhile, Boston Reds manager Irwin challenged the Beaneaters to a five-game series in San Francisco for the "world's championship," with the receipts to be divided 50–50 between the players and public charity. If his challenge wasn't accepted by November 1, the Reds would claim the title. The response of the imperious Soden was that the National League's champion couldn't meet a team from a league not governed by the National Agreement. When Zach Phelps, as Association president, made a similar overture to Nick Young, he was turned down on the same grounds.

Given that most former Players' Leaguers were in the Association in 1891, one could argue that the Reds won in the stronger league and thus were the stronger of the two Boston champions. No doubt it would have been a splendid match-up, but it wasn't to be. Boston baseball lovers would have to be satisfied that the city had three pennant winners in three leagues in two years. And Michael Joseph Kelly played for all three!

1. *Washington Post*, July 17, 1891, p. 6.
2. By the middle of 1891, Keefe and Behannon had closed the store. Behannon found work as a salesman for A. G. Spalding and Brothers!
3. *Sporting News*, July 4, 1891, p. 3; *Columbus Evening Dispatch*, July 15, 1891, p. 2.
4. *St. Louis Post-Dispatch*, July 25, 1891, p. 8.
5. *New York Clipper*, July 18, 1891, p. 319.
6. *Sporting News*, August 1, 1891, p. 5.
7. *Cleveland Plain Dealer*, July 29, 1891, p. 5; *Sporting News*, August 8, 1891, p. 1.
8. *Chicago Tribune*, August 1, 1891, p. 1.
9. *Sporting Life*, August 15, 1891, p. 12.
10. *Sporting News*, August 22, 1891, p. 4.
11. *Cincinnati Evening Post*, August 8, 1891, p. 4.
12. *Sporting Life*, August 1, 1891, p. 1; *St. Louis Post-Dispatch*, July 20, 1891, p. 8.
13. *New York Clipper*, August 8, 1891, p. 373.

14. *St. Louis Post-Dispatch*, August 15, 1891, p. 6.
15. The desertion of Milwaukee left only Denver, Sioux City, Omaha, and Kansas City in the Western Association. The transfer of the Cincinnati franchise to Milwaukee led to still more litigation. Von der Ahe, the Wagner brothers, and Baltimore president Harry von der Horst had signed a five-year lease at $1,200 per year on E. M. Pendleton's property. Pendleton now sued the lessees for back rent, which led to a six-year legal entanglement, finally resolved when the National League (in which all four lessees had become club owners) ruled on the amount the various parties owed Pendleton.
16. *Cincinnati Evening Post*, August 18, 1891, p. 3.
17. *Washington Post*, August 19, 1891, p. 6.
18. Marty Appel, *Slide, Kelly, Slide: The Wild Life and Times of Mike "King" Kelly, Baseball's First Superstar* (Lanham, Md.: Scarecrow Press, 1999), 162.
19. *Sporting News*, August 22, 1891, p. 1.
20. *St. Louis Post-Dispatch*, August 20, 1891, p. 8.
21. Bill Kling was the older brother of Johnny Kling, the outstanding catcher on the great Chicago Cubs teams of the early twentieth century.
22. *Sporting News*, August 29, 1891, p. 1.
23. *Washington Post*, August 26, 1891, p. 6. Ironically, John McGraw's successes managing the New York Giants under Brush's ownership (from 1903 to 1912) prompted the city's baseball writers to anoint him "the Little Napoleon."
24. Ibid.
25. *Columbus Evening Dispatch*, August 29, 1891, p. 2; *Sporting Life*, September 5, 1891, p. 1.
26. *Cleveland Plain Dealer*, August 28, 1891, p. 5.
27. *Sporting News*, August 29, 1891, p. 4; *St. Louis Post-Dispatch*, August 31, 1891, p. 3.
28. *Washington Post*, August 26, 1891, p. 6; *Sporting News*, September 5, 1891, p. 1.
29. *St. Louis Post-Dispatch*, August 26, 1891, p. 8.
30. *Chicago Tribune*, September 4, 1891, p. 6; David E. Porter, "Cap Anson of Marshalltown: Baseball's First Superstar," *Palimpsest*, 61 (July–August 1980), p. 104.
31. *Sporting News*, September 12, 1891, p. 1.
32. Harold Seymour and Dorothy Seymour Mills, *Baseball: The Early Years* (1960; reprint, Oxford University Press, 1989), 258.
33. *Washington Post*, September 24, 1891, p. 6.
34. *Boston Globe*, September 17, 1891, p. 3; *Sporting News*, September 22, 1891, p. 7. While Rogers was for war, Philadelphia co-owner Al Reach, whose firm supplied baseballs to the Association, favored peace.
35. *St. Louis Post-Dispatch*, September 22, 1891, p. 8.
36. *Washington Post*, October 7, 1891, p. 6.
37. *St. Louis Post-Dispatch*, September 28, 1891, p. 6.
38. David Nemec, *The Beer and Whiskey League: The Illustrated History of the American Association, Baseball's Renegade Major League* (Guilford, Conn.: Lyons Press, 2004), 231.
39. The following section, on the last month of the National League season, incorporates much material from my article, "Was the 1891 National League Pennant Thrown?" *Base Ball: A Journal of the Early Game*, 2 (Fall 2008), 5–17.
40. *Chicago Tribune*, September 16, 1891, p. 6; *Cleveland Plain Dealer*, September 15, 1891, p. 5; Alexander, "Was the 1891 National League Pennant Thrown?" 9. The Greenback Labor party, formed in 1878 in Toledo, espoused the cause of labor and advocated currency inflation to relieve agricultural debt. It made a good showing in the 1880 congressional elections but went into sharp decline thereafter.
41. *Boston Globe*, October 3, 1891, p. 1.
42. *Chicago Tribune*, September 20, 1891, p. 4.
43. *Columbus Evening Dispatch*, September 29, 1891, p. 2; Appel, *Slide, Kelly, Slide*, 164.
44. *Sporting News*, September 26, 1891, p. 1.
45. *Chicago Tribune*, October 1, 1891, p. 6; *Sporting Life*, October 10, 1891, p. 1.
46. *Sporting Life*, October 1, 1891, p. 3.
47. *New York Clipper*, October 24, 1891, p. 559.

48. *Sporting Life*, October 3, 1891, p. 3.
49. *Chicago Tribune*, October 1, 1891, p. 6.
50. Ibid.; *Chicago Tribune*, October 4, 1891, p. 13; *Sporting Life*, October 3, 1891, p. 1; October 10, 1891, p. 2.
51. *Chicago Tribune*, October 2, 1891, p. 6; *Sporting Life*, October 3, 1891, p. 10.
52. *Boston Globe*, October 3, 1891, p. 1.
53. *Sporting Life*, October 3, 1891, p. 1; *Chicago Tribune*, October 1, 1891, p. 6; Adrian Anson, *A Ballplayer's Career: Being the Personal Reminiscences of Adrian C. Anson, Late Manager of the Chicago Base Ball Club* (Chicago: Era Publishing Co., 1900), 297.
54. *Chicago Tribune*, October 3, 1891, p. 6.
55. Ibid., October 4, 1891, p. 4.
56. In whole or in part, Hart's fulmination appeared in several daily newspapers, as well as in the *Sporting News*, *New York Clipper*, and *Sporting Life*. The quotations here are from the *Cleveland Plain Dealer*, October 4, 1891, p. 2, and *Sporting Life*, October 10, 1891, p. 1.
57. *Columbus Evening Dispatch*, October 5, 1891, p. 2; *Cleveland Plain Dealer*, October 7, 1891, p. 2. Frank Robison's comment is from *Sporting News*, October 10, 1891, p. 1.
58. *New York Clipper*, October 24, 1891, p. 559.
59. Ibid.
60. Anson, *A Ballplayer's Career*, 297.

CHAPTER 8

1891–92: "Men of Money Have About Come to Their Senses"

Despite the attendance recovery in the National League and American Association in 1891, nearly every club claimed financial losses. Of course the club owners put the blame for that squarely on high payrolls necessitated by the inter-league competition for talent. Yet the war between the two baseball organizations continued, with no end in sight as the off-season began. The Association coveted the Chicago area. Three weeks before the end of the season, Julian Hart and the ubiquitous Bill Barnie—who had recently resigned as Baltimore manager after quarreling with Orioles president Harry von der Horst—went to Chicago with the aim of promoting an Association franchise. They were successful in getting a group of investors headed by George T. Williams to subscribe $50,000 in stock, and on October 9 the franchise was incorporated at Springfield, with Williams as its president. Besides Williams, who was in the lumber business, the other major investors were a brewer, a beer salesman, and a saloon keeper, so it seemed likely the Association would have Sunday ball and beer sales at the ballpark.

Fred Pfeffer was to be player-manager of the Chicago entry. Like many aging players, Pfeffer longed to have his own team; besides that, he had come to despise Cap Anson. After the late-season breakfast incident in Cleveland, Pfeffer told Joe Murphy, "I will get even for this, and there is no better place to do it than right here in Chicago."[1] Anson reportedly apologized to Pfeffer, but the veteran infielder was unappeased and refused to accompany the rest of the Colts on their postseason western tour.

Early in November, the New York Giants' board of directors voted 2–1 to fire forty-year-old Jim Mutrie and bring in Pat T. Powers, who had managed Buffalo in the Eastern Association the past season. John B. Day opposed the move, but J. Walter Spalding, Edward Talcott, and Edwin A. McAlpin were determined to get rid of the man who had worked for Day in the Association and the League for the past nine years. Mutrie had been popular with the Giants players. Said Jim O'Rourke, "Every player on the team had a deep affection for him and it was always a pleasure to do what he wanted."[2] Mutrie's dismissal only added to suspicions about the late-September New York-Boston games.

Mutrie now aligned himself with the Association. On November 9, Charles Prince, Barnie, and the Wagner brothers met at the Albemarle Hotel in Manhattan to discuss prospects for putting a franchise in New York City and reentering Brooklyn, where Charles Byrne was reportedly on the outs with his partners and wanted to return to the Association. They even tossed around the idea of expanding the Association into a twelve-team league (as it had been in 1884). The quartet wired Mutrie at his home on Staten Island, inviting him to join them to talk about forming and managing a team in New York. Mutrie caught the next ferry and, at the Albemarle, claimed he could get $50,000 in financial backing for a New York club. The next day, when the full complement of Association club owners assembled at the Grand Central Hotel for their regular meeting, Mutrie was much in evidence, as were George T. Williams and Fred Pfeffer. Again the subject of a twelve-team Association came up. Chris von der Ahe declared that although he wanted peace, he was absolutely opposed to a twelve-team setup. Like others in the Association, von der Ahe felt that in 1884 the League had manipulated the Association into adding four clubs to checkmate the Union Association. It had proved a losing proposition, while the League sacrificed nothing.

In the first two months of the off-season, both leagues aggressively worked to coax players into jumping from one to the other. The traffic was hard to keep up with. Bill Dahlen first signed for next season with Jim Hart and Anson for $1,200, then put his signature on an Association contract with Milwaukee for $3,000, with a $500 advance. Roger Connor and Danny Richardson jumped from the Giants and signed with the Athletics, who were to be managed by Barnie. Fred Pfeffer went to Indianapolis and offered Amos Rusie $6,000 to join his Chicago team; still only twenty, the pitcher had to get his father's consent before he signed, which he finally did and received a $2,000 advance. Pfeffer also tried unsuccessfully to persuade Pete Browning, his fellow Louisvillian, to join him in the Association. By mid-November, eleven players had left the National League for the Association; seven Association players had signed League contracts.

Of the seven captured by the League, the biggest catch was Charles Comiskey.

The *St. Louis Post-Dispatch* thought there was as much chance of Comiskey's leaving the Browns "as there is of the Mississippi River flowing toward Chicago." Von der Ahe offered him another $6,000 contract to continue as St. Louis's captain and first baseman, but Comiskey had had enough of "der boss President" as well as the Association. His old friend Ted Sullivan acted as his agent, and while John T. Brush made three trips from Indianapolis to St. Louis to court Comiskey, George W. Howe, vice president of the Cleveland club, did the negotiating with Sullivan on Brush's behalf. Sullivan told Howe whatever club Comiskey joined would have to give him a three-year contract. Instructed to use "franchise" as the code word for Comiskey, Sullivan early in November wired Howe, "You can get the franchise for three years for $21,000."[3] A few days later the acclaimed field leader visited Indianapolis, met again with Brush, and agreed to captain and manage the Cincinnati team under slightly different terms: three years for $20,000 plus a share of the Reds' profits. "Commy" had come a long way from the $75-per-month von der Ahe paid him in the Association's inaugural season.

Having earlier lost Tommy McCarthy and Jack Stivetts to Boston, Von der Ahe also said goodbye to Tip O'Neill, who followed Comiskey to Cincinnati, where, for better or worse, they would again team with Arlie Lathan. (In re-signing Latham right after the season ended, Brush specified that under no circumstances would Latham continue as Reds captain.) The outfield of O'Neill, Browning, and Bug Holiday was expected to be one of the best in baseball, at least in terms of batting proficiency. Von der Ahe also lost Jack Boyle, who was supposed to join Comiskey at Cincinnati but decided he preferred the Giants.

But the Browns' owner struck back at the League, getting two players from the New York Giants to join his St. Louis club. In Wheeling, he signed Jack Glasscock to a three-year contract to captain and play shortstop; subsequently von der Ahe lured catcher Dick Buckley from the Giants. Kid Gleason also joined the Browns, transferred to von der Ahe by the Wagner brothers after Gleason quit the Phillies and signed with the Athletics.

As rosters underwent shakeups, a shakeup also occurred in the ownership and management of the Pittsburgh club. Shortly after the National League's annual meeting in November (where J. Palmer O'Neill and the rest of the League's board of directors rejected Jim Hart's protest), O'Neill resigned from the Pittsburgh presidency and sold his stock to Mark Baldwin's father. William H. Temple and A. C. Scandrett became the new major stockholders. One of their first acts was to fire Bill McGunnigle, whose record after he took over the Pirates was 24–33, good for last place. Al Buckenberger, who had managed Sioux City to a pennant by default in the Western Association, was hired to replace him.

As the little world of professional baseball continued to turn on its rickety axis, Mike Kelly and his wife, accompanied by his father, were on the other side of the Atlantic, enjoying the all-expenses-paid European trip the Boston Triumvirs gave him to desert the Association. At the beginning of November the Kellys were in Ireland, where they visited Waterford, the birthplace of the King's father. The Kellys' itinerary then took them to London. The King remained confused about the currency and tipped in half-sovereigns rather than shillings, but he called London "a pretty good town" and bragged about coming in at six in the morning "with as fine a jag as you could get in any country in the world."[4] From England it was on to Italy and the Riviera.

A year earlier, National League and Players' League owners and investors had first talked about compromise, then moved on to enter into a series of franchise consolidations that left the players out in the cold. Now Brooklyn's Ferdinand Abell, proclaiming that something had to be done to end the wasteful inter-league conflict, raised the possibility of a different kind of consolidation, in which four Association franchises would join the League. Abell's partner Charles Byrne, along with Brush and Frank Robison, invited Francis Richter and four other baseball writers to dinner in New York and broached the subject of consolidation. Robison asked the writers whether, if everything were done fairly, they thought a twelve-club league would work; they agreed it might.

Von der Ahe would have none of it, declaring the Association would never combine with the National League in any form. Besides, he pointed out, the Association's president held in trust 51 percent of each club's stock, so nobody could consolidate without the consent of the rest of the Association. Barnie warned that a twelve-member League could drop back to eight at any time. "Were that little game played," Barnie said, "there is no doubt as to which clubs would be cast out, either."[5]

But events were already moving beyond von der Ahe and Barnie. Charles Prince, the biggest stockholder in the Boston Association franchise, was in financial trouble and ready to get out of baseball. At the League's November meeting, he got together at the Manhattan Athletic Club with Arthur Soden, J. Walter Spalding, Charles Byrne, John T. Brush, Al Reach, and Frank Robison. Western Association president Louis C. Krauthoff was also present. Prince left the meeting talking about a consolidated twelve-club organization. Now so was J. Earle Wagner, and Francis Richter brought the influence of *Sporting Life* to the cause of consolidation. The League owners even appointed a new peace committee, consisting of Brush, Byrne, and Frank Robison.

On November 11, Association president Zach Phelps arrived in Chicago from Louisville, denying that any kind of consolidation was going to happen and, like von der Ahe, noting that because he held 51 percent of each club's stock, everybody would have to consent to any member leaving the Association. But with Prince, the Wagners, and at least four League owners or co-owners in favor of consolidation, it began to look like a sure thing. The club owners' imperative in both leagues was to cut salaries, with which the *Washington Post* was in full sympathy. Commented the *Post*, "The most ordinary ball-tosser turns up his nose at an offer of $2,000, and with the utmost sang froid refuses to sign for less than $2,500 or $3,000. Now, that is all wrong, and it is gratifying to know that men of money have about come to their senses and are determined to take the bull by the horns."[6]

On December 10, Brush, Byrne, and Frank Robison arrived in St. Louis to talk to von der Ahe, without whose agreement to consolidate nothing could happen. According to the *Sporting News*, what brought von der Ahe around was the reality that he would have to help Charles Prince stay afloat. Moreover, for all his big-time ambitions, Milwaukee owner H. E. Gillette was also reported to be about out of money. The Browns' owner had had enough of putting his money into other clubs. J. Earle Wagner also refused to do anything for Prince or anybody else, although he and the League's peace committee assured von der Ahe they would help buy out the weaker Association clubs, so the twelve-team setup could be realized. Von der Ahe was also assured that in the new league, St. Louis and Louisville could continue to offer Sunday ball.

Now the Association appointed its own peace committee: Von der Ahe, Harry von der Horst, and Frank S. Elliott, attorney for the Wagners. "If there had been any doubt that the twelve club scheme would go through," the *Sporting News* observed, "it was dispelled now by the selection of the committee with no member of the Chicago Club on it." George T. Williams and his associates in Chicago were furious at the turn of events, but, as the St. Louis weekly put it, "The Windy City men found they were not 'in it.'"[7] Byrne drew up a preliminary peace agreement, and he and the other members of the two peace committees visited other club owners to sell the consolidation project. Von der

Ahe first talked with Ralph Lazarus and Aaron Cohen in Columbus, then traveled east to see Prince and M. B. Scanlon, Washington president—but he ignored Milwaukee and Chicago. Meanwhile, Byrne, Brush, and Robison succeeded in convincing the skeptical John I. Rogers, J. Walter Spalding (now the strongest figure in the New York franchise), and the Boston Triumvirs that consolidation would serve everybody's interest.

The full peace conference convened in Indianapolis on Tuesday, December 15, 1891, at the Bates House. Knowing they were to be left out of any consolidation arrangement, the Chicago investors arrived in a special railway car, set up shop in the Bates House, and prepared to fight, only to discover that von der Ahe, whom they had believed their ally, was ready to consolidate. When the club owners finally assembled, Williams spoke at length against consolidation, saying that at first he was lukewarm about getting into the Association, and that the prospect of a team in Chicago in 1892 "made the Association stock worth something, and that is why we were trapped into the thing. We are made the victims, and it is very shabby treatment from a crowd of men we supposed to be friends and partners." Fuming that Chicago hadn't joined the Association "to be dropped in two months," Williams left the meeting to tell reporters he was glad to be out of the company he'd been in.[8]

Williams's plea to his might-have-been peers was no use. It took almost three days to get everything agreed upon, but at 4:00 a.m. on December 18, the consolidation plan was adopted. Five Association franchises were bought out for a total of $118,000—what the *Washington Post* termed "funeral expenses." The Wagners received the biggest payment for the Athletics, $45,000; Boston got $35,000. Lazarus and Cohen were paid $18,000 for Columbus; the Chicago group got $14,000; and H. E. Gillette came out with only $6,000, which was the amount he paid the Association the previous August, after he had settled with von der Ahe for a like amount. The club owners agreed on a fifty-cent base admission, although clubs would have the option to charge twenty-five cents on special occasions; Sunday ball was approved in those cities (St. Louis and Louisville) where local laws allowed it. All twelve members of the consolidated circuit assumed the $118,000 debt and were to contribute 10 percent of gate receipts toward paying it off. The twelve were bound by a so-called ironclad agreement to maintain the league's membership intact for a ten-year period. All players' contracts were validated as they were at present; otherwise players would be parceled out among the twelve clubs, each of which would have a roster limit of fifteen. Francis Richter chortled that the coming of peace was the outcome "for which the best friends of base ball have contended, lo, these many years, and which only the shock of rebellion and the fire of revolution could force into permanent practice."[9]

Byrne and Brush had arrived in Indianapolis early to draw up a constitution for the "National League and American Association of Professional Base Ball Clubs." The Association went into separate session and dissolved its nine-club partnership, whereupon the five departing members resigned from the organization. The officials of St. Louis, Louisville, Baltimore, and Washington then signed the constitution and formally joined their franchises to the consolidated organization. Within a short time, M. B. Scanlon and associates sold a controlling interest in Washington to the Wagner brothers, who thus became owners of their third franchise in three years in three leagues. They named Bill Barnie to manage the Nationals.

At last, it seemed, baseball's peaceable kingdom had been achieved. But as Harold Seymour and Dorothy Seymour Mills have written, "The so-called consolidation . . . was not a consolidation at all. It was absorption. Although the Association formally dissolved, the League never took that step. The destruction of its once-great rival gave the National League an undisputed monopoly of professional baseball for an entire decade."[10] Indeed, the league's cumbersome name never caught on; from the beginning, everybody simply called it the National League—or in popular parlance, the "big league."

The *Milwaukee Sentinel* was unsparing in its contempt for the "throw down" of a franchise that had been major league for only four months: "Altogether the duplicity, treachery and mendacity which was developed at the meeting exceeds anything ever known in an alleged 'legitimate' business transaction, and it will be easier hereafter to convince the public that there is honor among thieves than to convince them that base ball men possess an iota of the same commodity."[11]

As far as is known, nobody involved with the Association held a wake at a saloon and raised a bitter toast to its demise, as John Ward had toasted the passing of the Players' League some ten months earlier. But somebody should have, because for ten seasons the Association had offered a high caliber of affordable, entertaining, often raucous baseball to people in nineteen different cities, varying in size from New York and Philadelphia to Toledo and Syracuse. National Leaguers might deride the Association as the "beer and whiskey league," but that intended insult only emphasized the Association's greater appeal to working-class customers, whose only day of leisure was Sunday and whose idea of enjoying themselves might involve taking some beer with their baseball.

If there had been a wake for the Association, it might have been held by some of the players who found themselves without jobs in the aftermath of the consolidation. In 1891, League and Association teams together had about 240 roster positions; for 1892 there were only 180 in the expanded twelve-club National League. After players from the five bought-out Association clubs were distributed, seventy-one men who had played in the two leagues in 1891 remained unclaimed, including such notables as Chicken Wolf, John O'Brien, John Reilly, Fred Dunlap, Henry Gruber, and Paul Hines. Some retired; most dropped down to the minor leagues, nine of which began the 1892 season. As usual, some leagues wouldn't finish.

Bill Dahlen, having signed a handsome deal with Milwaukee, found himself without a franchise to play for. Having no choice, he returned to Chicago's reserve, signing a new contract for $1,500, $300 more than the one he first signed with Jim Hart and Anson. Hart reimbursed H. E. Gillette for the $500 advance he gave Dahlen, then took that amount out of the young player's salary!

Asked about what would happen to payrolls under the new setup, Nick Young said they wouldn't be cut "unduly." "But," he went on, "those players who have been getting $4,000 and $5,000 will not get it any more, that's all." And while Charles Byrne had been one of the architects of the consolidation, Frederick Abell, his partner in Brooklyn, was pessimistic. Abell predicted nobody would make money under the twelve-club setup; the owners were going to have to come down hard on laggard players. "This year," he said, "no nonsense will be tolerated. If the players don't play good, fair ball, they will sit in the grand stand and pay their own expenses." A salary that averaged out to $30 per game, Abell added, was too much pay. The *Washington Post* didn't share Abell's pessimism. With lower salaries and an abundance of good players, "there should be plenty of opportunity to equalize the playing strength."[12] As for local prospects, the addition of such veterans as Dummy Hoy, Danny and Hardie Richardson, Henry Larkin, and Phil Knell, as well as Frank Killen, a young pitcher assigned from Milwaukee, was expected to make the Nationals a much stronger team.

Connie Mack's experience with the new Pittsburgh ownership was a harbinger of what awaited players in the coming season. Mack was paid $2,400 in 1891; when he received his new contract, it specified a $1,000 cut. In 1892, moreover, Mack and the other 179 or so National League players would have to work two extra weeks for their pay. The club owners drew up a schedule extending the season from 140 to 154 games, with the provision that the season would be split in half; the winner of the first half would play the winner of the second half in a postseason series to decide the pennant. That is, providing the second-half winner was a different team from the first-half winner. Given the extra money owners and players would make in a championship series, that was likely to happen.

The formation of one big league represented a triumph of the pursuit of peace over the exercise of common sense. Even with a split season, a twelve-team league meant that by Independence Day, half or more of the teams would be well out of the pennant race, and local interest was bound to flag over the remainder of the season. Operating in twelve cities with a schedule lengthened by fourteen games, the National League's total 1892 attendance was the greatest in its and the Association's history: 1,822,587. But that averaged out to a falloff of about 20,000 per club from 1891. St. Louis, again proving itself to be a fine baseball town, finished next to last but led the League with close to 200,000 paying customers; whereas Boston, which won the season's first half and dispatched Cleveland, second-half winners, in the postseason, attracted some 40,000 fewer people to the South End Grounds than in 1891. As for the *Washington Post*'s high hopes, Bill Barnie's Nationals lost ninety-three games and finished tenth.

Again, it was a losing season financially for most clubs, except that now the losers were all in one league. That happened even though the club owners slashed many players' salaries before the season, and instituted another round of cuts and reduced rosters by one player in midseason. To a greater extent than ever before, the owners had the upper hand; baseball feudalism was in full sway.

As in the winter of 1886–87, the owners assumed more offense would mean more ticket sales. Instead of modifying the balls and strikes count, they lengthened the pitching distance by another five feet to 60' 6", did away with the pitcher's box, and stipulated that in delivering the ball, the pitcher had to keep his back foot on a rubber slab 12" long and 4" wide (increased to 24" by 6" two years later). Within a short time (nobody knows exactly when) groundskeepers had set the slab in a pile of dirt in the center of the infield, pitchers were working off a "mound," and the essential features of the game as it has remained to the present were finally in place.

The change worked, both to boost offense and boost attendance. Batting averages soared; pitchers allowed more runs than ever. Oddly, the biggest batting surge came not in 1893 but the following year, when the whole National League (pitchers included) batted above .300. Hugh Duffy, who led the League with a .363 average in 1893, batted .440 in 1894—a mark considered the legitimate all-time high.[13] Power pitchers such as Cy Young, Amos Rusie, and Kid Nichols gave up more runs but continued to win at the same pace as before the lengthened pitching distance. But Bill Hutchinson, John Clarkson, George Haddock, and Gus Weyhing, among a number of others, lost much of their effectiveness. Attendance rose to about 2,225,000 in 1893, to more than 2,400,000 in 1894, and approached 3,000,000 over the next three years. The owners imposed a maximum salary of $2,400, and although particular owners often violated the maximum by a few hundred dollars, smaller payrolls and bigger crowds made for profitable operations for many if not most members of the League.

But it wasn't the equalization of competition the *Washington Post* anticipated consolidation would bring. Not only were Washington, Louisville, St. Louis, Chicago, and Pittsburgh chronic also-rans, but from 1891 through 1900, either Boston (1891–93, 1897–98), Baltimore (1894–96), or Brooklyn (1899–1900) won every pennant.

Of the three, by far the best known are the "Old Orioles," whose rowdy ways combined with their fast, inventive style to make that team figure prominently in baseball's vast lore and legend. Ned Hanlon signed to manage Baltimore during the 1892 season and began building the city's three-time pennant winners. He inherited John McGraw, who came up from Cedar Rapids in the Association's final year and, playing various infield and outfield positions, impressed no one. In a trade with Louisville, Hanlon acquired shortstop Hugh Jennings, who was batting .164 when he came to Baltimore. Those two blossomed under Hanlon's tutelage and their own close friendship. Together with such stalwarts as Dan Brouthers (for the 1894 season), catcher Wilbert Robinson, pitcher Sadie McMahon, and outfielders Joe Kelley, Steve Brodie, and Willie Keeler, the Orioles made Harry von der Horst one of the League's most-successful "magnates." Hanlon also managed the two Brooklyn pennant winners at the end of the decade, so he and Frank Selee won them all.

The National League could never come up with a postseason attraction equal to the World's Championship Series the League's and Association's winners played from 1884 to 1890. The split-season arrangement was abandoned after one try. In 1894, William H. Temple of Pittsburgh donated a huge loving cup to the winner of a postseason match-up of the first- and second-place teams. The inaugural Temple Cup Series went to runner-up New York, now led by John Ward, with Amos Rusie and Jouett Meekin throttling the Orioles in a four-game sweep. In 1895, Cy Young pitched two victories, as runner-up Cleveland beat the Orioles four games to one; but Baltimore finally took possession of the Temple Cup the next year, downing Cleveland four straight. The postseason match-ups generated little interest outside the cities involved, and even there, attendance was usually disappointing. After Baltimore defeated pennant-winner Boston in a listless 1897 Temple Cup series, the club owners voted to end it.

Brooklyn won its 1900 pennant in an eight-club National League. The misgiv-ings Bill Barnie expressed in 1891 proved almost exactly correct. When the League voted to cut back to eight franchises early in 1900, three former Association cities—Louisville, Washington, and Baltimore—were the ones lopped off, plus Cleveland. St. Louis remained in the League in 1899 because Frank and Stanley Robison bought St. Louis from a now-bankrupt Chris von der Ahe, transferred Cy Young and nearly every-body of ability from Cleveland to St. Louis, and left Cleveland baseball to wither and be abandoned by the League.

But by 1901, Cleveland, Washington, and Baltimore (but not Louisville) were oper-ating in the new American League, the principal architect of which was the same Ban Johnson who served as secretary of the aborted Cincinnati Association club and, as sports editor of the local *Commercial-Gazette*, feuded with Arlie Latham.[14] After two years of baseball's fifth inter-league war, the National and American leagues made peace and thus established the major leagues' enduring twofold structure. As popularly understood, the era of "modern" baseball had begun; what had gone before would be largely forgotten.

1. *Chicago Tribune*, October 10, 1891, p. 6.
2. John J. O'Malley, "James J. Mutrie," in Robert L. Tiemann and Mark Rucker, eds., *Nineteenth Century Stars* (Cleveland: Society for American Baseball Research, 1988), 98.
3. *St. Louis Post-Dispatch*, October 13, 1891, p. 10; clipping from *Sporting News*, n.d. (1912), in Charles Comiskey file, National Baseball Hall of Fame Library.
4. Marty Appel, *Slide, Kelly, Slide: The Wild Life and Times of Mike "King" Kelly, Baseball's First Superstar* (Lanham, Md.: Scarecrow Press, 1999), 165.
5. *New York Clipper*, December 19, 1891, p. 686.
6. *Washington Post*, December 6, 1891, p. 6.
7. *Sporting News*, December 19, 1891, p. 1.
8. *Washington Post*, December 19, 1891, p. 6; *New York Clipper*, December 19, 1891, p. 687; *Sporting News*, same date, p. 1.

9. *Sporting News*, December 19, 1891, p. 1; Harold Seymour and Dorothy Seymour Mills, *Baseball: The Early Years* (1960; reprint, New York: Oxford University Press, 1989), 261. Seymour and Mills put the buyout total at $130,000.

10. Seymour and Mills, *Baseball: The Early Years*, 262.

11. Quoted in *Sporting News*, December 19, 1891, p. 2.

12. *New York Clipper*, January 2, 1892, p. 720; February 6, 1892, p. 799; *Washington Post*, December 13, 1891, p. 3.

13. Recent research has revised the long-accepted .438 for Duffy to .440.

14. In 1903, Louisville joined Milwaukee, Minneapolis, St. Paul, Indianapolis, Kansas City, Columbus, and Toledo—all former major league cities except Minneapolis and St. Paul—to form the American Association, classified from its inception as a top-level minor league. Its membership remained intact for forty-nine seasons.

APPENDIX

Some Lives Afterward

Ban Johnson left baseball writing in 1894 to become president of the Western League (formerly the Western Association), which, after a bad 1892 season, hadn't operated at all in 1893. Johnson made the Western League into a well-run organization in which umpires were respected, players' rowdiness was curbed, and most clubs prospered. In 1900, Johnson seized the opportunity created by the National League's jettisoning of four franchises, renamed his circuit the American League and moved the St. Paul club into Chicago. The next year he proclaimed the American League a major organization and within two years, in baseball's fourth peace agreement, won recognition as an equal from the National League. For fifteen years, Johnson was the most powerful man in baseball, but he was never reconciled to the creation in 1920 of the office of Commissioner of Baseball and his relegation, under Commissioner Kenesaw Mountain Landis, to the presidency of the American League and nothing else. Forced out by his league's owners seven years later, he died an embittered man in 1931.

Charles Comiskey retired as a player at the end of his three-year contract with Cincinnati, following three unsuccessful seasons. Having become close friends with Ban Johnson, he purchased the Sioux City franchise in Johnson's Western League, moved it to St. Paul, and then moved into Chicago in 1900. The next year, under pitcher-manager Clark Griffith, the Chicago White Sox won the first American League pennant. They won another in 1906 and upset the crosstown Chicago Cubs in the third "modern" World Series. Comiskey became sufficiently prosperous that he built a new steel and concrete baseball facility across the street from where Brotherhood Park had stood. Opened in 1910, Comiskey Park hosted the 1917 and 1919 World Series. The scandal surrounding Chicago's defeat in the 1919 Series and the subsequent banishment of eight White Sox players left the White Sox a perennial second-division team.

Comiskey died seven months after his onetime pal Ban Johnson, with whom he had feuded for more than twenty years.

Connie Mack caught for Pittsburgh three years before spending another three years as the Pirates' player-manager. In 1897 he joined Ban Johnson's Western League as player-manager for Milwaukee, subsequently operating as one of Johnson's confederates in the American League enterprise. Mack became manager of the Philadelphia Athletics in 1901 and remained so for the next fifty years, eventually owning the franchise. In the pantheon of baseball's greatest managers, he rivaled John McGraw, although in appearance and temperament, the lanky and soft-spoken New Englander was the opposite of the stocky and pugnacious McGraw. Mack directed some of the finest teams in history and some of the worst. His Athletics won nine American League pennants and five World Series, but also finished last seventeen times. He finally retired in 1950 at age eighty-eight and lived until 1956.

John Montgomery Ward and Helen Dauvray finally divorced in the fall of 1893. By then Ward was back with the New York Giants, having led Brooklyn to a strong third-place finish in 1892. In 1894 the Giants rose from a sixth-place showing to second place and a four-game sweep of Baltimore in the first Temple Cup series. After that, Ward, perhaps sensing he would have trouble with Andrew Freedman, the Giants' new majority owner, left baseball at age thirty-four. He developed a lucrative law practice, served briefly as president of the Boston National League club, and was business manager of the Brooklyn club in the Federal League (an unsuccessful effort to operate a third major league in 1914–15). Ward became a good amateur golfer, remarried, and acquired a small estate on Long Island. He died in 1925, one day after his sixty-fifth birthday.

Cap Anson continued to captain and play first base for the Chicago team, although he could never get it above fourth place. After the 1897 season, Al Spalding and Jim Hart decided it was time for Anson to go. In June 1898 he signed to manage the New York Giants but left after a month, one of sixteen men who tried to manage for the overbearing Andrew Freedman during eight seasons. In 1900 Anson took part in a failed effort to revive the American Association, later served a term as Chicago city clerk, wrote an autobiography (most of which was an account of the 1888–89 global tour), and performed on the stage. Having made a succession of bad investments, he was broke when he died at seventy in 1922.

Albert G. Spalding continued to expand his sporting goods empire and occasionally took a hand in the operation of the Chicago franchise (as in the decision to fire Anson). In 1901 he helped thwart a scheme concocted by Andrew Freedman whereby the National League would become a syndicate dominated by New York. A few years later Spalding influenced the formation of a commission to inquire into the origins of baseball, which he always insisted was an indigenous American game. The 1907 report of the Mills Commission confirmed what Spalding believed, creating baseball's foremost myth: that the game was invented by young Abner Doubleday in 1839 at Cooperstown, New York. Four years later Spalding incorporated the myth into his weighty history of baseball (*Baseball: America's National Game*). He died in 1915 at Point Loma, California, where he had moved in 1901 with his longtime paramour, whom he married after the death of his first wife.

Mike Kelly went into rapid decline in 1892. He might still have been, as he was once described, "a great hand-shaker, a fine singer, a clever mimic, and one of the best story-tellers in the profession," but years of high living had taken their toll on both his skills and his waistline. As Boston won its second consecutive National League pennant, he participated in only seventy-eight games and batted a pathetic .189. At the end of his two-year contract, the Triumvirs weren't interested in re-signing him. After a brief return to the stage, he joined the New York Giants, but John Ward used him in only sixteen games from May to September before he received his release. Kelly drifted down to the minor leagues, dividing the 1894 season between Allentown (Pennsylvania State League) and Yonkers (Eastern League). That autumn he contracted pneumonia; on November 8 the erstwhile King of the Diamond died in Boston. He was thirty-six years old.

Chris von der Ahe fell on hard times in the expanded National League. Year after year his Browns finished at or near the bottom of the League, and he continued to meddle in on-field matters. Between 1891 and 1898, the Browns had twenty-two captains or managers, including three occasions when von der Ahe himself tried to direct the team. He even put a shoot-the-chute and a pond in the Sportsman's Park outfield and staged bicycle races, but nothing worked. In addition to his major losses in real estate, his wife accused him of adultery and won a handsome divorce settlement. In 1899, after a messy court fight, the mortgage company to which he was heavily in debt took over the Browns and sold the franchise to Frank and Stanley Robison. Von der Ahe lived in near-poverty for the next fifteen years, helped some by a charity game the National League's Cardinals and the American League's Browns played in 1908. Four years later the once rich and powerful "boss President" died in St. Louis.

Frank Selee lost his best players in defections to the American League's new Boston club. After a fifth-place finish with the Beaneaters in 1901, he took over the Chicago Cubs (as they were now called) and managed them until 1904. Suffering from tuberculosis, he had to turn the team over to first baseman Frank Chance midway through the season. As many others did in that time, Selee sought to improve his health by moving to a higher and drier climate. He was only forty-seven when he died in Denver four years later, although he lived to see the team he built win three pennants of the four the Cubs won in five seasons (1906–10). The gentlemanly, mild-mannered New Englander, one of the most successful managers in history, was finally elected to the National Baseball Hall of Fame in 1999.

John McGraw became Baltimore's player-manager in 1899 at the age of twenty-six and surprised most people by leading the Orioles to a fourth-place finish in the last year of the twelve-club National League. He played for St. Louis the next year, then joined Ban Johnson's American League as manager and part-owner of its Baltimore team. Allies at first, McGraw and Johnson became enemies when Johnson refused to tolerate the obstreperous behavior McGraw and his players carried over from National League days. In midseason 1902, McGraw jumped to the New York Giants, taking over a last-place team. With financial backing from John T. Brush (who bought out Andrew Freedman later that year), McGraw built the Giants into a consistent powerhouse. In the twenty years beginning in 1904, McGraw's teams won ten pennants, although they were successful in only four World Series. Until he resigned and retired early in the 1932 season, McGraw remained a contentious personality—admired by many, despised by some. But whatever one thought of him personally, he was one of the greatest managers in the game's history. McGraw was sixty when he died of prostate cancer in 1934.

John T. Brush had many disputes with Ban Johnson in the 1890s. Brush owned both the Cincinnati and Indianapolis franchises and persisted in shuttling players back and forth between the National League and Western League, depending on which team was doing better in the pennant races. A powerful figure in National League affairs in the 1890s, Brush formed a winning combination with John McGraw after buying control of the New York Giants. Afflicted with locomotor ataxia, a degenerative condition of the nervous system, Brush was wheelchair-bound during the last several years of his life. He died in his private railway car en route to California shortly after the Giants' defeat in the 1912 World Series. He was sixty-seven.

John B. Day's influence in his beloved Giants waned after 1890. Two years later he ceded the franchise presidency to Cornelius C. Van Cott and sold his stock. Day owned a tobacco factory on Manhattan's Lower East Side, but a few years later he had to sell it. In 1899, in one of his many switches, Andrew Freedman hired Day to manage the Giants. He lasted sixty-four games before being dismissed. The National League paid him a small salary to be inspector of umpires, but failing health forced him to resign in the early 1920s. He was living in straitened circumstances when he died early in 1926.

Hugh Duffy followed his stunning 1894 season (for which the Boston Triumvirs awarded him a $200 raise) with .352, .300, and .340 batting averages. In 1901, Duffy became one of the players Frank Selee lost, when he signed as player-manager with Milwaukee in the American League. The team finished last and drew poorly, so Ban Johnson moved the franchise to St. Louis (where it revived the nickname Browns). Duffy stayed on at Milwaukee, which returned to the Western League (soon to be reorganized as the minor league American Association). After another season there, he again became a National Leaguer, signing to manage the Philadelphia Phillies. Three years in Philadelphia preceded managerial stints with the Chicago White Sox and various minor league clubs. Duffy served two years as a scout for the Boston Braves and a year managing in the International League before taking over the Boston Red Sox, who finished fifth and last in their two years (1921–22) under his direction. A "baseball lifer," Duffy settled into scouting for the Red Sox, a job he still held at the time of his death at age eighty-seven in 1954.

Harry Stovey had seen his best days by 1891, when he batted only .279 and led the National League in strikeouts (69). He divided the next two seasons among Boston, Baltimore, and Brooklyn, playing in only fifty-six games in 1893, after which he retired from baseball. Though a native Philadelphian, he resided in Bedford, Massachusetts, where he joined the police force, eventually rising to captain. A regular at the Methodist church, "Captain Harry" was one of Bedford's most-respected citizens. He died there in 1937, two months shy of his eightieth birthday.

Amos Rusie won 133 games for the Giants between 1892 and 1894 and struck out 1,040 batters. But his career started downhill when Andrew Freedman took over the

New York franchise. Freedman fined Rusie $100 on two separate occasions during the 1895 season; when he wouldn't refund the fines, Rusie sat out all of 1896 and retained John Ward to represent him in a $5,000 suit against Freedman. The Giants' president was obdurate, but the other National League owners got together to pay Rusie what he demanded. In 1897 the big pitcher came back to win twenty-eight games. He hurt his arm late in the following season, and when he couldn't pitch, Freedman spitefully suspended him without pay for all of 1899 and 1900. At the end of the 1900 season, John T. Brush, still Cincinnati owner, obtained Rusie from New York in exchange for a twenty-two-year-old right-hander named Christy Mathewson. Rusie was hit hard in three starts for the Reds and quit, having pitched only ten full seasons. He finished with 241 wins, 158 losses. Life after baseball was a struggle for the onetime "Hoosier Thunderbolt." Rusie was down and out when John McGraw gave him a job as Polo Grounds park superintendent, which he held for eight years. After that he moved to Washington State and ran a chicken ranch, which failed in the Great Depression. Rusie never fully recovered from injuries he suffered in 1934 in an automobile accident; he died eight years later in Seattle at age seventy-one.

Charles Radbourn, after leaving the Cincinnati Reds in August 1891, assumed fulltime operation of a saloon and billiard parlor he owned in Bloomington, Illinois. Three years later Radbourn wrote Chris von der Ahe seeking to return to baseball, but that prospect came to naught after a hunting accident destroyed his left eye. Suffering from syphilis, he became a recluse, cared for by his wife Carrie. He collapsed on February 5, 1897, and died two days later. The Ol' Hoss was forty-two.

Cy Young had won 219 games for Cleveland when, in 1899, Frank and Stanley Robison bought the St. Louis franchise and moved the Spiders' top players there. Unhappy working for the penurious Robisons, Young put in twenty-six and twenty-win seasons for St. Louis, then jumped to the Boston Americans for a $3,500 salary. After winning thirty-three and thirty-two games in his first two American League seasons, Young pitched twenty-eight victories in Boston's pennant drive and two more in its upset of Pittsburgh in the first twentieth-century World Series. Although he posted a 22–15 mark in 1908, John I. Taylor, Boston's young owner, judged him too old and sold him to Cleveland for $12,500. There he racked up another nineteen wins. Released after winning only ten times in the next two years, he signed with the run-of-the-mill Boston National Leaguers. In his swan-song season he pitched in eleven games, winning four, losing five. At forty-four, he went back to his farm in Ohio's Tuscarawas Valley, having pitched 906 times, worked 7,377 innings, and won 511 games, including three no-hitters, one of which was a perfect game. Venerated throughout baseball, Young lived eighty-eight years. The year after his death, major league baseball established the Cy Young Award, given to the season's outstanding pitcher (beginning in 1967, to a pitcher in each league).

John Clarkson, after winning thirty-three games for Boston in 1891, developed arm trouble and was abruptly released. Joining Cleveland, he still managed to end the season with twenty-three victories, but the wear and tear of so many innings, together with the lengthened pitching distance, reduced his 1893 record to 16–17. Never an easy man to get along with, he apparently became unpopular with his Spiders teammates. In mid-season 1894, after winning eight games and losing a like number, he was traded to Baltimore for Tony Mullane, but by then he was ready to retire. His lifetime record was 328–178. Clarkson moved to Bay City, Michigan, and ran a cigar store, but in 1895, for unknown reasons, he entered a mental hospital in Flint. He remained there for the next thirteen years, until members of his family moved him to his native Boston area. Early in 1909, Clarkson died in a mental facility in Belmont, Massachusetts. He was forty-seven.

Kid Nichols pitched his last game in the major leagues in 1906. It was a loss, which put his career record at 361 wins against 208 defeats. He topped thirty victories eight times. At the end of the 1901 season, at age thirty-two, he left Boston to manage the Western League's club in Kansas City, his off-season residence. After pitching and directing the Blues to a pennant and a third-place finish, he returned to the National League, signing with the Robison brothers to manage and pitch for St. Louis, where he compiled a 21–13 record. But his team finished fifth, and in July of the next year he was fired as manager and released as a player. Nichols caught on with Philadelphia; in 1906, after four appearances for the Phillies, he retired. He returned to Kansas City, where he became active in civic affairs and took up bowling, winning a local championship when he was sixty-four. Clean-living and personable, he died in 1953 at age eighty-three.

Fred Pfeffer, John Clarkson's teammate on Chicago's National League champions in the 1880s and a Brotherhood activist, didn't get to be player-manager of an American Association team in Chicago (nor did Amos Rusie get to pitch for it) and thus never had his chance to get even with Anson. Chicago traded him to Louisville before the 1892 season. During Pfeffer's four years playing in his hometown, the Colonels finished seventh, eleventh, and last twice under four managers, including Pfeffer for part of the 1892 season. In 1896, Pfeffer played with New York and Chicago before being released by the Colts in June 1897. After baseball, he coached at the University of Wisconsin, managed a year in the Three-I League, and operated a saloon in Chicago until the advent of Prohibition closed him down. Pfeffer spent his last decade tending press boxes at local race tracks. He died in Chicago in 1932 at age seventy-two.

Arlie Latham spent four more years with mediocre Cincinnati teams, under Comiskey and then Buck Ewing. He continued to be an often-irritating prankster and tease, and to perform his crowd-pleasing antics on the ball field. But he also remained a good player, batting .282, .314, and .311 from 1893 to 1895 and stealing more than two hundred bases. Except for eight games he played in 1896 for St. Louis, he spent the next thirteen years as a player and manager in the minors, although he made a cameo appearance with Washington in 1899. In 1909, John McGraw hired him as the game's first professional coach. He also played in four games that season and stole a base at age forty-nine, thus becoming the oldest man in major league history to do that. Later Latham spent seventeen years in England overseeing that country's unsuccessful national baseball program, followed by sixteen years working as a park attendant and press-box custodian for the Giants and New York Yankees. He lived to be ninety-two, dying in November 1952 in Garden City, New York.

Buck Ewing came back from injuries that limited his playing time in 1890 and 1891, to bat .320 in 105 games in his last year with New York. Just before the start of the 1893 season, the Giants traded him to Cleveland for George Davis, who became one of the decade's finest players. Abandoning catching for right field, Ewing put in another good year, playing 116 games, batting .344, and driving in 122 runs. The next year he appeared in only fifty-three of the Spiders' games, received his release, and signed to succeed Comiskey in Cincinnati, his hometown. Moving to first base, he could still bat .318, drive in ninety-four runs, and steal thirty-four bases. Ewing played only about half the time in 1896 but directed the Reds to a third-place finish, their best showing so far in the National League. A single game was the extent of his playing time in 1897. As a bench manager in his last two years with the Reds, he guided them to third place and sixth place before resigning. Unwisely agreeing to manage the Giants in 1900, he endured half a season with Andrew Freedman before turning the last-place outfit over to George Davis. Returning to Cincinnati, Ewing managed in the amateur leagues and coached at a nearby military academy. Afflicted with Bright's Disease, he died at his home in Cincinnati in October 1906, just before his forty-seventh birthday. Then and for long afterward, those who saw the hard-hitting, versatile Cincinnatian in action proclaimed him the finest player of his time.

Tony Mullane wouldn't take a $700 pay cut John T. Brush imposed in midseason 1892 and spent the rest of the year with Butte in the Montana State League. He returned to the Reds for 1893 but was traded to Baltimore in June. Traded to Cleveland a year later, Mullane completed the season with an 8–11 record, received his release, and spent the next four years in the Western League, followed by a four-game stopover in the International League. Turning to umpiring, he was working in the Pacific Northwest League when, at age forty-three, he signed to pitch for Spokane and won all three of his decisions. He went back to Chicago, joined the police force, and pitched in local semi-pro leagues until he was about fifty. Mullane lived to be eighty-five, dying in Chicago in 1944. He was a multi-talented player, often positioned in the outfield or infield when he wasn't pitching. Ambidextrous, he sometimes pitched both left- and right-handed in the same game. In the American Association, the "Count" won thirty or more times five years in a row. Mullane's 285 major league victories are the most of any pitcher not in the National Baseball Hall of Fame.

Jack O'Connor was expelled from the American Association in 1891, but by 1892 there was no Association, so he was free to sign with Cleveland. It was a good fit for a man considered the dirtiest player in the Association. With the exception of the easygoing Cy Young, the Spiders were a truculent, umpire-baiting crew whose behavior rivaled that of the fabled Orioles. As a catcher, infielder, and first baseman, O'Connor spent seven years with Cleveland. In 1900, he went with Young and the Spiders to St. Louis, but the Robisons sold him to Pittsburgh early in the season. O'Connor was a part-time player on the Pirates' pennant winners in 1901 and 1902; he also worked as Ban Johnson's agent in getting four teammates to jump to the American League's New York Highlanders, as did O'Connor himself. He couldn't get along with Highlanders manager Clark Griffith, who sent him to the St. Louis Browns in 1904. There he continued as a part-time player until 1910, when he succeeded Jimmy McAleer as the Browns' manager under a two-year contract. On the last day of the 1910 season, the last-place Browns played a doubleheader with Cleveland, whose well-liked Napoleon Lajoie was in a tight battle for the batting championship with much-disliked Ty Cobb. Not only the batting title but an expensive automobile, to be awarded to the winner by the Chalmers Motor Car Company, were at stake. O'Connor directed his rookie third baseman to play on the outfield grass, and Lajoie obligingly bunted that way for seven base hits. He also hit a legitimate triple, so that his eight-for-nine day apparently gave the Cleveland star the title and the Chalmers. Ban Johnson would have none of it. He declared Cobb the winner, ordered the Browns to fire O'Conner, and used his influence to have him blacklisted throughout Organized Baseball. Subsequently O'Connor won a lawsuit for the $5,000 St. Louis was to pay him in 1911. He worked for St. Louis's Federal League club in 1914, then became a boxing promoter in St. Louis. O'Connor died in 1937 at age sixty-eight, having been kicked out of two major leagues—a unique distinction in an otherwise undistinguished career.

Pete Browning, after dividing the 1891 season between Pittsburgh and Cincinnati, split 1892 between the Reds and Louisville, where he once vowed never to play again. It was Browning's last full season; in 104 games he batted only .292. He hit .369 in 1893 but played only fifty-seven times. Released after that, he was briefly a teammate of Mike Kelly's at Allentown in the Pennsylvania State League, played three games with St. Louis and Brooklyn, and finished his career in 1896 with twenty-six games in the Western League with Columbus. For the next nine years, Browning worked at odd jobs in Louisville, lived in pain caused by his mastoiditis, and continued to drink heavily. Finally he underwent surgery, but that left him with severe brain damage. His strange subsequent behavior, presumed to be insanity, led to a brief confinement in the Central Kentucky Lunatic Asylum. He had several stays at Louisville's City Hospital, where he died in September 1905 at the age of forty-four. Although Browning was often a liability in the outfield, his lifetime major league average—generally accepted to be .343—puts him among the elite who ever stood in a batter's box.

Willie McGill, the American Association's *enfant terrible* in 1891, signed with Comiskey's Cincinnati club for 1892 but pitched only three times before leaving, supposedly because of a lame arm, although it may have been that Comiskey suspended him for bad behavior. The next year McGill joined Cap Anson's lackluster Chicago team and, working from the new 60' 6" distance, won seventeen games but lost eighteen, giving up 311 hits in 303 innings. In 1894 his record was 7–19, and he allowed nearly six earned runs per nine innings. McGill was with Philadelphia in 1895 and 1896, where his combined record was 15–12. After that, except for a short stint with Chicago at the end of the decade, he pitched in the Western, Three-I, and Connecticut State leagues and the minor league American Association, never winning as many as he lost. He ended his professional career in 1905 in the Wisconsin State League. The lengthened pitching distance—as well as his own lack of self-discipline—kept the diminutive left-hander from equaling what he had done as a teenage major leaguer. McGill pitched several years in strong Chicago semipro competition and later became, of all things, an athletic trainer. He lived to be seventy, dying in Indianapolis in 1944.

Bibliography

Archival Resources

Files for the following were examined in the National Baseball Hall of Fame Library, Cooperstown, New York.

Anson, Adrian
Brouthers, Dan
Browning, Louis R.
Clarkson, John
Comiskey, Charles
Connor, Roger
Duffy, Hugh
Ewing, William
Glasscock, Jack
Gore, George
Kelly, Michael J.

Latham, Walter Arlington
McGunnigle, William
Nichols, Charles
O'Connor, Jack
O'Rourke, James
Pfeffer, Fred
Selee, Frank
Stovey, Harry
Tiernan, Mike
Ward, John Montgomery

Newspapers

Boston Globe, 1890–92
Chicago Tribune, 1890–92
Cincinnati Evening Post, 1891–92
Cleveland Plain Dealer, 1890–92
Columbus Evening Dispatch, 1890–92
New York Clipper, 1889–92

New York Times, 1890–92
Sporting Life, 1889–92
Sporting News, 1889–92
St. Louis Post-Dispatch, 1889–92
Washington Post, 1891–92

Official Publications

Players' National League Official Guide for 1890. Chicago: F. H. Brunell, 1890. Reprint, Horton Publishing Co., 1989.

Reach's Official American Association Guides, 1890–1891. Philadelphia: A. J. Reach Company, 1891–92.

Spalding's Official Base Ball Guides, 1889, 1890, 1891. Chicago: n.p., 1890, 1891, 1892.

Books

Abrams, Roger I. *The Dark Side of the Diamond: Gambling, Violence, Drugs, and Alcoholism in the National Pastime.* Burlington, Mass.: Rounder Books, 2007.

Achorn, Edward. *Fifty-nine in '84: Old Hoss Radbourn, Barehanded Baseball, and the Greatest Season a Pitcher Ever Had.* Washington, D. C.: Smithsonian Books, 2010.

Alexander, Charles C. *John McGraw.* 1988. Reprint, Lincoln: University of Nebraska Press, 1995.

———. *Our Game: An American Baseball History.* New York: Henry Holt, 1991.

Allen, Lee. *The Cincinnati Reds.* 1948. Reprint, Kent, Ohio: Kent State University Press, 2006.

Anson, Adrian. *A Ball Player's Career: Being the Personal Reminiscences of Adrian C. Anson, Late Manager of the Chicago Base Ball Club.* Chicago: Era Publishing Co., 1900.

Appel, Marty. *Slide, Kelly, Slide: The Wild Life and Times of Mike 'King' Kelly, Baseball's First Superstar.* Lanham, Md.: Scarecrow Press, 1996.

Ardell, Jean Hastings. *Breaking into Baseball: Women and the National Pastime.* Carbondale: Southern Illinois University Press, 2005.

Axelson, Gustav. *"COMMY": The Life Story of Charles A. Comiskey.* 1919. Reprint, Jefferson, N.C.: McFarland, 2003.

The Baseball Encyclopedia, 10th ed. New York: Macmillan, 1996.

Bevis, Charlie. *The New England League: A Baseball History, 1885–1949.* Jefferson, N.C.: McFarland, 2008.

———. *Sunday Baseball: The Major Leagues' Struggle to Play Baseball on the Lord's Day, 1876–1934.* Jefferson, N.C.: McFarland, 2003.

Bowman, Larry G. *Before the World Series: Pride, Profits, and Baseball's First Championships.* DeKalb: Northern Illinois University Press, 2003.

Brown, Bob, ed. *Monumental Baseball.* Cleveland: Society for American Baseball Research, 2009.

Brown, Warren. *The Chicago Cubs.* New York: Putnam's, 1946.

Browning, Reed. *Cy Young: A Baseball Life.* Amherst: University of Massachusetts Press, 2000.

Burk, Robert F. *Never Just a Game: Players, Owners, and American Baseball to 1920.* Chapel Hill: University of North Carolina Press, 1994.

Cash, Jon David. *Before They Were Cardinals: Major League Baseball in Nineteenth-Century St. Louis.* Columbia: University of Missouri Press, 2002.

Casway, Jerrold. *Ed Delahanty and the Emerald Age of Baseball.* Notre Dame, Ind.: University of Notre Dame Press, 2004.

Cook, William A. *The Louisville Scandal of 1877: The Taint of Gambling at the Dawn of the National League.* Jefferson, N.C.: McFarland, 2005.

Curran, William. *Mitts: A Celebration of Fielding.* New York: William Morrow, 1984.

———. *Strikeout: A Celebration of the Art of Pitching.* New York: Crown, 1995.

Devine, Christopher. *Harry Wright: The Father of Professional Base Ball.* Jefferson, N.C.: McFarland, 2003.

Di Salvatore, Bryan. *A Clever Base-Ballist: The Life and Times of John Montgomery Ward.* New York: Pantheon Books, 1999.

Duren, Don. *Boiling Out at the Springs: A History of Major League Baseball at Hot Springs, Arkansas.* Dallas: self-published, 2006.

Egan, James M., Jr. *Base Ball on the Western Reserve: The Early Game in Cleveland and Northeast Ohio . . . 1865–1900.* Jefferson N.C.: McFarland, 2008.

Ellard, Harry. *Base Ball in Cincinnati: A History.* 1907. Reprint, Cincinnati: Ohio Book Store, 1987.

Fleitz, David L. *Cap Anson: The Grand Old Man of Baseball.* Jefferson, N.C.: McFarland, 2005.

Frommer, Frederic J. *The Washington Nationals: 1859 to Today.* Lanham, Md.: Taylor Trade Publishers, 2006.

Frommer, Harvey. *Old Time Baseball: America's Pastime in the Gilded Age.* Lanham, Md.: Taylor Trade Publishers, 2006.

Ginsburg, Daniel E. *The Fix Is In: A History of Baseball Gambling and Game-Fixing Scandals.* Jefferson, N.C.: McFarland, 1995.

Graham, Frank. *The Brooklyn Dodgers.* 1945. Reprint, Carbondale: Southern Illinois University Press, 2002.

———. *The New York Giants.* New York: Putnam's, 1952.

Hardy, James D. *The New York Giants Base Ball Club: The Growth of a Team and Sport, 1870–1900.* Jefferson, N.C.: McFarland, 1996.

Hetrick, J. Thomas. *Chris von der Ahe and the St. Louis Browns.* Lanham, Md.: Scarecrow Press, 1999.

Hubbard, Donald. *The Heavenly Twins of Baseball: A Dual Biography of Hugh Duffy and Tommy McCarthy.* Jefferson, N.C.: McFarland, 2008.

Ivor-Campbell, Frederic, et al., eds. *Baseball's First Stars.* Cleveland: Society for American Baseball Research, 1996.

James, Bill. *Baseball Managers from 1870 to the Present.* New York: Scribner's, 1997.

Jordan, David M. *Occasional Glory: The History of the Philadelphia Phillies.* Jefferson, N.C.: McFarland, 2002.

Kaese, Harold. *The Boston Braves, 1871–1953.* 1948, 1954. Reprint, Boston: Northeastern University Press, 2004.

Koszarek, Ed. *The Players' League: History, Clubs, Ballplayers and Statistics.* Jefferson, N.C.: McFarland, 2006.

Lambster, Mark. *Spalding's World Tour: The Epic Adventures That Took Baseball around the World and Made It America's Game.* New York: Public Affairs Press, 2006.

Lansche, Jerry. *The Forgotten Championships: Postseason Baseball, 1882–1981.* Jefferson, N.C.: McFarland, 1989.

Lee, Bill. *The Baseball Necrology: The Post-Baseball Lives and Deaths of Over 7,000 Major League Players and Others.* Jefferson, N.C.: McFarland, 2003.

Levine, Peter. *A. G. Spalding and the Rise of Baseball.* New York: Oxford University Press, 1985.

Lewis, Franklin. *The Cleveland Indians.* 1949. Reprint, Kent, Ohio: Kent State University Press, 2006.

Lieb, Fred. *The Pittsburgh Pirates.* New York: Putnam's, 1948.

Lieb, Fred, and Stan Baumgartner. *The Philadelphia Phillies.* New York: Putnam's, 1953.

Lowry, Philip J. *Green Cathedrals: The Ultimate Celebration of Major League and Negro League Ballparks.* New York: Walker and Co., 2006.

Macht, Norman I. *Connie Mack and the Early Years of Baseball.* Lincoln: University of Nebraska Press, 2006.

Martin, Robert F. *Hero of the Heartland: Billy Sunday and the Transformation of American Society, 1862–1935.* Bloomington: Indiana University Press, 2002.

McNeill, William F. *The Evolution of Pitching in Major League Baseball.* Jefferson, N.C.: McFarland, 2006.

Morris, Peter. *Catcher: How the Man Behind the Plate Became an American Folk Hero.* Chicago: Ivan Dee, 2009.

Murdock, Eugene C. *Ban Johnson: Czar of Baseball.* Westport, Conn.: Greenwood Press, 1982.

Neft, David S. et al., eds. *The Sports Encyclopedia: Baseball,* 24th ed. New York: St. Martin's Griffin, 2004.

Nemec, David. *The Beer and Whiskey League: The Illustrated History of the American Association, Baseball's Renegade League.* Guilford, Conn.: Lyons Press, 2004.

———. *The Great Encyclopedia of Nineteenth Century Baseball.* New York: Donald I. Fine Books, 1997.

Pearson, Daniel M. *Baseball in 1889: Players vs. Owners.* Bowling Green, Ohio: Bowling Green University Popular Press, 1993.

Peterson, Richard "Pete," ed. *The St. Louis Baseball Reader.* Columbia: University of Missouri Press, 2006.

Pitoniak, Scott. *Baseball in Rochester.* Charleston, S.C.: Acadia Publishing, 2003.

Riess, Steven. *City Games: The Evolution of American Society and the Rise of Sports.* Urbana: University of Illinois Press, 1989.

———. *Touching Base: Professional Baseball and American Culture in the Progressive Era.* Westport, Conn.: Greenwood Press, 1980.

Roer, Mike. *Orator O'Rourke: The Life of a Baseball Radical.* Jefferson, N.C.: McFarland, 2005.

Schiff, Andrew J. *"The Father of Baseball": A Biography of Henry Chadwick.* Jefferson, N.C.: McFarland, 2008.

Schiffert, John. *Base Ball in Philadelphia: A History of the Early Game, 1831–1900.* Jefferson, N.C.: McFarland, 2006.

Seymour, Harold, and Dorothy Seymour Mills. *Baseball: The Early Years.* 1960. Reprint, New York: Oxford University Press, 1989.

Skipper, John C. *A Biographical Dictionary of Major League Baseball Managers.* Jefferson, N.C.: McFarland, 2003.

Solomon, Burt. *Where They Ain't: The Fabled Life and Untimely Death of the Original Baltimore Orioles.* New York: Free Press, 1999.

Soos, Troy. *Before the Curse: The Glory Days of New England Baseball, 1858–1918.* Jefferson, N.C.: McFarland, 2006.

Spalding, Albert Goodwill. *Baseball: America's National Game.* New York: American Sports Publishing, 1911.

Spatz, Lyle. *Bad Bill Dahlen: The Rollicking Life and Times of an Early Baseball Star.* Jefferson, N.C.: McFarland, 2004.

Stein, Fred. *A History of the Baseball Fan.* Jefferson, N.C.: McFarland, 2005.

Stevens, David. *Baseball's Radical for All Seasons: A Biography of John Montgomery Ward.* Lanham, Md.: Scarecrow Press, 1998.

Sullivan, Neil J. *The Minors: The Struggle and Triumph of Baseball's Poor Relation.* New York: St. Martin's Press, 1990.

Thorn, John, et al., eds. *Total Baseball*, 7th ed. Kingston, N.Y.: Total Sports Publishing, 2001.

Tiemann, Robert L., and Mark Rucker, eds. *Nineteenth Century Stars*. Cleveland: Society for American Baseball Research, 1989.

Tootle, James R. *Baseball in Columbus*. Charleston, S.C.: Acadia, 2003.

Voigt, David Q. *American Baseball: From Gentleman's Sport to the Commissioner System*. Norman: University of Oklahoma Press, 1966.

———. *The League That Failed*. Lanham, Md.: Scarecrow Press, 1998.

Von Borries, Philip. *Legends of Louisville: Major League Baseball in Louisville, 1876–1899*. West Bloomfield, Mich.: Altwanger & Mandell, 1992.

Ward, John Montgomery. *Base-Ball: How to Become a Player, with the Origin, History, and Explanation of the Game*. Philadelphia: Athletic Publishing Co., 1888.

Wilbert, Warren. *A Cunning Kind of Play: The Cubs-Giants Rivalry, 1876–1932*. Jefferson, N.C.: McFarland, 2002.

Wood, Gerald C., and Andrew Hazucha. *Northsiders: Essays on the History and Culture of the Chicago Cubs*. Jefferson, N.C.: McFarland, 2008.

Zeiler, Thomas. *Ambassadors in Pinstripes: The Spalding World Tour and the Birth of the American Empire*. Lanham, Md.: Rowman and Littlefield, 2006.

Articles

Akin, William E. "Bare Hands and Kid Gloves: The Best Fielders, 1880–1899." *Baseball Research Journal*, no. 10 (1981), 60–65.

Alexander, Charles C. "Was the 1891 National League Pennant Thrown?" *Base Ball: A Journal of the Early Game*, 2 (Fall 2008), 5–17.

Anson, "Pop," et al. "Interviews with the Old Timers: Comments on Past Events in Baseball History." *Baseball Magazine*, 21 (June 1918), 227.

Ball, David. "The National Agreement and Its Discontents: The Difficult Origins and Rugged Development of the Reserve Clause." *Base Ball: A Journal of the Early Game*, 3 (Spring 2009), 7–22.

Bowman, Larry G. "The Helen Dauvray Cup." *National Pastime*, no. 17 (1997), 73–76.

Casway, Jerrold. "Baseball's Hibernian Collaboration." *Base Ball: A Journal of the Early Game*, 3 (Fall 2009), 67–75.

Dunbar, William H. "Baseball Salaries Thirty Years Ago." *Baseball Magazine*, 21 (July 1918), 291–99.

Haupert, Michael. "Take Me Out to the Ball Game: The Pursuit of Pleasure and Profit on the Ball Field." *Base Ball: A Journal of the Early Game*, 4 (Spring 2010), 28–43.

Holst, David L. "Charles H. Radbourne: The Greatest Pitcher of the Nineteenth Century." *Illinois Historical Journal*, 81 (Winter 1988), 255–68.

Jensen, Don. "Everyone Went to Nick's: High and Low Life in Manhattan's First Sports Bar." *Base Ball: A Journal of the Early Game*, 3 (Spring 2009), 94–106.

Kane, Robert A. "Billy McGunnigle: Baseball's Forgotten Pioneer." *Baseball Research Journal*, 28 (1999), 17–22.

Lamb, William F. "A Fearsome Collaboration: The Alliance of Andrew Freedman and John T. Brush." *Base Ball: A Journal of the Early Game*, 3 (Fall 2008), 5–20.

————. "George Davis: A Look at a Forgotten Star." *National Pastime*, 17 (1997), 3–8.

Lipset, Lew. "'Granpa' Was Harry Stovey." *National Pastime*, 4 (Winter 1985), 84–85.

McShane, Clay, and Joel A. Tarr. "Living Machines: The Horse in Ohio Cities." *Timeline*, 27 (January–March 2010), 34–53.

Morris, Peter. "A Motion as Near Flying as Any Human Could Attain: The Nineteenth-Century Umpire as Sprinter." *Base Ball: A Journal of the Early Game*, 2 (Fall 2008), 18–25.

Moses, Ralph C. "Bid McPhee." *National Pastime*, 14 (1994), 48–50.

Porter, David E. "Cap Anson of Marshalltown: Baseball's First Superstar." *Palimpsest*, 61 (July–August 1980), 100–107.

Schaefer, Robert H. "The Wiman Trophy, and the Man for Whom It Was Named." *Base Ball: A Journal of the Early Game*, 1 (Fall 2007), 44–54.

Schwartz, John. "From One Ump to Two." *Baseball Research Journal*, 30 (2001), 85–86.

Suehsdorf, A. L. "Frank Selee, Dynasty Builder." *National Pastime*, 4 (Winter 1985), 35–44.

Tiemann, Robert. "The Forgotten Winning Streak of 1891." *Baseball Research Journal*, no. 19 (1989), 2–5.

Torangeau, Dixie. "Remembering the Congress Street Grounds." *National Pastime*, n. 24 (2004), 71–78.

Ward, John M. "Is the Base Ball Player a Chattell?" *Lippincott's Magazine*, 40 (August 1887), 310–19.

Index

Charles C. Alexander, Distinguished Professor Emeritus of History, Ohio University, has authored biographies of Ty Cobb, John McGraw, Rogers Hornsby, and Tris Speaker, as well as *Our Game: An American Baseball History* and *Breaking the Slump: Baseball in the Depression Era*. *Turbulent Seasons: Baseball in 1890–1891* is his thirteenth book. He now lives in Hamilton, Ohio.

Annie Morris